MY GENTLE BARN

My Gentle Barn

Creating a Sanctuary
Where Animals Heal and
Children Learn to Hope

Ellie Laks

WITH NOMI ISAK

HARMONY
BOOKS · NEW YORK

Copyright © 2014 by Ellie Laks

All rights reserved.

Published in the United States by Harmony Books,
an imprint of the Crown Publishing Group,
a division of Random House LLC,
a Penguin Random House Company, New York.

www.crownpublishing.com

Harmony Books is a registered trademark,
and the Circle colophon is a trademark of Random House LLC.

Library of Congress Cataloging-in-Publication Data
Laks, Ellie, author.
My Gentle Barn: Creating a sanctuary where animals heal and children learn to hope/
Ellie Laks with Nomi Isak.—First edition.
pages cm
1. Human-animal relationships—California. 2. Animal shelters—California. 3. Animal rescue—
California. 4. Laks, Ellie. I. Isak, Nomi, author. II. Title.
QL85.L27 2014
636.08'3209794—dc23   2013042589

ISBN 978-0-385-34766-2
eISBN 978-0-385-34767-9

PRINTED IN THE UNITED STATES OF AMERICA

Book design and illustrations by Jaclyn Reyes
Photograph opposite title page courtesy of the Gentle Barn
Jacket design by Nupoor Gordon
Jacket photography: front/Zack Cordner; back/(wood, straw) Shutterstock,
(animals) courtesy of author

1   3   5   7   9   10   8   6   4   2

First Edition

For the animals. May all beings know peace!

Author's Note

Memory is a crazy thing. Some memories come in full pictures; others come in snapshots or blurs. Sometimes all there is, is a smell or a feeling. Two people can have the same experience, yet later when recalling it they tell two different stories. This book is my attempt to share *my* memories and include all the smells, tastes, feelings, and flavors that came with them.

We all parent the way we were parented unless we learn some other way. Even though I recall my childhood as lonely, I don't think it is anyone else's fault. I believe that the people in my life loved me and tried their best to raise me properly. I love my family, especially my parents, whom I've gotten so many good qualities from. My father dedicated his whole life to healing people—people who were too old, too young, or too risky for other surgeons to operate on. I think I learned my work ethic and my desire to serve and have purpose from him. My mom is the most generous person in the world; when she made a meal she made extra in case someone unexpected showed up, and she always invited people who had nowhere else to go. My mom was always driving someone to the hospital or making a meal for another family or listening to someone else's problems. I think I got my generosity from her.

When you read the depiction of my early years, remember that it is from a child's perspective and the way I felt inside at that time, not necessarily the way my parents felt toward me. Our childhoods shape the people we become as adults, and I wanted to truthfully share my experiences that made me the woman I am today. This book is not about blame; the reason I am sharing my story with you is so I can explain why the Gentle Barn is so important to me, why I've worked so hard, and why I've sacrificed everything for it.

———

Most of the names and identities in this book have been changed to protect the privacy of the people depicted.

PROLOGUE

When I was a child in St. Louis, there was a field behind our Orthodox Jewish synagogue that held my attention far better than what
was happening inside the sanctuary. While the women sat in their
segregated section and gossiped for the entire two-hour service, I
would squirm in my seat, unable to follow the command to sit still
and be quiet. Eventually, I would tell my mother I had to go to the
bathroom and instead would slip out the back door of the temple
and into the field. I would crawl through the tall grass looking for
beetles and giant grasshoppers. I would tunnel through the bushes,
hollowing out hidden forts. Sometimes I'd just lie in the grass and
watch the clouds float across the sky. The time would pass so quickly
I'd end up scurrying back to the temple right when services were

ending, trying to brush the burs and foxtails off my dress and tights as I ran.

One Saturday in the fall, when I'd snuck out into the field, I noticed some big butterflies glimmering in the sunlight as they flitted from one weed to the next. I lay down in the field to get a closer look at their orange wings struck through with black veins. When I rolled onto my back I saw that the sky was filled with them—their wings, tiny stained-glass windows lit by the sun. Lying in the grass transfixed, far more still and quiet than I ever was in temple, I felt a tiny touch on my arm, then on my hand, then on my face. One after another, butterflies were landing on me, until I was covered entirely, head to toe—a mirror of the orange, fluttering sky.

In that moment, I felt—for the first time in my young life—a sense of peace and stillness inside me.

That stillness and well-being never came to me from being around humans—not at home, not at school, not with the few friends I had. Animals—whether a tiny winged insect or the horses at the stables down the road—were the only ones who could provide me with that depth of calm and happiness. They ushered me through my childhood and through my life—calling me back again and again to a place of peace and purpose.

Years later, when I went on to start the Gentle Barn—rescuing, rehabilitating, and offering sanctuary to abused animals—many people misunderstood what it was all about. At the beginning, some viewed it as a hobby or an obsession. With time there were many who saw it differently and thanked me for rescuing all these animals—viewing my work as an act of selfless devotion.

To all of those people, I wanted to say, "You don't understand. I'm not saving the animals; they're saving me."

Now there are those who understand even this, for they, too, have been saved by the animals. Thousands of at-risk and special-needs kids who have participated in our youth program—as well as the adults who have come to volunteer—have been touched and transformed by the animal residents of the Gentle Barn.

What started off as a personal quest for peace and wholeness has blossomed into something so much bigger than that little girl covered in butterflies ever could have imagined.

My Gentle Barn

CHAPTER 1

They say that two people can have the same kind of childhood—raised in the same crazy, dysfunctional environment—and one can become a psychopath while the other grows into a normal, functioning adult. The distinguishing factor is that the normal person had a witness as a child. Without a witness, abuse or neglect will drive a person over the edge.

I made it to adulthood intact because animals were my witness. Not that there weren't bumps along the road to my healthy, functional behavior, but always the animals were there to witness my every step.

I was forever escaping to the lake down the road or into the woods behind our house in search of peace and a place where I mattered. I would sit on the leafy ground under the trees and wait for the wild bunnies to come see me. They'd sniff at me and eventually hop into my lap, and I'd spend hours talking with them and petting them. My absence from the house was rarely noticed, except on my return, when my mom would call for me to change out of my filthy clothes before dinner. I didn't fit the mold that Orthodox Judaism had cut out for me—I was to help my mom with housework, grow up to have lots of babies, and keep my mouth shut. It didn't seem fair that my brothers never had to help with the dishes or that their voices were acknowledged while mine was ignored or silenced. The only ones who noticed me were the baby-sitters. Two of our babysitters were young men, and they paid far too much of the wrong kind of attention to me. One made me sit on his lap when I didn't want to, and the other would wait until my little brothers were napping, and then he'd take me into the bathroom where he said he had something to show me. He would take down my pants and force me onto the cold tiles. I learned very quickly how not to look at him, but instead to look out the window to the trees, to the sky, to the nature that held me close. Out there I was free. When he was done, he would give me little plastic animals. My reward for not telling.

When he set me loose, I would run to my beautiful lake with my Australian shepherd, Simon, where we'd muck around in the shallows and all was right again in my world. Simon and I would watch the tadpoles turn to frogs and track salamanders so I could hold their cool, slimy bodies until they wriggled away between my fingers. I loved that lake; it was my sanctuary, just like the field behind our synagogue and the woods behind our house. But on one particular visit to the lake, something different happened. A man I had never seen approached me and gave me candy and money to do things a seven-year-old girl should never be asked to do. I'd been taught by the babysitters to say yes and wait patiently until it was over. So that's what I did with this man.

When I got home I told my brother, who told my parents. My father was furious—not at the man, but at me. He banned me from ever going to the lake again. No one ever thought to hunt the man down; I was the one to blame. For me that was the day my father joined the other side, the adults who did me wrong. The young men used me, my mother didn't know what to do with me, and now my father had gone from merely favoring my brothers to shutting me out entirely, and on top of it taking away the one place that could give me solace. Without my lake, the emptiness inside me was too vast and too bleak. There was no one to love me and nowhere to turn, and I knew I must be horribly broken to be so invisible. The only solution I could come up with, the only thing I had the power to do, was to leave this world for good. Maybe then, I thought, they would notice me in my absence.

But I didn't know yet what it took to die, so I failed miserably at trying to leave this world. First I tried to smash my head in with a shoe; needless to say, that didn't work. Then I ran sobbing up to the second floor of our house, intending to jump out the window, but I couldn't break the glass. Frustrated and hopeless, I went down into the garden for refuge. As I sat crying on the brick path, I received a message that would change the course of my life. A hummingbird dove to within inches of my face, and there he hovered for minutes upon minutes, his thrumming wings filling my ears with vibration, his eyes—tiny beads of ink—taking in my face. It was as though he were suspended in time, allowing me to absorb every one of his shimmering colors. Gold, red, purple, blue, green. An entire rainbow rolled up into one tiny being, and this one being was seeing me, was interested in me, and was reminding me that I was anything but alone. The world surrounding me was teeming with life—life that noticed me and beckoned me to stay.

It was this diminutive messenger who gave me the courage to tell my mother everything. That the babysitters had been doing things to me for a very long time, wrong things. I even told her about the plastic animals.

"Oh, don't be ridiculous," my mother said, her shrill voice a slap in the face.

"But it happened," I insisted. "It did happen. It happens all the time."

My mom went back to cleaning up the house, doing the laundry, her jaw set on edge.

I followed her around, trying to explain—no one ever saw, the babysitters made sure of that. "They told me not to tell, but I'm telling you."

She put down the laundry basket and held up her hand: *Silence.*

The discussion was over. There was nothing more I could say. Nothing more she would hear.

I fled to my room, slammed the door, and sprawled on my bed sobbing, irate. "It did happen!" I yelled. I pounded the bed with my fists and kicked at the wall, yelling at the top of my lungs. One very hard kick sent my foot straight through the plaster. Seeing the gaping hole in the wall, I jumped from my bed and ran outside, ran until I was sure no one would find me. Out of breath, I fell to my knees under a birch tree, the leaves crunching under my weight.

I was wrong that I wouldn't be found; moments later my dog, Simon, was licking at my tears. I threw my arms around his neck. "It did happen, right, Simon? It happens all the time. You believe me, don't you?"

He nuzzled at my face, and I felt a little less alone. A little less crazy. Simon always seemed to know when I needed him most. Just when I felt the most alone, he would find me and lift me up out of my darkness.

Although nothing more was said about the subject, we only had female babysitters after that. The young men would never again make me sit on their laps, never force me onto the bathroom floor, banging my head on the shower tiles. I would never again have to hold my breath so I wouldn't cry out. It was over.

For years I wouldn't piece together the cause and effect, that my telling had had anything to do with the disappearance of the young men. I felt my mother had dismissed me, and I hated her for it. She hung a poster over the hole above my bed and told me it was our little secret. We didn't have to tell my father I'd ruined my bedroom wall.

For the next several years, my life was a series of camouflaged holes. Chunks kicked out of the fabric of my life and hastily patched over. My mother brushing off my protests with annoyance. "Ellie, stop your nonsense." My heart broken again and again.

On the occasion when my parents remembered my birthday I got to pick out my gift. A trip to the pet store was my default. I'd walk up and down the rows of cages housing hamsters and lizards and finches, and I'd feel a magical sense of possibility filling my being. I'd gaze at the animals and wait until one of them seemed to call to me, silently asking me to choose him or her. By the time we got home, that animal would have a name. I'd set up a cage or aquarium with soft bedding or water and sand and sit with my new friend for hours, letting them crawl all over me, and feeding them special treats. My hamsters were like little powder puffs they smelled so good, and a dove I got for finding the afikomen at Passover would fly to me when I cooed to her. One year I was even given riding lessons at the stables near our house. I bonded deeply with all these animals, better than I ever bonded with humans. I'd run home after school and go straight to my new animal or I'd go to the stables, and the horses would greet me with a toss of their head and we'd say hello by breathing each other in.

Inevitably, though, the pets disappeared—sometimes after a few months, sometimes after only a couple of weeks. There was never a warning and never an apology. My mother simply would grow tired of them, and the animals would be gone. Even the riding lessons were taken away when I made friends at the stables with a non-Jewish boy. I'd sob and I'd mourn but, with a sweep of her hand, she would issue her pronouncement: "Ellie, stop your nonsense. They're just animals."

One very cold winter night, a couple of weeks after I'd received two bunnies for my January birthday, I brought the rabbits into my room before bed. Except for our dog, Simon, animals were not generally welcome in the house, but I would sneak them in whenever I could. And on this particular night I knew it was far too cold outside for these young bunnies.

"Ellie," my mom said from my bedroom doorway. And she pointed to where the cage was almost hidden behind my bed. "Out."

I pretended not to know what she was talking about.

"The rabbits. Outside."

"But they'll freeze," I said.

"They'll be fine. They're animals. They live outdoors."

"But Mom, it's too cold tonight."

She marched into my room and lifted the cage. I ran after her to the front door, pleading with her to let them stay inside just for this night. She opened the door, and I screamed, "They're going to die! Please just let them stay in the living room."

"No. They're going on the porch."

"Just inside here," I pleaded, and pointed to the spot next to the front door. "It's almost the porch."

With the door open, the frigid air filled the front entryway and I hugged myself for warmth, tears streaming down my face. My mother set the cage down outside, then looked at me and said, "Enough. Now go to bed. You'll go see your rabbits in the morning."

I hardly slept that night, and as soon as my window glowed with the faintest morning light, I ran out onto the porch.

Both rabbits were on their sides, little furry blocks of ice.

When my mother saw me sobbing and shivering over the cage, she stood in the doorway and said, "Ellie, what's wrong with you? You're going to freeze out there."

"They're dead!" I screamed.

"You're being ridiculous. They're just rabbits; we'll get you more. Now stop your nonsense and come inside."

The force that drove me to be with animals defied all reason. I was compelled to have them near me no matter what. I began feeling little whispers deep inside—not in words, just in knowing. *Go to the stream. Cross the bridge. Now turn right.* I would follow this invisible force right to a bird who had fallen from her nest or to a turtle in the woods who had cracked his shell, and I would nurse those animals back to health the best I could, sneaking them into my room and making a nest out of straw and mud or setting up a box with a bowl of water and lettuce pilfered from the fridge. It never occurred to me to question how or why this guidance came. For me it was just like breathing or feeling hungry. I didn't question how or why I needed to breathe; I just breathed. When I was hungry, I followed that hunger to food. In the same way, I followed my inner knowing to the animals that needed help. The shock would come later when I learned that others did not experience this type of connection to animals. I had thought it came with the package—sight, smell, hearing, inner whispers from the animal world.

One time the whispers led me to the lake, where a whole flock of ducks had frozen in the ice-covered water. Only one duck remained unglued to the surface of the lake. That big, white duck bobbed and weaved her head as she stood on the shore, clearly distraught by the loss of her whole community. I dug in my pocket for the bread I'd grabbed on my way out the door and I fed her tiny pieces, luring her all the way home.

I named my new duck Snow White and made a nest for her in the garage. Everywhere I went after that, Snow White came along. Simon would be on one side of me, and this big, white, waddling duck would be on the other. The Three Musketeers, traipsing around the suburbs of St. Louis.

But of course, Snow White's story ended no more happily than all the others. My parents forced me to take her back to the lake and, after much protest, I grudgingly obeyed. The next morning, when I ran down to check on her, I found her on the frozen shore with a halo of red snow around her head. The neighborhood gang of rogue boys had found her before I did.

"It's all your fault!" I yelled that evening as my mom hurried around the kitchen preparing dinner. "You're the one who's making all my animals die."

"Don't you talk to your mother that way," my father called from the living room. A moment later he appeared in the doorway to the kitchen. "You apologize right now."

"You keep sending them away and making them die!"

"That's it. Out you go," my father said, and he grabbed my arm and ushered me out the back door and locked it after me.

It was freezing outside and nearly dark.

"You'll see," I shouted at the locked door, my breath making white puffs in the air. "When I grow up I'll have a huge place full of animals and I'll show the world how beautiful they are!" I would heal all their hurts and they would heal mine, and anyone who was lonely could come be with us and be healed too.

Bursting with anger and tears, I ran around to the side of the house, where the big sliding glass window glowed orange with the warmth inside. I could see my dad laughing with my mom, then my little brothers running into the dining room and sitting at the table. *I hate them,* I thought. *I hate my family.* I bent down and pushed the icy snow aside until I found a rock small enough to fit in my hand but heavy enough to break glass. I lifted the rock up and took aim, but then something stopped me. And that something was this thought: *They're not worth it.*

I dropped my hand and the rock fell back into the snow. Those people inside were a family I lived with, but clearly I was not a part of them. I was not a part of the orange, warm glow. I was not a part of the laughter and joy. I was alone, on the outside looking in, and I would need to figure out how to live this life without their love.

———

I made a decision when I was eleven that proved to my parents yet again what an odd child I was, and it pushed me even further from the center of my family's warmth. I came home one day from school very upset. There had been a chicken at school who had sat trembling in a cat carrier in the corner of the room as the screaming kids ran around playing. I knelt down next to the carrier and glanced around, hoping the teachers wouldn't mind, then I gently brought the terrified chicken out and cradled her in my lap. "It's OK, girl. You're all right." As I petted her and told her how beautiful she was and reassured her that she was safe, she finally began to settle down.

But soon the principal came in shouting, "Don't pet that chicken!" She ran over to me and whisked the hen out of my arms. "We've got to get it to the slaughterhouse." She stuffed the chicken back in the cat carrier and rushed out of the room with her. In that moment my whole world changed, for I suddenly understood that it wasn't a coincidence that *chicken and rice* had the same word in it as *chicken that clucks*.

At dinner that night, still upset, I announced my decision. "I'm not going to eat animals anymore."

"OK, dear," my mom said. "Now, please eat your chicken soup. It's getting cold."

"Didn't you just hear me? I'm not going to eat the chicken soup. I don't want to eat animals anymore."

"It's not an animal. It's soup," my dad said, and my brothers started giggling.

"It *was* an animal, and I'm not eating them anymore."

My mom sighed. "Fine. But I'm not going to make you anything special."

"OK," I said. I would make do with pasta and lettuce.

After a couple of weeks, my parents realized I was actually serious about this, and they started panicking. "You're not going to get enough protein," they said. "You're going to get sick, and you're not going to grow."

If being short was the price to pay for not eating my friends, so be it.

———

When I was fourteen—still not eating meat and getting quite tall—my dad announced we were moving to California. He'd gotten a prestigious job in Los Angeles, and we were moving in the middle of the school year. Simon, our beloved family dog, would come with us. But my parents tried to convince me that my blue parakeet, Puff—who'd become my closest friend alongside Simon—should not make the trip.

"A bird can't go on an airplane," my dad said.

"Yes, she can. I asked the vet." And I brought out the cardboard carrying case I'd gotten as evidence.

Both my parents tried to talk "sense" into me, but I was having none of their "logic."

I looked each of them in the eye and said, simply: "If she's not going, I'm not going."

Apparently I'd become a force to be reckoned with, because they both finally gave in. Puff would make the trip with us.

On the day of our departure, the whole family sat in the huge, noisy airport dressed in our travel clothes and looking like we were going to temple. Our carry-ons and packages took up a whole bank of benches, but I kept the box that held my parakeet carefully balanced on my knees, and I spoke softly through the air holes, reassuring Puff that there was nothing to be afraid of. People were racing every which way, and the loudspeaker was going off every two minutes, yet I could barely make out what the scratchy voice was saying. After one such announcement my dad said, "That's us," and he and my mom jumped up and started gathering our bags and packages and reining in my brothers. As I stood up, I saw a blue blur fly in front of my face, and my stomach sank. I weighed the box in my hands, and it felt very light. Then I saw the hole in the side of the carrier. Puff had chewed her way out.

"Come on, Ellie," my mom said. "They called our plane."

"I can't," I said, and held out the empty box. "Puff is gone."

"Oh, Ellie, she'll be fine."

I looked up at the high ceiling of this enormous, crowded airport, and I burst into tears. "I have to find my parakeet!"

My dad stopped and circled back to us. "What's going on? We're going to miss our plane."

"I'm not going without Puff," I said.

"Puff?" my dad said, as though he'd never heard the name before.

"My parakeet flew away."

"It's a bird," my dad said. "It'll be fine. Let's just go now."

"No!" I yelled, and I started sobbing uncontrollably. "We have to find Puff. I'm not leaving her."

At this point, a man who worked at the airport came up and asked what the trouble was. I explained as best I could through my tears, and the man ran off, then reappeared a moment later with a long ladder.

"I think she went that way," I said, and the man headed toward the far wall with the ladder, and I ran after him across the airport.

I spotted Puff on the ledge just below the ceiling, and the man set up the ladder and extended it to its full length. By now a small crowd had gathered around us and watched as the man climbed up the ladder.

"This is absurd," my father said.

The man climbed right up to where Puff was perched and reached toward her. But millimeters from his grasp, she let out a small squawk and flew off along the high ceiling in the opposite direction.

The man took down the ladder, and off we flew after her, with my parents trailing us, yelling, "Forget the bird! We're going to miss our plane," and me screaming that I wouldn't leave without her. And now the crowd was running after us too and calling, "Let her keep the bird!"

At the opposite side of the airport, the man again extended the ladder up to the ledge below the ceiling, and as he got close to her, I held my breath, and there was a hush in the crowd, like everyone was reaching with him toward my parakeet. Even my parents had stopped yelling for a minute.

But again, Puff escaped his grasp and flew back toward the opposite wall, chirping and squawking along the high ceiling.

Down the ladder came, and off we all ran across the airport, the man and me and my parents and my brothers and the crowd. And one more time, up went the ladder and up went the man, and again a moment of hush.

"Puff," I said quietly, and I closed my eyes, almost like I was praying, "please, please let this nice man bring you back to me."

As he reached toward my parakeet, she extended her wings, but then she folded them back in. And the man closed his hand around her.

He climbed down the ladder, parakeet in hand, and the crowd applauded. We put Puff back into the box and taped over the hole. "Thank you so much," I said, and I hugged the man. "Thank you for saving my bird."

My mom grabbed my arm, and off we ran, this time toward the plane.

Disheveled and out of breath, we boarded the plane at the last possible instant. But Puff was with me, and she made the move with us to California.

Puff and Simon and the countless other animals who passed through my life helped me get through the social inferno of high school. It was a religious all-girls school within a tight-knit Jewish community, and I was the new kid in the middle of ninth grade. Not only was I an outsider to this community, but I was an alien to this faith. I had never understood the god my parents prayed to, never understood how standing and sitting in temple and swearing to obey narrow, rigid rules connected us to something bigger. The only thing that connected me to something outside my humanness was the warm, honey-hay scent of a horse's breath or a blue iris poking up through the snow in spring or a field full of butterflies.

My feelings about God and religion were sealed one Saturday during that first year in Los Angeles. I was walking with my mother to temple, and a dark fluttering drew my eye to the gutter. On the pavement a pigeon was flapping, lopsided and frantic. When I picked her up, my mother said, "Ellie, put it down. You don't know where it's been."

"But she's been hit by a car," I said. "We have to get her to a doctor." The vet was nearby and I thought the pigeon just might make it if we took her straight there.

"We have no time to take it to the vet," my mother said. "We'll be late for temple."

My mother's words didn't compute. Wasn't the purpose of temple to help us be good people? Why would I go sit in a building to learn to be good when the opportunity to be good was right here in my hands? "Wouldn't God want us to help this hurt bird first?"

"No," my mother said. "Put that bird down and let's go."

"No," I said, and I planted my feet on the sidewalk. My mother stormed off to temple to learn to be good without me, and I walked with the pigeon to the vet. The poor bird was in horrible shape and didn't make it, but I could live with myself for the decision I'd made.

After that I found as many excuses as I could on Saturdays—sore throats, menstrual cramps, whatever I could think up—and went to temple only when my mom called my bluff.

Those first couple of years in Los Angeles, I spent most of my free time isolated in my room. I'd get home and Puff would fly to me and climb all over my head and give me parakeet kisses, and the awkwardness and angst of my day would be lifted. But all lives eventually come to an end, and the life spans of small animals tend to match the size of their bodies. Two years after our arrival in Los Angeles, Puff died, and I was inconsolable. I couldn't stop crying, even at school. All day, one girl after another asked what was wrong. Some instinct kept me silent. "I'm fine" is all I would say, but they could see I wasn't fine. Their questions finally wore me down and by the end of the day, I revealed the source of my pain.

"Puff passed away," I said.

"Who's Puff?"

I hesitated before saying, "My parakeet."

As soon as I'd said it, I was flooded with regret. The girls exploded in laughter, and as I watched them double over in delight at my expense, some door inside me slammed shut. I got it like a punch in the stomach: I couldn't talk about animals—not at all. If I did, I'd keep being seen as a freak.

So I packed my special bond with animals away deep inside me and sealed it tight. From now on, I vowed, I would keep those two worlds separate. My animals were my secret. Other humans didn't have to know.

I applied myself to my new task of creating a normal life and a normal personality for myself, where I spent more time with my own species. I never stopped finding a deep comfort and peace with animals and was never without a pet—or two or three—but I thought the only way I could survive would be if the four-leggeds stopped being the sole center of my world. What rushed in to share that space was boys, or rather the attention I got from them. In high school I seemed suddenly to become visible to the opposite sex, or was it perhaps that they had become visible to me? Everywhere I went I noticed boys noticing me—on my walk home from school; at Saturday services, where the boys were not supposed to be noticing girls but they always did; and at the beach, where I fled when I began ditching school. I even had a partner in crime, my classmate Liza. The two of us would sneak out of the dank, dark school that shared a basement with cockroaches and teachers who wore wigs and skirts down to the floor, and we'd hop on a bus headed west. The moment the brakes released and the bus was rumbling toward the ocean, I was free. Free of the false beliefs that were crammed down our throats, free of rules and regulations that did not allow someone to turn on a light or even rescue a dog from a burning building on the Sabbath, free of the box I was much too big to fit in.

Liza and I would hike up our skirts and descend from the bus at the boardwalk. Venice Beach was a smorgasbord of male attention—in every flavor, color, and culture—and it was delicious, especially for someone as emotionally starving as I was. After the beach, we'd head to the mall and add to our secret wardrobes of short skirts and blouses that showed cleavage. On Saturday night I'd change at Liza's house and we'd sneak out to the Comedy Club to meet guys or down to Gladstones, where we didn't get carded on the margaritas we ordered.

It wasn't long before I turned from boys to men much older than me. They treated me better than I'd ever been treated, fawning over me as though I were an exotic princess. I was willing to give a man anything he wanted in exchange for adoration. What I wasn't yet equipped to understand was that it wasn't adoration at all. These men didn't want me, they wanted something from me. But I was so hungry for love I was willing, even eager, to take it personally.

<hr />

By the time I was twenty-two I had left my upbringing far behind in the dust. I saw my parents on Saturdays for lunch but didn't talk much about my life. I was taking acting classes (which they didn't approve of) and sleeping with whoever I wanted (which they didn't know about). My life was going to be much larger than anything they could have planned for me. I had friends and a social life and a promising career as an actress.

One day my acting teacher couldn't make it to class, and a talented actor and director named Don showed up to teach instead. Don was tall, stunningly handsome, and thirteen years my senior. He began coming around after that to watch my scenes, and a playful flirtation blossomed between us. Eventually he invited me to lunch at his house, but when I got there, there was no lunch anywhere in sight. An afternoon of kissing turned into spending all our free time together. He'd take me out with him to the theater and introduce me to all his actor friends and bring me backstage, and he even took me out of town to his beach house. I felt honored that someone so talented would choose me, and I felt safe and protected in his presence and in his arms, and I wanted to be with no one else.

But for all my newly acquired worldliness, my sheltered Orthodox upbringing kept me from understanding what was happening when, a year into our relationship, Don began acting very strange. He would say he'd call me right back and I wouldn't hear from him for a week. He'd tell me he was on his way over, but then wouldn't show up for days. I finally demanded an explanation, and he broke down in tears and confessed that he'd been fighting a drug problem. He said he wanted to quit but he didn't know how. I had no point of reference for understanding such a thing. Why couldn't he just decide to stop?

I loved Don, and I promised to stay with him and to help him. But I was puzzled by the power a substance could have over someone. In order to help, I reasoned, I needed to try his drug so I could understand his experience from the inside out. Don fought me on it, but I was like a dog with a bone and wouldn't let go.

"Fine," he finally said one day, "try it." And he reached into his pocket and pulled out his crack pipe.

It's called freebasing, and it hits your brain in a couple of seconds. And that's exactly how long it took me to become a crack addict.

When I took my first puff, my ears rang and everything stopped. The chatter in my mind evaporated. Leaving only stillness. Time replaced by a vast field of nothing. No past to overcome, no future to deal with, no self to like or dislike. Movement slowed like an underwater dive, silent explosions of euphoria in every cell of my being. The moment so full that nothing outside it existed—a lot like being covered in butterflies.

But twenty minutes later, the thoughts slammed back in. Judgments. Self-hating. *What the hell have I done? My parents. My friends. What would they think?* The noise in my head like a brick being thrown through glass. Don held out his pipe and I gratefully reached for it. I wanted that peace and stillness back more than anything I'd ever wanted. And the rest of the night went just like that—suspension in pure quiet until the noise slammed back in and I reached for the pipe—again and again until my blood was pumped so full of crack cocaine that my heart started pounding triple-time.

"Oh God, Don, I don't know what's happening." I couldn't catch my breath. "I think I'm having a heart attack."

He gently led me to the door, and we walked barefoot into the cold night. Walked and walked until my heart calmed down and I could take a full breath—an emergency room visit averted.

I wish my drug tale ended there—scared straight and back on track with my life—but it didn't. I soon was willing to do anything to have more of that feeling—the euphoria of that first puff. My life disappeared into the drug as I chased, and never quite captured, that fresh, first hit. Don and I scored in dark alleyways in the worst neighborhoods and binged for weeks at a time without sleeping or bathing or eating, until all our money was gone. Each sunrise cracking me over the head like a two-by-four with the reality of what I had done, again, which made me reach once more for relief. I stopped seeing my family altogether, I had no job, and my friends fell away one after another.

Don was the only person I talked to, and week by week he got stranger and stranger.

In the middle of the night during a binge he returned from the liquor store with a bottle of vodka. He slammed it down on the table. "You poisoned it," he said.

"What are you talking about?"

"You poisoned my vodka."

I looked at the clear liquid, still sloshing in the sealed bottle. "It's not open," I said.

Don lunged for me and threw me down on the carpet, his hands grasping my throat. He held me there, and everything began to fade to white. *Kill me,* I thought. *Please, just kill me. Release me from this insanity.* But he finally let go, and I automatically gasped for breath.

I couldn't leave. The drug cycle had sucked me deep inside it and Don and I were inextricably tied together at its center.

Each time we ran out of money, we'd be left with absolutely nothing. Even the euphoria was out of reach. All that remained was a feeling of failure and hopelessness darker than anything I'd ever known. Disgusted with myself, I'd finally swear off crack . . . for a month, or four, if I was lucky. Then we'd have a reason to celebrate—a gig landed or one left behind—and Don would hand me the pipe, and it started all over again.

After running this cycle over and over for three years, I found myself alone one day in the apartment at the end of a binge. At ninety pounds, my hair greasy and matted, I was crawling around the floor searching for crumbs of the drug in the carpet. In that dim room—the blinds drawn at noon—I abruptly stopped and sat up.

"Oh—my—God," I said out loud. "What are you doing?"

It was suddenly so clear. I was not a *middle* kind of person. I had always been sort of an extremist. And yet, this was not *life* and this was not *death*. It was in the *middle*.

"You can't stay in the middle, girl," I told myself, "so why don't you just end it?" And I crawled into the corner of the room and sat hunched against the wall, where I could see out over all that remained of my world, and from there I began planning my exit.

I thought long and hard and considered all the possible ways I might end it. But after a couple of hours of scheming and plotting the perfect exit strategy, there was an opening through which a thought was born: *In the spectrum of life–middle–death, there isn't only one extreme; there are two.*

My ancestors were not middle kind of people either. Some of them had been lined up along a European river by the Nazis and shot dead just for being Jewish; others had been orphaned by tuberculosis and had sung in the streets of London for money. And yet out of that dark soil, new lives had grown and blossomed. My orphaned grandfather had grown up to lead the Jewish brigade to free people from the concentration camps, then went on to become the chief rabbi of South Africa. An entire nation of Jews traveled miles just to seek his advice. That was not a middle kind of life. Neither was my father's. Despite a terrible childhood, he'd grown up to be the top cardiac surgeon in the world.

And you, I thought to myself, *you're going to do crack for three years and then kill yourself? What a pathetic attempt at being an extremist. Look at your ancestors! Look what you've descended from.*

What might I become if I chose life? Really *chose* it?

What a shock this was. I'd spent my whole life hating myself, hating life, wanting to be numb, wanting out, and here I was at a moment when I could slip easily out life's back door, and I wanted to live? But how on earth was I supposed to do that? I couldn't even remember how to live. I sat there for a long while absorbing and integrating this unexpected twist.

Eventually I got myself up off the floor and went into the bathroom to brush my teeth and take a shower. I combed the snarls out of my hair and then ate a good meal, the first in a very long time. Then I found the closest Narcotics Anonymous meeting and broke up with Don. I moved to an apartment on the other side of town and began the slow, painful climb out of addiction.

It would be nearly twenty years before I would come to understand that what had gotten me up off the floor that day was not just me on my own making a decision to give life another shot. I'd been caught in a powerful undertow, and the strength it took to reverse that tide could not possibly have come from my small, misguided self. No. I was not alone in the room that day. That room was packed with my ancestors and guides and spirits come to lift me up. To lead me away from the abyss and set me right on my path so I could do what I had come here to do.

I spent that first year off crack at the edge of *impossible*. Every moment of every day brought the craving for the drug, a physiological desire now as innate as thirst or hunger or the need to sleep. I had to meticulously plan every day, where I would go, who I would see, who I would not see. Craving was worse by association: a location, the quality of light, the air temperature, certain types of people. For the first three months I went to an NA meeting every single day. Then I found a therapist. And even with all this support, that deep desire for escape— either in a puff of silver-white smoke or by death—never once left me, and never would, not entirely. But something had shifted in me that day on the floor, that moment when I'd gotten up off the carpet and chosen to bathe rather than to die. That moment had changed me on a cellular level and was silently guiding me back to life, always back to life.

I enrolled in college and signed up for every psychology course I could find. If the world thought it too strange to make a life of helping animals, I would help people. I started seeing my parents again on Saturdays, and they helped me out financially. I got a dog to keep me company while I studied, and we visited the dog park daily. There I met professional dog walkers who made their living playing with dogs. It felt like the perfect side stream of income while I went to school. Before long, I had a pickup truck with a camper shell, business cards, and a handful of clients. Soon I expanded from merely walking dogs to grooming and training as well, and then I moved to a larger place so I could board dogs too.

But before I had even walked my first dog, I knew in my heart that this new business would not be an end but a means. The profits would be redirected toward another endeavor: rescuing animals from the pound. On some level of my being, I knew that was what I had to do if I wanted to keep choosing life.

With the cash from my first substantial paycheck in hand, I headed to the animal shelter with my heart racing, knowing that a whole new chapter of my life was about to unfold. Standing at the front desk, I could hear the barking echoing off the walls back in the kennels. It sounded like there were hundreds of dogs back there. This was not the solid, full-bodied bark of a dog behind the door of his house warning you not to trespass. This was a chorus of yelping with a high-pitched edge, the kind that said, "Oh please, oh please, help me leave this place." I took a deep breath and walked through the door to the kennels, and an odor unlike no other flooded over me—the sour smell of pee on cement. Everything in this place was concrete and metal. No soft edges. When the dogs saw me, their yelps turned to whining and howling and many of them jumped up against the cage doors, sticking their paws out between the bars as I passed. Cage after cage of canines imprisoned for doing no wrong. I walked up one side, looking in at each and every dog, trying not to let the smell and sight of the filthy kennels overwhelm me. But halfway down the other side I burst into tears. Every dog was whining and begging and pleading to be chosen. How on earth would I make such a choice? If I took only one, would I be choosing the one who got to live or would I be choosing the thirty who would die? Maybe I'd underestimated what it took to be a rescuer. Maybe I wasn't cut out to do this after all. I closed my eyes and tried to pull it together and found myself praying to some unknown force. *Please, please help me. Show me who I'm supposed to take home, because I can't make this decision by myself.* When I opened my eyes I saw that a big, black dog to my right was not alone in her kennel as I'd thought. She was partially hiding a litter of puppies—perhaps a week or two old and squirming on the concrete to get closer to her warmth. I hadn't expected to see such young puppies at the shelter.

This mama dog was trying her best to look after her babies, but she was trembling and whimpering and hunched against the back of her kennel.

I wiped at my tears before I approached the warden.

"Can you tell me about that black Lab mother and her puppies?"

"They're being put down today," he said matter-of-factly.

"All of them?"

"Uh-huh."

"But they're just babies."

"Well, no one's adopting them. We need to make space. That one family is taking up a whole kennel. There could be five adult dogs in there."

It turned out the mother had been confiscated from a man brought up on animal cruelty charges. He'd been running a puppy mill, keeping this dog in a cage to have litter after litter. She had given birth to this last set there at the shelter.

"Well, that's who I'm taking home," I said.

"So you want the mother, then?"

"And her puppies. I want all of them."

I pulled my pickup around to the back door, and the shelter workers loaded the mom and her seven puppies into the truck bed.

As I was driving home I realized I was trembling. It wasn't fear, and it wasn't exactly excitement. It was more like a flood of life force bigger than I could contain, a powerful sense of purpose and drive pumping through my body. This was what I was supposed to be doing, and now no one could stop me. No one would get rid of the animals I brought home. No one would interfere with my efforts to nurse them back to health. And I no longer cared if anyone laughed at me. It was a matter of life and death—my own life and death.

On that drive back from the pound, I got my first glimpse in a very long time of who Ellie was, and who Ellie was meant to be.

CHAPTER 2

I decided on the name Rover Rescue, and for the first four years I wore every hat there was to wear—rescuer, rehabilitator, fund-raiser, and director of adoptions. I went regularly to the local animal shelter and chose the saddest, sickest, most scared dogs and cats and brought them home to heal them physically and emotionally, with the goal of placing them in a loving home. Each time I went to the pound I relied on the same inner guidance that had helped me with my very first rescue— the black Lab mama I'd ended up naming China. That guidance was something like the inner whispers that had connected me to the natural world as a child, and I was grateful to feel it rising up in me again.

After that first rescue, I had made a pact with the universe. *If you keep guiding me, if you keep showing me who to rescue, I'll keep doing this work.* Each time I visited the pound, I'd silently say, *OK, show me which one.* And every time, something drew me to the dog or cat who was supposed to come home with me that day. One time the guidance had even told me not to go inside the shelter at all, so I'd waited just outside the front door, and five minutes later a couple had shown up with the sweetest toy poodle who was going to be put down just for being old.

Most rescuers took only the young dogs with no health or behavioral problems because they were the easiest to adopt out, and the supervisor at the shelter tried again and again to convince me that was the only route to being a responsible rescuer.

"You're giving valuable time to these old, unplaceable animals," he'd said more than once. "You're not going to be able to rehabilitate them. Then you're going to be stuck with them." But who was I to say no to the universe? I kept being guided to the animals no one else would ever choose. I knew that without me they had no chance at all.

The spirit that guided me didn't abandon me after the rescue itself. It led me every step of the way until the animal was placed in a new home. One eleven-year-old German shepherd had been brought to the pound by her elderly owner, who was going in for an open-heart surgery she thought she might not survive. As an older, owner-surrendered dog, the shepherd was first in line to be euthanized.

"She's not up for adoption," the shelter supervisor said when I asked to take her home.

But the dog was a sweet, gentle soul and had no health problems. "I know I can find her a home," I insisted.

The supervisor would not budge. "I don't want you using your resources on an old dog."

Now he'd overstepped the line. "How I use my resources is none of your concern. That's my job, not yours." I fixed my gaze on him. "How can you euthanize a dog when someone is standing right in front of you wanting to give that animal a home?"

He said nothing, but his jaw was clenched and his feet were planted firm.

I sat down in front of the shepherd's cage and said, "I intend to sit right here until you give me this dog."

He walked away but came back every fifteen minutes to check whether the stubborn rescuer was still sitting on the concrete floor. And sure enough, I was. Finally he returned with some papers and a pen. "You can't have the dog unless you sign a waiver."

"Sure," I said, reaching for the pen. "I'm happy to sign any paperwork you need."

At my next dog adoption day, which I held the following weekend at a pet store, the end of the day arrived and the German shepherd had not been adopted. As I started packing up, a fit woman in her sixties approached me and told me she'd really like a dog as a companion. Her husband had died, and she had lots of time and no one to share it with. She walked a lot, but was worried she wouldn't be able to keep up with a young dog.

My eyes filled with tears, and a smile broke out across my face. "I have your friend right here," I said, and led her to the German shepherd. The two made an instant connection; the shepherd was adopted less than a week after I'd pulled her from the pound.

I loved this work and was good at it, and perhaps the part I excelled at most was this final phase—placing an animal in a loving home. I had a knack for making successful matches. Of the five hundred animals I would ultimately place in new homes, I had only five of them returned—an extremely low number for a rescue operation.

Most of the dogs and cats I pulled were in bad shape and required extensive rehabilitation. This started with healing the animal's body, and I saw every type of disease and injury imaginable, the saddest being those inflicted by abusive owners. If the animal was sick, we'd start off with a vet visit, and then I'd take it from there with daily medicine, supplements, fluids, and wound flushing. Knowing I had a small nonprofit, the vets patiently taught me all I needed to know in order to carry out home treatments and keep my visits—and my costs—to a minimum. Once the dog's or cat's body was healed, the longer, more challenging process of emotional healing began.

The most important part of the rehabilitation process was listening to what an animal told me. If a dog was terrified 24/7, he was telling me that the abuse had been erratic, coming at him from unexpected sources or for no apparent reason. If a dog gets yelled at and sent outside for peeing on the floor, he learns not to pee in the house. But if he gets yelled at, hit, or kicked as a result of someone's unpredictable anger and abuse, the dog learns to fear every human all of the time.

One small terrier was so petrified of people when I first met her at the shelter, her body shook so hard she was practically convulsing. When I arrived home with her, I opened the back of my camper truck, and she was sitting with her nose in the far corner, her body quaking violently. I climbed slowly into the truck bed and shut the door, sitting as far from her as possible with my back toward her. I knew this was a one-shot deal. If I didn't win her trust before I took her in the house, she'd escape under a couch or a bed and remain a feral shadow from there on out. I wasn't going to let that happen, and I was willing to sit out there for as long as it took. I followed my instincts and this dog's cues every step of the way. I began inching toward her at a glacial pace, my back to her the entire time, never daring to look at her or even to turn around, so as not to convey dominance or any kind of threat. Forty-five minutes later, I finally was within arm's distance of her. Listening not only with my ears but with my whole body so I could sense any signs of increased distress, I reached slowly behind me and touched her, then very gently stroked her wiry fur. For the next hour, I did just that; I pet this shaking dog with my back turned. Finally, when I was sure she wasn't going to feel trapped or try to bite me, I gently brought her around and held her loosely in my lap. With my face turned away, I stroked her and quietly told her all about the second chance at life that lay before her. "I'm never going to give up on you," I said to her. "I want to be your safety and your warmth. I'm going to love you day and night." After an hour of cradling her and talking to her, I finally felt her body begin to relax, and I was able for the first time to look at her. Eventually she even dared to steal glances at me. Four hours after pulling up in front of my home, I knew I'd won her trust and brought her inside to begin our next three years of rehabilitative work.

The longer a rehabilitation took, the harder it was for me to give an animal up. It was clear that first day that this little terrier was going to stay with me indefinitely. So I named her Rover after my nonprofit and gave her the job of mascot.

Every time I rescued a dog or cat, every time I proved to her that she could trust me, I felt one more small corner of my lonely childhood mending.

For the first couple of years, almost all of the funding for Rover Rescue came from my business of walking, training, grooming, and boarding dogs. I also charged an adoption fee when a new family took in a dog or cat, and that helped cover some of the vet costs. My dad had helped me buy a house a year and a half into my rescuing career when I'd convinced him that to properly run both a business and a nonprofit I had to have a place of my own with a large backyard. It was a beautiful little half-acre in Tarzana, which is part of the San Fernando Valley in Southern California. This corner of the Valley was a crazy quilt of new tract housing with swimming pools and tennis courts, side by side with barns and stables behind old ranch houses, and it was still agriculturally zoned. My place had a small grassy backyard, and beyond that a large dirt barnyard and the original barn. There was a variety of fruit and nut trees as well as fruitless mulberry trees that canvassed the yard in dappled light. The barnyard gave the dogs plenty of room to roam between walks and dog-park runs.

But even with all this space, it was tricky business housing rescues and boarders on one property. To make sure all the animals stayed healthy, I had to keep newly rescued dogs or cats in quarantine in one of the bedrooms until the vet had cleared them of infectious disease. Rescued pregnant dogs were given a room to themselves to give birth and nurse their pups. Litters with parvo had yet another room. And all the animals had to be inside for the night—which meant that even my own bedroom was brimming with dogs and cats.

This was the environment I lived in when I met Scott at the dog park.

I had just gotten all the dogs into my truck after a good romp in the park, and I noticed two big dogs in the back of a Jeep parked next to me. They were staring at me in the most intense way, and I felt a deep pull to go say hello to them. As I was petting them, the driver hopped out and watched me for a moment.

"They're beautiful," I said.

"Thanks," he said. "They're a Lab-ridgeback mix." Then he stuck out his hand. "I'm Scott."

After that we saw each other often at the dog park and talked while our dogs sped around the grounds, kicking up wood chips and vying for tennis balls.

Finally one day he asked me out to dinner.

"Sorry," I said. "Thank you, but I've got a litter of puppies with parvo at home. I can't leave for longer than a half hour." I had rescued eight puppies with the dreaded parvovirus—referred to in the dog community as "the P word." Parvo spreads like wildfire. Although adult dogs have a halfway decent survival rate, when it comes to puppies, more often than not the virus wins. But I'd discovered that if you could keep the puppies hydrated with subcutaneous fluids, they had a better chance of making it. If the litter was large, by the time I finished treating the last of the puppies, I had no more than thirty minutes before I had to start all over again with the first dog.

"Well," Scott said, "how about if I come over and sit with you while you take care of them?"

This got my attention. A man who was willing to sit in a sick-puppy room while I gave injections? "OK," I said, "if you want to. Sure."

I didn't expect him to stick around long. I worked hard to keep my place clean, jumping up every time a puppy had an accident as well as cleaning the yard and hosing down the patio twice every day. But I knew how most people felt about animals. One or two pets was acceptable, perhaps even quaint. Five, ten, twenty animals was considered an obsession and planted you firmly in the category of freak—eccentric, at best. I had finally allowed animals to take their proper place in the center of my life, where they ruled my schedule and delineated my lifestyle. If that made me eccentric, then so be it. But there were no movies or dinner dates for me.

My tight treatment schedule, together with the practicality of wearing something that could get peed on, didn't allow for a change out of my fur-covered sweatshirt before Scott showed up. Besides, I figured he would only last an hour, two at most. It never occurred to me that he might stick around solely because he liked who I was. I believed I had to work hard to win a man's attention; I had to be witty, charming, or at the very least wear a miniskirt. And I didn't have the time, setting, or frame of mind to do any of these. But at three in the morning, after hours of talking with me, watching me take care of sick puppies, and even holding them while I gave injections, Scott stood on the front porch and said, "That was fun."

Yeah right, I thought. *He's probably thinking, "That was the strangest date I've ever had."*

But two days later, he came back for a second round. And this time he asked me to show him how to give the fluid injections. And with that, he pretty much stole my heart.

———

Within a year, Scott and I were married, and I was amazed at how unflappable he was at the center of the four-legged whirlwind that filled our life. My favorite time of the day was when he'd come home from work and together we'd take all the dogs out for a walk and tell each other about our day. On weekends he'd even help me with the pet adoptions that we held at local pet stores and malls, where we brought the dogs and cats who were healthy and ready for a new home. I felt like the luckiest animal-rescuing woman in the world to have found such a man.

My parents were another story. They didn't understand why I didn't give up my activities with animals now that I had a husband to support me. My parents were divorced by this point, but they were a unified front in their opinions about my life. "You've got to be more attentive to your husband," my mom would say. Sometimes my dad would ask why I didn't just volunteer a couple of days a week instead of having my own nonprofit . . . now that I was married. Although my parents had come back into my life when I'd gotten off crack, my relationship with them was no less complex than it had always been. I knew they loved me, in their own crazy way, and I'd appreciated their financial support when I'd needed it. But after all these years, they still had no clue who I was or what made me tick. When they gave me advice, it was as though they were talking not to me but to some role they'd been waiting all these years for me to step into. The good, compliant daughter role. The has-none-of-her-own-opinions role. But that was not—and neither could it ever be—me. And I still responded, deep inside, in knee-jerk rebellion to any advice they offered. That said, they were still my parents and I'd still been raised in a rule-laden tradition where children obeyed their elders. What they said mattered a lot more than I wanted it to.

I got that they wanted me to live a normal life and act like a normal person. And it's not like I'd never wanted that for myself. But I'd pushed animals out of the center of my world and had ended up on the floor in the corner of a room plotting my own demise. What my parents couldn't understand was that Rover Rescue was not just some crazy hobby I'd picked up. It was my lifeline. And dropping my lifeline would have grave consequences, not only for me but for everyone in my life. In the end, it didn't matter how much they thought I should be normal. I needed—for my very survival—not to be.

Until I got pregnant.

The moment I found out a new little life was growing inside me, my awareness pulled inward, and my life force settled down—literally down, as though rooting me to the ground—and all I wanted to do was nest. Just as a mama bird weaves bits of foliage or wool into her nest to make a soft landing for the eggs and insulation for the naked pink hatchlings, I wanted to create a home environment suitable for receiving a vulnerable new life. Having a house overrun with sick and recovering animals did not seem a suitable environment for my baby. My baby would be my new focus, my new sense of purpose, my reason to stick around on the planet and stay clean. I was going to create the most beautiful life for this new human being, and to do that I intended to stay home and enjoy the fact that my husband made a good enough living for me to be a full-time mother.

From this new vantage point, I slowly began to admit to myself that my rescue operation had begun to go just a bit awry. Perhaps the rescuing itself had become sort of an addiction; it had grown more and more difficult for me to adopt the animals out. I knew a long rehabilitation period could result in my getting attached, but I'd begun to get a little too attached even when rehab took only weeks. No matter the length of time, I'd pour my heart into bringing the animals around, convincing them they could trust me. What kind of message was I giving them when I then turned around and abandoned them to someone else? Since my MO always was to rescue animals no one else wanted—sick, mangy, toothless, and terrified—they were not immediately placeable even if I could bring myself to give them up. The result: a growing pack of dogs in every room of my house and a cat on every chair. A rescuer has a moving stream of animals, equal parts ebb and flow. An animal hoarder's flow gets backlogged, with an ever-growing collection of animals. After more than four years of successfully rescuing and placing dogs and cats, I was beginning to move a little too close to that line between rescuer and hoarder.

With my new sense of purpose leading me belly-first into the world, I did something I couldn't even have imagined doing just a couple of months earlier: I shut down Rover Rescue and vowed to bring in no more animals. It felt a lot like cutting off one of my limbs. But I was determined to create normalcy for my child, so I bit the bullet and adopted out all but eight of the dogs—not a large number to keep when you've been living with two dozen. Among the eight I kept were the little terrier, Rover, and China, the mama black Lab who'd been my first rescue. Because most of the cats were not the cuddly kind or were too old to be placed or had positive test results for feline HIV, twenty cats remained with us.

I turned my attention toward preparing for the baby's arrival. I transformed one of the freed-up rooms into a nursery and filled it with all the baby furniture I was sure I would need. And once the last of the adoptions had taken place, I had my weekends wide open to spend with my husband, affirming our bond before our baby's arrival.

⸻

Nine months of nesting, seventeen hours of labor, and a C-section later, we welcomed our beautiful baby boy, Jesse, into the world. When I looked for the first time into his little face, I knew I was looking at a piece of my own soul. We belonged to each other inextricably. And my whole being was flooded with a love unlike anything I had ever felt.

Over the next days and weeks, I could not take my eyes off my gorgeous, perfect baby. I cooed over him and watched him sleep, his eyes darting under his tiny eyelids. And just when I thought I'd felt as much love as a person could tolerate, Jesse would make some new sound or facial expression, and my heart would swell till I thought it might explode. I was terrified of something happening to him, because I knew if it did, I wouldn't be able to go on living. So I put every ounce of my being into nurturing and protecting him and attending to his every need.

Of course, I still had a menagerie of animals who also had needs. It wasn't easy juggling their needs with Jesse's, and because of Scott's long work hours, much of the time I was alone to manage it all. Inevitably, when I went to feed the animals, Jesse would cry. And when I went to calm Jesse, one of the dogs would barf or pee on the floor. Just taking the dogs out for a walk became a feat of maneuvering. I'd designed two special leashes so that I could walk up to eight dogs at a time: each leash had one handle but split into four sub-leashes. I thought it was pretty brilliant . . . except that by the time I'd gotten the fourth dog clipped onto one of my elaborate leashes, the other three dogs were already tangled up. And by the time I'd clipped the second set of four dogs onto the other leash, the whole thing looked more like an intricate spiderweb than a dog-walking system. Add to this picture a crying baby harnessed onto me in a sling; this is what we looked like when we went out into the neighborhood daily.

I had a new understanding of why most rescuers didn't have children, and why most parents weren't rescuers. Every day spent with my beautiful new son, I was further reassured that I'd made the right decision in shutting down my rescue operation.

While *I* had pulled inward in response to the new little being in our home, wanting to spend every available moment watching our son, Scott had the opposite—and very male—response of turning into an "über-provider." In his effort to protect and provide for our baby he took on extra jobs, adding to his already long workdays and even working some weekends. He came home at night absolutely spent and had no desire to participate in our nightly ritual of walking the dogs. I understood that he was exhausted working to provide for us, but I missed him on the nightly dog walks. The world of animals that we had shared was now mine alone, and I felt more and more abandoned to deal with the needs of all of these beings—human and animal—on my own. Scott, in turn, started to feel annoyed by my constant requests that he join me in dog duties when he was so tired. And before Jesse was three months old, a distance began growing between Scott and me—a gap that would prove difficult to bridge.

As Jesse grew, I saw that he was a particularly strong little boy, climbing and pulling himself up onto chairs before he could even walk. He started walking early, at ten months, and soon he was strutting around the house or yard with his tummy sticking out, shoulders back, and a look of determination on his face. *The world is my oyster. Ready or not, here I come.* He would gather up sticks and rocks all over the yard and make little piles of his booty. He would climb into or on top of anything that stood still, occasionally including the dogs. And he'd always try to help out with whatever tasks I was trying to accomplish. When Jesse was nearly a year old, I took several days to dismantle a low brick wall that surrounded the patio. The first day, Jesse watched for a while from the baby carrier on my back, then he demanded to be put down. Once on his feet, he picked up a brick with his pudgy but very strong little arms and carried it to the small garden-wheelbarrow I was using to cart the bricks to a stack behind the barn. He half-lifted, half-pushed the brick up into the wheelbarrow. Then he went back for more. The bricks and the wheelbarrow became his favorite new toys. As soon as we went out into the yard in the morning, he would squirm until I set him down, and he'd strut to the empty wheelbarrow and climb in, waiting for his favorite game to begin. The game consisted of me pushing the wheelbarrow as fast as I could around the barnyard as Jesse squealed in delight, his dog "siblings" chasing alongside. The game ended when I began huffing and puffing and could push the wheelbarrow no farther, at which point Jesse climbed out and went in search of bricks.

I loved watching him explore and learn about his environment, but the more he began to individuate from me—starting to communicate what he liked and didn't like and wanting to walk more than to be carried—the more I grew restless. When he'd been a tiny baby, his helplessness had made me feel so absolutely necessary to his survival. A lioness prepared to lay down my own life to protect him. Once he started becoming his own little person, with such an air of independence, I started feeling an old familiar tug, the same tug I'd always felt once a rescued dog was happy and well adjusted. *Mission accomplished, let's go rescue another.* I couldn't just coast. I wasn't wired that way. I yearned for something to fill me with purpose, to make me feel necessary, like I wasn't just taking up space on the planet. I began daydreaming about visiting the animal shelter, just to see who was there.

Yet an equally strong pull was keeping me away from the pound. I finally, for the first time ever, was having a normal life. Sure, I still had a bunch of dogs and cats, but they were no longer the driving force. Having and raising a child had thrown me into the midst of ordinary women who were married and raising families. I hung out with other mothers when I took Jesse to the park, and I played with the dogs at the dog park and did projects in the yard with Jesse on my hip or playing nearby. I was amazed I'd been able to be normal for this long, while still in one piece, and I was determined to stay on track. So I tried as best I could to rein in these feelings of restlessness and stuff them deep in a box at the back of my heart.

It was right around this time, when Jesse was a year old and I was fighting to protect my new normalcy, that I was running an errand one morning with Jesse and saw something I'd never seen before. We were driving across the sprawling San Fernando Valley, which is flat and stretches to the ends of the earth in a monotonous grid of tract housing and strip malls. The orange orchards and farmland that had once filled this basin had left behind only vestiges, a stand of orange trees here, a scrap of field there. The Valley could be baking hot in the middle of winter, and this was one of those days, so the windows of the car were rolled down in an effort to stir up some semblance of a breeze. At one point as we drove along I began to smell something foul, like fertilizer but much worse. Then I saw a stretch of chain-link fence that spanned an entire city block, and behind the fence was an odd assortment of old wood sheds. I slowed, and the stench filled the entire car. Then I saw the animals. Goats, sheep, pigs, chickens, ducks, as well as a circle of ponies attached to a red metal carousel. The place was crammed with animals.

I told myself to just keep driving. I was a rescuer in recovery, and this was just the sort of thing that could knock me off my track. But I found myself pulling over to the curb. I got out and took Jesse out of his car seat and grabbed the baby sling. "We're just going to have a little look," I told him. "Then we'll be on our way."

As soon as we walked under the peeling, painted sign that said PETTING ZOO, I saw the source of the stench. There was animal excrement everywhere—not just the usual zoo poop, but days and days of accumulated excrement. The animals themselves were listless. The pigs were lying in their own feces because there was nowhere clean for them to be. Despite the heat there was no drinking water out for any of the animals, and the entire time my nostrils were filled with a stench so thick I could hardly breathe. To my amazement, tourists were everywhere, snapping pictures of their kids left and right—standing in front of a llama with horribly matted fur or petting a starving goat. Didn't these people smell the stink or recognize the suffering? Then we came to the horses, who were being beaten into giving pony rides as the kids' parents captured it on film.

I swallowed back my nausea, knowing that I was on shaky ground. I was angry at how these animals were being treated, but I also knew I couldn't take this on. I had a one-year-old and a husband and a new, normal life. I couldn't save a whole zoo full of animals.

"OK, Jess, let's go now," I said, and I picked him up and headed toward the front gate. But before I could get there, before I could put this whole sad, miserable mess of a zoo safely behind me, I saw this one particular goat.

She had a big belly—like she was about to give birth—and hooves so overgrown she could barely walk. Her legs were bowed because of those wild, curling hooves, and her coat was a filthy, matted gray. On her back leg was a tumor that was oozing pus and blood. Like all the other animals, her despondency was palpable, but this goat was different somehow. She looked me right in the eye, as though some hope still remained in her wracked little body. And with those soulful eyes she reached inside me and put a stranglehold on my heart. I could just hear her craggy, Eeyore-like voice in my head. *Oh . . . thanks for noticing me.*

At that moment I knew I was done for. I was going to be taking home a goat.

CHAPTER 3

As I headed to the front kiosk of the petting zoo, I wasn't planning or scheming or even thinking about my childhood vision of having a place where animals and people healed one another. In fact, that vision had been sealed tight and tucked away at the back of my heart time and time again and had sort of gotten stuck there. All I knew was that this goat needed help and that I needed to be the one to help her.

It's just one little goat, I told myself. *It'll be like having one more dog—nine dogs instead of eight . . . ten if she's pregnant.*

But the owner didn't see it the way I saw it. "I ain't sellin' my animals," she said in a voice rough as gravel. She was a big woman with unkempt hair and disheveled clothes, and she kept her arms crossed over her chest.

At first I'd asked if I could *have* the goat, figuring they would be happy to get rid of an animal this bad off. When the owner had re-fused, I'd offered to pay.

Jesse squirmed, and I patted his back and shifted him in his sling. "What's her name?" I asked.

The owner reluctantly revealed that this sad little creature was called Mary.

"Well," I said, and I paused a second, knowing there would be no turning back, "the problem is, I told Mary I would help her. I can't leave without her, so I'm going to stay here till you say yes." I could feel my heart pumping fast and strong, as though my whole body were fill-ing with fresh new blood, fresh new life. This was what I'd felt every time I'd found a bird fallen from her nest or taken the saddest, most broken dog home from the pound. I was being the voice for the voice-less. I was seeing this poor soul and speaking up for her. I was doing what no one else would do, what no one had ever done for me. Trem-bling with this surging life force, I knew I'd found my way back to that peculiar groove that had been carved out especially for me.

This aliveness carried me through the rest of the day as Jesse and I sat by Mary's side, with tourists taking our picture. At closing time I asked the owner again if I could have or buy the goat.

Again the woman said no.

"OK," I said. "I'll be back to see Mary in the morning."

At the crack of dawn the next day I got myself and Jesse dressed and we showed up once again at the petting zoo. We sat all day by Mary's side, petting her and talking to her and giving her water from a bottle and a bowl that I'd snuck inside in my purse.

"Where's Mary's nose?" I would ask Jesse, and he would touch her soft nose with his little fingers. "Where is your nose?" I would then ask, and he'd touch his own nose. "Where are Mary's feet?" I'd ask. We'd move on to stomach and chin and ears, and this was how our day went, with my son climbing in and out of my lap and Mary helping me teach him about himself and the world around him.

All through the day, Mary would find my eyes and lock her gaze onto mine. Those yellow goat eyes with pupils that narrow into thin, horizontal rectangles, like little mail slots for secret messages. She'd gaze at me again and again and send me tiny messages that beseeched me to please get her the hell out of there.

This went on day after day, with us showing up in the morning, sitting by Mary's side for the entire day—leaving her only to take little side trips to the other animals to keep Jesse engaged. Every evening at closing time, I'd ask again to take the goat home, and each and every evening the woman said no. Jesse would conk out in the car on the way home, and I'd put him straight to bed. Scott would return late in the evening, and I tried more than once to explain what I was up to, warning him I might be bringing home a goat. But I didn't get the sense that he believed me, even knowing what he did about my tendencies.

This zoo vigil lasted twelve days. On the thirteenth morning, the owner finally cracked. As soon as she spotted me, she practically yelled, "Fine, OK, take the goat!" and a cigarette cough shook her body. "But just get the hell out of here!"

With my heart full up to the brim, I carried Mary to my Ford Explorer with Jesse on my back. When we got home I shut the gate between the grassy yard and the barnyard, and carried Mary into the barn. All eight of my dogs lined up at the fence, yipping with tails wagging, eager to meet the new "dog."

"Sorry, guys," I told them. "Mary is very sick and very weak. She's in no shape to play with you."

I didn't know a thing about taking care of a goat, but that was a small hurdle compared to the vigil I'd just carried out. I would learn about goats the way I'd learned about dogs and cats and birds and rabbits—through intuition, and by asking lots of questions. I called around for a referral for a veterinarian who treated goats and found one who made house calls with his mobile vet truck. When he arrived, I opened my big side gate, and he drove right into the barnyard and set up shop. Dr. Geissen agreed that Mary looked pregnant, but after a thorough examination he determined otherwise.

"There are no fetuses," he said. "She's just been bred so many times, her belly has assumed that shape and stayed that way."

I was relieved; not that I would have minded baby goats, but Mary's body was in such bad shape, she needed all her energy for healing.

"Now, let's have a look at that tumor," the vet said, and he asked me to hold on to Mary so he could get a proper look.

The tumor was large and oozing and awful to look at, but it turned out to have a fairly small point of attachment to her leg. While Dr. Geissen collected his surgical gear from the truck, depositing it into large metal buckets, I waited with Mary, trying not to picture what he was about to do. For all my bravery in flushing wounds and administering subcutaneous fluids, I was actually quite squeamish. If I was the only one around, the force that drove me to help a hurting animal overrode my queasiness, but when there was a qualified professional present, I was more than happy to check out. I watched as far as the injections of anesthesia at several sites around the tumor, and then we waited about ten minutes for the area to get numb. But what the vet did next I can only guess at because I had my eyes squeezed shut, even as I kept Mary from walking away. By the time Dr. Geissen said, "OK, you can open your eyes now," there was a clean, white bandage over the area where the tumor had been. I couldn't go anywhere near the thought of what he had done with the thing once he'd removed it.

"Are there stitches?" I asked.

"Yes. I'll come back in a couple of weeks to take the sutures out. Just make sure the area stays dry." Dr. Geissen took a step back and cocked his head this way and that as he looked at Mary's feet. "Of course, you're going to have to trim those hooves."

Well, I didn't know the first thing about trimming hooves and asked if he could show me how to do it.

He went back to his truck and brought out some large clippers with a wide jaw. "These are hoof nippers," he said. "They're for horse hooves." And he explained that I wouldn't even need to get a pair of these if I kept up with trimming. Once he'd cut off the bulk of the overgrowth—a good twelve inches of twisted hoof material—he said, "Do you have wire cutters?"

Yes, I had wire cutters. He instructed me to retrieve them so he could teach me to do it with my own tools.

Dr. Geissen trimmed the first hoof. It took a while because even with me trying to hold her still, Mary fought him all the way through it. Since she'd clearly never had her hooves trimmed, she wasn't used to having her foot lifted and held and didn't like it one bit.

"The more you do this, the more she'll get used to it," he said. And sure enough, by the second leg, she was already fighting a little bit less. Dr. Geissen pointed out the different parts of Mary's foot. Goats have cloven hooves, which means the hoof is split into two halves. Looking from the bottom, each half has a teardrop-shaped toe, surrounded by hoof material, which protects the toes, just like human toenails. The toe and the surrounding toenail are both supposed to touch the ground, but Mary's toe had not touched the ground in a very long time. Her toenails had long ago grown over the toe, obscuring it completely, and then twisted out to the front, making it very difficult for her to walk. After the second hoof was trimmed, the vet let Mary amble around a bit. She tested out her new hooves, lifting one and setting it back down, then another. When we brought her back for the third foot, she was more settled—like she had approved of the test drive and was ready to have all of her feet back in contact with the earth.

Dr. Geissen handed me the wire cutters. "Your turn," he said.

I lifted Mary's leg while he held her still. Even after I'd watched him trim the first two hooves, I worked slowly, unsure where the toenail ended and the toe began. The last thing I wanted to do was cut this poor goat; she had already been to hell and back and didn't need any more pain inflicted on her.

When all four hooves were finally trimmed, Mary looked like a different goat. She walked more freely and began to explore the yard, as though the procedure had returned to her a goat's natural curiosity. But she was malnourished and quite weak, and her legs were still bowed from having walked around on those crazy hooves for so long. She also seemed to have a back problem, with one of her hind legs shorter than the other.

"There's nothing really we can do for her legs and back," the vet said. "You just give her good food and all this space to wander in and hopefully it rights itself over time."

Gauging Mary to be an elderly goat, the vet suggested a diet of Bermuda hay (the usual goat diet) with a little alfalfa hay each day to supplement (for extra calories and minerals). Oat straw would serve as the best bedding, he said, since the straw fibers were tube-shaped and would hold heat. As soon as Dr. Geissen left, I made a trip with Jesse to the local feed store to buy bales of hay and straw. I scattered some hay out for Mary, and she happily began to munch. Then I pulled clumps of straw from the bale and shook it out over the floor of one of the stalls in the barn, fluffing it up so it would be nice and soft. After two minutes of this, the air was filled with straw dust, making me sneeze over and over. For the rest of the day and night I kept finding straw fibers in my hair, in my ears, and even in my underwear.

The next day I made calls to report the petting zoo. It wasn't enough to save one animal. I wanted that place to fly right or be shut down.

"We have a file three feet high," the guy at Animal Control said. "We're working on it."

The SPCA said pretty much the same thing.

Satisfied that the zoo was being taken care of, I settled in with my new goat, focusing on getting her healthy. To boost her immune system, I began her on a supplement of algae superfood. I had discovered this superfood a year and a half before when my dog China seemed to be on her last legs—incontinent, losing her fur, riddled with arthritis, and barely able to see because of cataracts. I had lamented about China's decline to a friend, who had suggested I give her the algae. With nothing to lose, I gave it a shot, and within three months China's cataracts were gone, her fur had grown back, she had stopped peeing on herself, and she was hiking five miles a day with me. This miracle cure was now a staple in all of my dogs' and cats' diets, as well as in my family's. Because it was an all-natural food, it could be fed—like any greens—to any animal. Now it was Mary's turn to reap the benefits of the miracle algae.

On one of my feed-store runs to buy Mary more hay, I also learned about grain mash—a mix of bran, oats, corn, barley, alfalfa, molasses, and a little water—that would add minerals and calories to Mary's diet and give her just a little extra plumpness. This was how I liked all my rescued animals to be. That *just a little extra* told everyone involved— especially the animal herself—that now she was living the good life. Now there was plenty and she'd never want for anything.

In the first few days after I'd brought Mary home, I brushed the mats out of her hair. Once her leg had healed, I washed her filthy coat, revealing that she was indeed white, not gray. With all the great supplementation, before long her coat grew in soft and shiny.

Although Scott was a little surprised that I'd actually won out in the goat standoff, he took it all more or less in stride. Mary wasn't in the house, after all, and he rarely went out into the backyard since he got home so late from work. Scott's and Mary's lives didn't often intersect.

One morning I sat in the yard with Jesse and watched Mary meandering through the dappled sunlight. Three months had passed since I'd brought her home, and Mary had reached a new level of vitality. She moved with ease. Her eyes shone. And she had attained the perfection of *a little bit extra.*

Wow, I thought. *I did that.* Somehow I had forgotten just how good

I was at nurturing animals back to health. But there before me, in the form of a happy, healthy goat, was proof that my gift was alive and well.

I ran inside and got my camera and took several pictures of Mary in my yard. I needed to show the owner of the petting zoo just how healthy this goat was now.

I don't know what grand delusion led me to think the big, gruff woman would be happy to see that I'd healed Mary, but an hour later when I stood in front of her with Jesse on my hip and handed her one photo after another, the woman simply grunted. I was even more disappointed to see that Animal Control and the SPCA had not made any headway at all; the zoo still looked and smelled just as dreadful, the animals were just as unhappy, and the tourists seemed just as oblivious. I noticed one baby goat, in particular, who was really sick. Delicate and white with spindly legs, he had green mucus running from his nose and seemed to be struggling just to breathe. I asked the owner what was going on with the little goat.

"I don't know," the big, gravel-voiced woman said. "He's sick."

"He needs medical attention," I said.

To that the owner simply shrugged and swatted at a fly.

"Well, you saw how I healed Mary." I paused, thinking, *Scott will understand; it's just a baby.* "So, um, I'm going to take that little goat home and heal him too, OK?"

The woman shook her head, more in resignation than refusal. She'd probably never met anyone before who'd stood their ground with her like I did.

"How old is he?" I asked, and shifted Jesse to my other hip.

"I don't know." The woman frowned. "Maybe three months."

"Where's the mom? I mean, he's probably too young to be separated from her."

"Who knows where she is. Just take the baby."

"But you do have the mom here?"

The woman heaved a deep sigh. "She doesn't care about him. They don't care about their babies. They're just goats."

I knew this wasn't true. I'd seen mama animals in all kinds of species—from ducks to dogs to horses—nurture their babies and grieve when they were taken away; it couldn't be any less true for goats. But I didn't get the sense the owner was going to give in on this one, at least not that day, and that little goat needed medical help right away. I went back to the car and got the baby carrier and secured Jesse onto my back, then returned to the petting zoo. I picked up the tiny white goat, feeling his fragile ribs against my fingertips, and carried him back toward my car, but as I walked out the entrance I heard a frantic baaing behind me, followed by a crashing sound. I didn't have to turn around to know it was the mom. She was running at the fence, bleating and baaing. One baby on my back and another one in my arms, I watched as a big brown-and-white goat tried to get out the gate, then under the fence, then over the fence, baaing frantically all the while.

I approached the fence, where the owner was trying to secure the she-goat with a lead. But the goat wouldn't have it; she was trying to get through the fence to me, or rather to the little white goat in my arms. I understood; I would be just as furious if anyone ever tried to take Jesse from me.

"That's the mom," I said. A statement, not a question.

Reluctantly the woman nodded.

I loaded both the baby goat and the mama goat into my Ford Explorer. By this point, the owner understood that if she didn't let the mom come home with me, she'd have a crazy woman camping out with her goats again.

When I got the two new goats back to my barn, the dogs lined up at the fence, their favorite place ever since the dividing gate had been shut. They wagged their tails and jumped and barked but, alas, they were deprived of two more potential playmates. Mary and the mama goat greeted each other with gentle "I know *you*" head bonks, and both the mama and Mary fussed over the frail little baby.

When Dr. Geissen came out, he told me the baby goat had pneumonia. We gave him antibiotics and lots of fresh water, and the mama goat was at his side the whole time, nursing him and licking him. I started him right away on the superfood algae; by this point the stuff had worked miracles not only with dozens of dogs and cats, but also with Mary the goat, and I prayed it would help this baby, too.

I trimmed the mama goat's nails. They weren't as bad as Mary's had been, since this mama was a relatively young goat, but her hooves had been neglected too. I filled more stalls with lots of fresh, fluffed-up straw (and more straw fibers got in my hair and ears and underwear). I made a run to the feed store to make sure this malnourished, nursing mama would have plenty of good nutrition to support both her body and her baby's. Unlike Mary, these two goats had not been named, so when I finished getting them settled in, I sat for a long while and watched them explore their new home, and eventually the name Billy rose to the surface for the delicate white baby, and the name Sophie felt just right for the mama.

That night, I made sure to have a nice dinner ready before Scott got home. After we ate, I said, "I've got something to tell you."

Scott's face shifted through about three different emotions in half a second.

"It's not bad," I rushed to tell him, and he looked relieved. "I brought home another goat, but he's just a tiny baby."

Scott nodded cautiously.

"He's super sick. I knew he'd die if I didn't take him home. Turns out he has pneumonia."

"You went back to the petting zoo."

"Yeah. They haven't shut it down yet."

Scott went into the living room and turned on the TV.

I followed after him, saying, "I have one other thing to tell you."

He gently shoved two cats and a dog off the couch so he could sit down. He slid back into the couch and said, "What's that?"

"Well, I kind of brought home the baby goat's mom, too."

"Kind of?" Scott said.

"Did," I said. "I did bring home the mom, too."

Within a couple of weeks Scott relaxed into the fact that we now had three goats. In reality, since he hardly ever saw them, I think he kind of forgot they were there. Jesse and I, on the other hand, spent practically the whole day, every day, with the goats. Jesse traveled around the barnyard on my hip or secured to my back in the baby carrier. We'd enter the barnyard in the morning with Jesse running ahead calling out, "Aminals! Aminals!" to our four-legged residents. He watched from his perch on my back as I mucked out the barn, fed the goats, and gave little Billy his supplements and medicine. I gave Billy superfood algae twice a day and marveled at what a good mother Sophie was, constantly nursing and grooming her baby. In just a few weeks, the team effort turned Billy's pneumonia around, and he was soon romping around the yard, full of life and mischief. Now I had three happy, healthy goats, all of whom had attained the perfection of *just a little bit extra.*

So of course I ended up back at the petting zoo.

This time I was not going there to show the owner how well I had healed her sick animals. Neither was I going merely to check whether the zoo had brought up its standards or been shut down; I knew in my gut it had not. This time, when I went back to the zoo, I was on a mission. Ever since my first visit to that dreadful place, I'd been haunted by images of those miserable animals and I hadn't been able to get the ache out of my heart. How could I sit idly by when so many animals were suffering and I had the space to take them in and the ability to make them well? If Animal Control and the SPCA couldn't get it together to shut the place down, I had to do what I could to help relieve some of the suffering.

"Do you have any other animals that need healing?" I asked when I'd found the owner. "I know you're overwhelmed. No questions asked. I'll take the sick ones off your hands."

It was even hotter out than that first time I'd shown up at the zoo.

There were still mountains of poop and lots of flies. Still there was no drinking water out for the animals. And more tourists than ever were looking but not seeing the suffering right in front of them. Why on earth had the authorities not shut this place down yet?

To my surprise there was no fight in the owner's response. In fact, the woman didn't say a word. She simply went to the back of the zoo, behind a closed gate, and she brought out one animal after another. First, Nonie the sheep and her son, Josh, both terrified of humans. Then Katie, an elderly horse who whinnied and tossed her head, pulling against her lead—clearly no longer willing to be a pony-ride horse. Then came the goat Zena, who—the owner explained—had begun ramming the visitors, and she was followed by her baby, Amy. And finally there was Grandpa Goat, who could not even get up because his legs were so deformed. The goats and sheep all had overgrown hooves, and all of the animals were filthy. It was the saddest parade I had ever seen.

This group of animals was larger than I'd expected, and I certainly wasn't going to fit a horse in my car. So I went home and called around until I found a trailer I could borrow.

I returned later that day with the trailer, ready to take my new babies home. With Jesse on my back, I led or carried each animal out to the parking lot and walked them slowly into the trailer. At one point two men who worked at the zoo came out to help me. To my dismay, they each grabbed a terrified sheep by the wool and threw them into the trailer.

"That's OK," I said, wincing. "Thanks for your help, but I can do this on my own."

When all the goats and sheep were in the trailer, I went back into the zoo and slowly approached Katie, the old pony-ride horse, and saw that she had scar tissue on her face that directly outlined the shape of the halter. Clearly her halter was too tight and had never been removed. I gently took hold of her lead, and she raised her head and bared her big teeth, and instinctively I took a step back and looked down. Not looking at her but still holding her lead, I turned my back and slowly walked out toward the parking lot, and she followed me the whole way, right up into the trailer.

When I got home, I opened my big side gate and backed the trailer right up to it. I let the animals walk down into the yard at their own pace, except for Grandpa Goat, who had to be carried. Once they were all in the barnyard and the gate was closed, I let the dogs out and they lined up at their usual post along the dividing fence, wagging their tails, but this time they didn't bark. By now they understood the setup; the farm animals were for show, not for touch (or chase).

Before I called Dr. Geissen out, there was one thing I needed to do. I wanted to take Katie's halter off. I approached her slowly, not looking at her directly. "We're going to take that thing off," I said. Mostly looking down, I reached for her halter, and she went for my hand, trying to bite me.

"OK," I said, taking a step back. "I get it. You're really angry."

I had to walk away several times, and finally, moving slowly with my feet but quickly with my hands, I managed to get the halter off without getting bitten.

"You don't have to wear that awful thing ever again," I told her.

I understood why Katie didn't want attention, or even to be looked at. Throughout her life she had carried thousands of crying kids on her back, making hundreds of thousands of trips around a metal post.

"I don't want a thing from you," I promised her. I knew it would take some time, but I figured if I didn't pay any attention to Katie—other than feeding her without looking at her—she'd slowly come to believe that my promise was true.

When Dr. Geissen arrived, he examined all of the goats and sheep, and we started the process of wound washing, deworming, and ear cleaning. He prescribed anti-inflammatories for Grandpa, who he said had severe arthritis. When Dr. Geissen left I made a run to the feed store, set up more stalls in the barn with loads of straw, trimmed the goats' and sheep's overgrown hooves, and of course started all of the animals on the miracle algae.

When I finally was finished in the barnyard, my back was aching, I was utterly exhausted, and I had straw fibers in every imaginable nook and cranny. But I scrubbed myself and Jesse clean, fed Jesse and put him to bed, and then set to work on cooking up Scott's favorite meal—fettuccini Alfredo with nondairy cream sauce and portobello mushrooms. I even put wineglasses on the table.

When Scott returned from work, he came into the dining room and smiled. "Mm," he said. "That smells good." But a moment later the smile dropped and he rolled his eyes.

"What did you bring home this time, Ellie?"

Maybe he was starting to get it that I couldn't help myself, that this was just the way I was wired. Not that he was happy; it was more like quiet resignation. Back in the days when he was helping out with the dog adoptions, he might have been excited to engage with farm animals too. But he'd long ago shifted away from the world of animals that we had shared and was concerned only with providing for our family—of humans. He seemed like a different person from the Scott who had sat up half the night with me giving sick puppies injections. I wished he would join me, at least a little, in the excitement of saving these poor creatures, or at least be happy for me that I was doing something I loved. But instead he seemed to grow grumpier by the day.

One night, about a week after this last visit to the petting zoo, I came in from the barnyard later than usual. Scott had already arrived home and was waiting for me on the couch. "Come sit down," he said.

"Let me just wash my hands."

When I finally sat down next to him, he said, "I feel like I have to stand in line just to get a little attention from you."

"I'm sorry, Scott. It'll settle down. It's just that these new animals are still healing."

"And when they get healthy, you'll go get more."

I didn't respond. I didn't want to lie.

"Why can't you just be a normal, available wife?" he said.

"I'm trying," I said. But at that moment I realized I'd completely lost sight of my goal to maintain the normalcy I'd found after Jesse's birth. Normalcy had escaped me once again. "I *tried*," I corrected myself. "But I'm not normal, Scott. I'm just not."

Scott seemed to have joined my parents' camp, the people who wanted me to act like a normal person. And although I now knew that this was just never going to be possible, the last thing I wanted was to ruin my marriage. So I vowed to put my rescuing on pause for a while, to just take care of the animals I had. I made it my priority to show up for Scott and Jesse. But with nine farm animals, eight dogs, twenty cats, a toddler, and a husband, I was beginning to feel more than a little strain handling it all on my own. I had a barnyard to clean up daily, a baby's diapers to change (several times a day), and a husband who needed some attention after a very long day of work. I finally broke down and hired a Mommy's Helper for part of the day; she could at least watch Jesse while I took care of the rest of the crew. But I could see myself starting to slip. When I played with Jesse, I felt like I was neglecting the new sickly animals in the barnyard. When I tended to the animals a bit too long, Jesse threw a fit. And sometimes I forgot to get dinner on the table. I had forty-nine mouths to feed—fifty if I remembered to eat, myself.

As best I could, I ignored the old familiar pull to help any and all animals who needed me. But the whispers I'd felt deep inside me as a child were in full force once again. And despite my best efforts to block them out, a few weeks after the final petting zoo rescue, the whispers led me down a side road to a woman who'd lost her house and was living in her car with her collection of pets. Two dogs, several cats, a handful of ducks, a goose, and thirty chickens all had taken up residence with her in her white sedan. *I'm sorry, Scott,* I thought. *You're just going to have to understand.* I told the woman about my place, and she broke into tears and handed over all but her two dogs.

By July, three potbellied pigs, a big farm pig, and another horse had made their way into the mix. The place began to look like Old MacDonald's Farm. My days were spent running back and forth from the barnyard to the phone to ask the vet a question or driving to the library to do research or to a feed store to gather information from the people who worked there. I was learning much faster than I would have had I gone to vet school or a master's program. I was on fire and loving every minute of it.

But every ounce of joy and aliveness that I was experiencing was matched by equal amounts of disgruntlement in Scott. With each new pig or horse I rescued, he would groan that now we had one more mouth to feed. Although I'd begun dipping into a trust fund that had been granted to me in my parents' divorce settlement, Scott's income was still covering much of the barnyard costs. Each month, I was buying two dozen bales of hay, six bales of straw, six bags of grain, and five bags of potbellied-pig feed. And the vet visits had grown in direct proportion to the number of animals in the barnyard.

But in truth, Scott cared much less about the money than about my waning attentiveness. I tried hard to wrap up my chores in the barnyard and make dinner before he got home from work. But a barnyard is not always a predictable operation, and the chores can't always be squeezed into a preordained block of time, especially for someone like me, who reaches for perfection in everything I do. Add to that a toddler's needs, and you've got the antithesis of predictability and punctuality.

One afternoon, Jesse needed my undivided attention on into the evening. By the time Scott got home, I hadn't had a minute to get dinner ready for anyone—neither for the animals nor for the humans.

I gave Scott a kiss and said, "Do you mind watching Jesse while I run out and feed the animals? I'll be really quick."

"Sure," he said.

Just fifteen minutes, I told myself as I rushed out into the barnyard, and I had every intention of sticking to that. Then I'd be back in to give Jesse a bath and put him to bed before making dinner for Scott and me.

In the tack room, I mixed up the pigs' dinner—pig feed pellets, bran, and superfood algae mixed with water until it turned into a kind of porridge. As usual, our big white farm pig, Duncan, was right outside the door to the tack room, squealing and grunting and trying to get the door open. But his big pig efforts resulted only in him blocking my exit with his dinner.

"Duncan, back up," I called through the door.

Duncan, as was the case every night, did not back up. All twelve hundred pounds of him kept pushing up against the door trying to get it open. The door, of course, opened out, not in. I turned my back, the pigs' bowls stacked in my arms, and tried to push the door open with my back. After two minutes of this—and waiting for just the right moment, between Duncan's assaults on the door—I managed to get out the door with the pigs' food.

"If you just waited, it would actually go a lot faster," I told Duncan as I set the four bowls down in the yard for the pigs. But of course he was far too busy with his dinner to hear me.

My next task was to keep the goats away from the pigs' dinner with scattered grain and a push broom. "You guys are next," I told the goats. "I promise."

And so it went, feeding one group of animals at a time, cleaning up along the way, sweeping off the barn's patio or cleaning up the mess in the chickens' area of the barn. Each time I was back in the tack room, I'd wipe down the counters or turn all the trash bins in the same direction so that everything looked neat and tidy, sparkling and orderly.

Once everyone had been fed, and every last surface was raked or swept or wiped down, I could stop and take a breath. I inhaled the wonderful, sweet smell of hay, listened to the pigs snoring in their pig pile, and looked up at the stars, knowing there was no better, richer life for me.

"Um, can we talk?" Scott said as soon as I walked back into the living room, and I was jarred back into my other reality. An hour had passed. It was past Jesse's bedtime, and he hadn't even had his bath. Scott hadn't eaten, and he was hungry. No one was smiling.

"Yes," I said. "Just let me give Jesse his bath and get him to bed first. OK?"

When Jesse was bathed, I put him in his jammies, nursed him, and sang him to sleep. By the time I walked back into the living room, another hour had passed.

"This is crazy," Scott said, looking at his watch. "What the hell's going on here?"

"I'm sorry. I'm here now."

"*Now*," he said.

"I'm trying to be a good wife and mother. It's a lot—"

"Well, why don't you stop all this crazy stuff with the animals, then? Just look at you."

I looked down at my jeans and T-shirt, caked with mud and manure, and realized my face must be just as dirty. "Scott," I said, "that"—I motioned toward the back door and the barnyard beyond it—"that crazy yard full of sick and sad animals on the mend. That's what I live for. Telling me to stop . . . that'd be like me telling *you* to stop eating food or drinking water. It feeds me more deeply than anything else in the world."

"Clearly," Scott said, standing up, "it feeds you more than I ever could." And he walked out of the room.

I felt his hurt like a punch in my own stomach, but I didn't see any way to go backward. If I stopped doing what I was doing, I'd be horribly unhappy. Yet if I kept it up, he would be equally miserable.

Scott had always known about me and animals. I'd told him all about my childhood and the way I'd brought home hurt animals and tried to make them well. I'd told him how animals had been my only true friends, my only true family. And I'd told him—more than once—about my vision of having a haven where animals and people healed one another. He'd always smiled and nodded, but apparently he hadn't been listening. Or maybe he'd just figured I would never actually follow through.

Truth be told, I was not thinking my way through some grand design to create my vision; I just kept following my impulses, sniffing after those whispers that had always led me. I'd stashed that dream away so many times it had sort of gotten lodged at the back of my heart. Frozen in place and forgotten. But little by little, with each new animal I brought home to the barnyard, my heart had melted just a little bit more. Until finally, two months after the last petting-zoo rescues and just a couple of weeks after our second horse, Shy, had arrived, that frozen dream was fully thawed. And it dislodged and fell with a thud at my feet.

"Oh my God," I said out loud. I was standing amid my now-healthy farm animals—fifty in all—and there at my feet, laid out before me and filling my yard in full, glorious color, was my vision, plain as day. The baby goats springing around the yard, the chickens scratching and pecking at the dirt for bugs, the pigs in their pig pile in the barn, the horses and goats and sheep commingling in harmony. "This is it. This is my haven." I had healed all these beautiful beings, and they were healing me, daily. How I'd not seen what I'd been up to was beyond me, but finally I was in on the secret.

It's time to share this with other people, I thought. The name The Gentle Barn came to me in a rush, traveling the same pathways as the whispers that connected me to the animal world. I snapped up the name, saying, "Thank you!" to the sky. "Genius!"

"You're going to open to the public?" Scott said. "Our house will be open to strangers?"

"Not the house," I assured him. "They can come in through the side gate." Then I added, thinking it would ease his concerns about the growing cost of caring for the animals, "After the grand opening I'm going to ask for a donation to get in, every Sunday, to help with food and vet fees. Eventually we'll be self-supporting, and I'll even earn a salary."

But Scott wasn't the least bit assured. "Strangers in our house?" he said again.

Slowly, limpingly, Scott joined the parade. Not that he ever got on the bandwagon, but grudgingly he followed along behind it.

I spread the word about the grand opening in every way I could think of. I took out an ad in a local parenting magazine and I papered the town with fliers. The event even appeared in the calendar section of the *L.A. Times*. In preparation for the big day I bought extra brushes so people could try their hand at grooming the animals. I bought popcorn to pop and lots of drinks, as well as extra treats for the animals. Five neighbor kids signed on as volunteers, to remind people: "When a sheep or chicken walks away, he's saying *no*." The kids would be stationed in various sections of the barnyard to help teach "animal-speak" and to be sure all the animals, as well as the people, were safe.

The day before the grand opening, I scrubbed the barn top to bottom and spread sand over the dirt in the barnyard to make it softer on the animals' hooves. Early the next morning I covered the picnic tables in the grassy part of the yard with red-and-white checked tablecloths and tied pink bows in the two horses' manes and tails. I also re-raked the barnyard every time an animal relieved himself. My barnyard was going to be spotless.

The grand opening was held on August 25, 1999. Though Scott wasn't anywhere close to thrilled, he tried to be supportive and helped out by taking care of Jesse so I was free to interact with the visitors. I was planning to open the doors at ten, and by nine thirty there was already a crowd of people waiting outside. When I finally opened the gate, a flood of kids and their parents filled the small grassy yard just behind my house. Before I ushered them past the second gate and into the barnyard, I introduced myself and the Gentle Barn and talked about the animals they were going to meet; I explained the signals an animal gave when they wanted to be left alone and asked people to pay attention to their cues and to please not chase them. Then I led everyone into the barnyard and toured them around. As I told each animal's story, it occurred to me that my barnyard was like a giant walk-through storybook; everywhere you turned, there was an incredible character with an awe-inspiring tale of courage and triumph.

By now almost all the animals were comfortable with humans and wandered happily from child to child, nibbling treats. In the heat of the afternoon, I brought out a huge basin and a hose, and the kids gave our horse Shy a bath. And Katie, who was still not terribly happy with people, was used as an example of animal-speak: When a horse puts her ears back, she's saying, *Back off.*

The entire day I had a huge grin plastered on my face, until my cheeks hurt too much to keep smiling. I kept looking around, my eyes wide, not quite believing so many people had shown up. Some small part of me didn't believe it was real. I'd created something that I thought was the most beautiful thing in the world. But for years, everyone in my life had shot this dream down, had scolded me for bringing animals home, had gotten rid of them when I wasn't around, had begged me to just stop that "nonsense" and be a normal human being, and yet here was a crowd of people praising me and congratulating me and asking all kinds of questions about the animals. These strangers cared about what I cared about. What a shock. What a thrill.

The day filled me up with so much excitement and so much joy, I wasn't just walking; I was hovering. I floated to the gate to shut it after the last visitor had left. I floated through the cleanup of the yard. I floated to recoup Jesse from Scott, who had been on parenting duty all day long.

OK, Ellie, I told myself as I gave my son a hug. *Now it's time to be present with Jesse.* But I kept catching my mind wandering back to the opening, wanting to replay scenes from the day. I'd pull myself back into the moment, back into my son's world. *Be in present-time now. Jesse is just as important as this morning was.* But again I'd catch my mind wanting to drift.

The entire afternoon and evening was like a tug-of-war with myself. The Gentle Barn Ellie on one side and Ellie the mom on the other.

By the time Jesse was fed and bathed and put to bed, I was exhausted. I found the guestbook and sank into the couch to read over the names. I counted 150 visitors in all. What an amazing start!

When I finally went to bed, Scott was already asleep. I slid under the covers next to him, my body weary but my heart brimming. I let the bed have my weight, but for a long time I lay there awake, replaying the day over and over in my head.

Just a few months before, when Mary's gaze had locked onto mine at that godforsaken petting zoo, I'd had no intention of changing my life, or of stealing time away from my little boy or putting a strain on my marriage. But that little goat had nudged at my sunken dream and had begun buoying it to the surface. Each animal who followed had joined in, urging me on and bringing back to light my very reason for being. What I didn't yet see, however (and wouldn't fully see for years to come), was that the more my dream became a reality, the further it would edge Scott's dream—and his needs—out of the picture.

CHAPTER 4

The Gentle Barn puzzle was coming together. Two major pieces were now in place: the animals, and the public who were coming to meet them and learn their stories. But there was one more critical piece that needed to be snapped into the puzzle. The at-risk kids.

I'd done an internship with at-risk youth back in college, and I'd recognized myself in them right away. Most of them had been abused or neglected. Many had tried to commit suicide or were addicted to drugs. I'd seen one teen after another whose eyes were blank, like the light had gone out; they'd experienced so much pain that it had just been easier to shut down entirely. And just as I'd always been drawn to the most damaged animals, the ones no one else wanted, I was drawn to the kids no one else knew how to help. Many of those kids ended up in the juvenile justice system. Some of them ended up dead. Most had had people give up on them. I wanted to act as witness to these children. I wanted to tell them, "I see you, and I see that you're good. I see that you're whole and likable and have something to offer the world." And I wanted to let my animals help me with that task.

Now I finally had the chance to bring animals to those kids, or rather to bring those kids to the animals. I could finally put this idea into action. So, right after the grand opening, I started calling around to rehab centers, group homes, and schools in at-risk neighborhoods. I also called facilities for special-needs kids. I expected to run into resistance or at least a little red tape, but one facility after another said, "Great! When can we come?"

Oh, I thought. *Wow. Wonderful.* And yet, some part of me froze. I expected to have time to prepare—like months . . . or a year. Not that I needed to prepare the barnyard; the animals were ready to meet these kids. *I* was the one who wasn't entirely ready. As soon as I penciled the first group of at-risk teens into the schedule, just a few weeks away, I started to panic. What would I do with these teenagers? Would they even listen to me? Maybe they'd think the barnyard was boring. And what if something went wrong? What if an animal spooked and kicked or bit someone?

This first scheduled group was from Daybreak House—a local probation camp; these kids were tough. Maybe they'd get out of control and I wouldn't be able to rein them back in. And the worst possibility of all: maybe they'd laugh at me or even hate me.

Over the coming weeks, I planned and replanned the first session of my first group. Every step of the way, I questioned and doubted. I'd always been so sure animals could help these kids, but maybe it was just a misguided fantasy. Maybe it wouldn't work at all. The night before the group was to visit, I went over my plan again, tweaking this or that part of it, then second-guessing myself and changing it back. *We'll start with the horses; kids love horses. Or maybe it would be better to start with the smaller animals and work our way up. Some of the kids might be scared of big animals.* I'd written down the lines I would speak, like a script. I wanted to be sure to come off as wise, and maybe even witty. I wrote down facts about the animals I wanted to share, as well as each of the animals' stories. When I finally went to bed that night, I set my papers and a pen on the bed next to me, just in case I got any good ideas in the middle of the night.

The next morning I woke up before my alarm went off and jumped out of bed to feed Jesse and get the barnyard ready. The group wasn't coming until the afternoon, but I wanted to be certain everything was just right. With Jesse on my back, I fed the pigs and goats and chickens and ducks, and the entire time, inside my head, I was going over and over my plan for the session, practicing various lines. I wanted so badly for this first group to go well. I wanted to connect with these kids and to show them there was a path out of the darkness.

When the barnyard was spotless, I gave Jesse lunch and got him ready for the Mommy's Helper. Finally, at ten minutes to one, I slipped out the gate to await the van from the probation camp. As I waited I tried to read over my plan one last time, but I was so nervous I wasn't able to focus on what I was reading. And besides, so many things were crossed out, with little scribbles in the margins, I couldn't make all of it out.

One o'clock came and went, and I began pacing alongside the fence. Finally I ran in to get my cell phone. When I'd dialed the number for Daybreak House, the woman who answered said she didn't have anything on her schedule about a barn. Disappointment replaced the panic. I knew it had all seemed to fall into place too easily. It had been too good to be true. And yet there was also a feeling of relief as the nervousness drained out of me.

I went back into the barnyard and started sweeping off the barn's patio, even though I'd done it just an hour before. When I moved to raking through the sand, I heard a car pull up outside. Then I heard the boys' voices as they piled out of the van.

It was 1:45 and no one had called to say they were running late.

This would turn out to be a common scenario with a lot of the groups, from a lot of different agencies.

I opened the gate, and eight boys—twelve to sixteen years old—filed in with their eyes cast downward and their shoulders rolled forward, their hearts well out of reach. Most had short-cropped hair and oversize pants hanging low on their hips; some had tattoos, and not one of them looked me in the eye when I said hello. Most didn't even say hello back.

I led them and their two counselors to the picnic tables in the grassy yard next to the barnyard. But most of the boys remained standing.

"Hi, welcome to the Gentle Barn. My name is Ellie," I said, trying to keep my voice even. My nervousness had returned full force the moment the boys had walked in. "How are you all doing today?"

A few of the boys shrugged or grunted. One said, "OK," but didn't look up.

"You guys can sit down," I said, "if you want to." And two more boys sat, but the rest stayed on their feet.

"OK," I said, touching the folded-up notes in my pocket but not pulling them out. "The Gentle Barn was my dream since I was seven years old. I didn't live on a farm. I didn't know anything about these kinds of animals."

Most of the boys turned away to look at the animals.

"We're going to talk here for a little bit," I said. "Then we'll go over and meet the animals." But the boys were still looking over the fence, not at me.

"Hey, guys," one of the counselors said. "Sit down and listen to the lady." And slowly the boys made their way to the benches and sat.

"Thank you," I said, and I really meant it. I swallowed hard and my mouth was dry, but I managed to get my next line out. "The animals—these and others before that—they saved me."

At this point, one of the older boys perked up and said, "I thought *you* saved the animals," and I was so grateful to this boy for speaking to me.

I nodded. "Yes," I said. "I rescued them, but they also rescued me. They rescue me every day."

"How?" the boy said.

"Thank you for asking." I could feel myself beginning to relax, just a bit.

I told the boys about the animals, how they had survived abuse and neglect, how they'd healed and were such good models of resilience and hope. And how working with them gave me such a deep sense of purpose. "They're my heroes," I said. "I'm touched every day by their courage. By their forgiveness and trust."

Even though most of the boys were staring down at the table or off into space, I could see that some of them were listening to what I was saying.

"Now," I said, "I'd really like to know your names." And I turned to the boy nearest me. "Let's start with you."

Some of the boys mumbled their names so quietly I had to strain to hear them. I suspected they'd been practicing for a long time at being unheard and unseen; it had probably been safer that way.

After they'd all told me their names, I said, "OK, let's go meet the animals now." And I walked to the gate in the chain-link fence and held it open for them. But the boys were just as slow to stand up as they'd been to take a seat. I took a breath and tried to relax, to give them as much time and space as they needed. But I was so anxious to have this all go well and to fit everything in that I wanted to do; I could feel myself straining against my own impatience, like a horse against her reins.

When the boys finally were all in the barnyard, I had the impulse to take them first to meet Mary, since she was the founding animal, but that wasn't how I'd planned it. It made me nervous to second-guess myself, and I decided to stick with the plan I'd mapped out; somehow that made me feel safer. I led the boys across the barnyard to where Rudy the goose was drinking, making that quick slapping sound she made in the bowl as she snapped at the water.

When the boys had finally gathered around, I told them how Rudy had come to me from living in a car with a homeless woman and dozens of other animals. Then I shared how this goose had taught me an important lesson. For her first few weeks in my barnyard, she had stood in my way and gotten underfoot as I'd tried to do my morning chores. I sometimes stopped to pat her and say hello, but then I'd continue on with my chores as Rudy honked and stuck her long neck out this way and that, making odd, curling shapes with it. Each morning, I chugged along with my chores, ignoring Rudy's fuss, until one morning when she bit me right on the butt.

At this the boys laughed, as I knew they would. And the sound of their laughter made me relax a little bit more.

"I was mad at first," I said.

"Damn right," said one of the boys.

"But then I realized that maybe she was just trying to tell me something." I paused and looked around at the group. "You know how sometimes people can do something that seems mean, but it's just because their quiet request got ignored?"

I could see in the boys' faces that they were taking this in and thinking it over.

"What do you think she was trying to tell me?"

A couple of the boys shrugged, and one said, "Who knows? How would you know what a duck wants?"

"She's a goose, stupid," one of the other boys said.

"You're right, she's a goose," I said, "but I'd like to ask that we talk to each other with kinder words, especially while you're here. Remember, this is the *Gentle* Barn. Let's try to be gentle, even with each other."

The other boys laughed and taunted, and the boy who'd said "stupid" kicked at the ground.

"All of us," I said. "This is a place to practice kindness." I took a breath and then continued with my story. "So, I'm going to show you how I found out what Rudy wanted." And I sat right down on the ground in front of my goose, and she climbed straight into my lap and wrapped her neck around me.

"Whoa," said one of the boys, and some of the others laughed.

With this big, warm goose in my lap, I took my first really deep breath of the day.

"Thanks, Rudy," I said before I took the boys to meet the next animal.

I introduced the boys to all of the chickens and ducks, and then the goats and pigs, encouraging them to pet and interact with the animals, and telling them each animal's story. After a half hour in the barnyard, I passed out grooming brushes, and the boys took turns brushing Shy the horse. Then I took them across the barnyard to meet our other horse, Katie. "Katie's different from Shy," I told them. "We have to walk very slowly and listen to her." As we approached, Katie laid her ears back. "There," I said. "Did you hear that?"

"Hear what?" one of the boys said.

"Let's take a step back," I told them, and we all backed up and Katie's ears relaxed forward. "Did you see that?"

A couple of the boys shook their heads.

"We're going to take a step forward again, and this time watch Katie's ears."

We all took a step forward, and on cue, Katie laid her ears back again.

"She moved her ears down," one of the boys said.

"Yes, good. Let's back up." When we'd taken a step back, I said, "She's talking to us when she lays her ears back like that. What do you think she's telling us?"

"She doesn't like us," another boy said.

"Well, she doesn't know everyone here, so she doesn't know yet if she likes you or not. But she is saying, 'Don't come any closer.' I'm teaching her she doesn't have to yell for me to hear her—yelling in Horse is biting or kicking—she just has to whisper—like putting her ears back."

"Do all animals put their ears back?" one of the smaller boys asked.

"Great question," I said. "All animals have a way of communicating. Not all of them put their ears back, but all of them have their way of saying, 'Back off' or 'I'm hungry' or 'I love you.'"

"Animals say 'I love you'?" the boy said, incredulous, and the other boys mocked him in false, high voices: *"I love you, I love you."*

"You have great questions," I said, ignoring the other boys' taunting. "Yeah, animals say 'I love you.' That's what Rudy was telling me when she climbed into my lap." I knew the taunting and mocking these boys did was their defense against being vulnerable. If a subject made them uncomfortable, they acted fake or macho to cover it up. "Rudy was being real," I said. "She knows she's safe here, so she doesn't have to put on an act. She can show her real feelings."

For our last half hour, I suggested that each of the boys go back and spend time with their favorite animal. Some went straight to a particular goat or to Shy, but others seemed uncertain and wandered around the barnyard or hung back, undecided. Eventually they all found their way to an animal or two. I sat and watched as these "tough" guys slowly began to let down their guard, interacting gently, almost tenderly with the goats and chickens and pigs.

At the end of the visit, I thanked the boys for being so kind and trustworthy with the animals, and I shook each one's hand. The kids who walked out the gate looked like different people from the withdrawn teenagers who'd walked in just two hours before. Most of them had begun looking me in the eye when they spoke to me. They were standing taller, their chests less sunken and their heads held a bit higher.

"I knew it!" I said after the van had pulled away. I shut the gate and walked into the house with a huge grin on my face. It was true, I *had* suspected that some kind of transformation would take place in these kids, but it was something else to see it in action.

That night when I said good night to all the animals, I told them how great they'd been with the kids that day, and how proud I was of them. I sat down in front of my big white goose. "Rudy, you're a star," I said. When I got to Katie, I kept a respectful distance, as I did every night. "Katie, your timing is impeccable. You're the best teacher. One day, I'm going to kiss that soft nose of yours and scratch you under your beautiful mane."

When I went inside the house, I wanted nothing more than to tell Scott all about my first day with the at-risk kids—how amazing it was to see them slowly come out of themselves and open up to the animals and even begin to open up to me—but I knew I wouldn't get much of a response from Scott, so I held myself back, saying only that it had gone very well.

Daybreak House called me within days of this initial field trip to sign on to a once-monthly schedule of visits. They said the boys couldn't stop talking about the animals. The counselors had been amazed at how much the boys had transformed in such a short time, how quickly they'd dropped their usual guardedness. The director said they'd been looking for something like this for a while, an alternative to traditional therapy that would reach inside the toughest of the kids and open them up.

I wanted the groups to come as often as the agencies could bring them. With consistency we could really make some headway with the kids. By the end of the first month I had different groups visiting three days a week, and I was still getting calls from more places. I had kids signed on to come regularly from probation camps, foster-care facilities, and special-needs classes. I also started getting one-time field trips from local schools; I'd sent brochures to every school within a fifty-mile radius of the Gentle Barn, but I'd had no idea so many would take me up on my offer to come visit.

I continued to be a nervous wreck before each new group of kids arrived. Did I really know what I was doing? I was, after all, making all of this up. I hadn't learned it from some authority in the field; I didn't even know if there was an authority in the field. Was my theory about animals healing kids really viable? But slowly I began to see miracles taking place in my barnyard.

One such miracle happened on the very first visit from Evergreen Foster Care Facility. A lot of these children had been pulled out of severely abusive homes. Because of their emotional issues many didn't go to regular schools but were schooled in the facility where they lived. On this first visit from Evergreen, fifteen boys and girls—ages six to fourteen—arrived at the barn. I could hear the excited chatter as they walked up the driveway from the bus. Five seconds after their arrival, one boy stopped and picked up a rock and threw it at the rain gutter of my house.

A counselor was immediately at his side. "Joey, stop! What are you doing?"

"A spider," I heard him say. He bent to pick up another rock.

The counselor grabbed his arm and said, "I knew you weren't going to behave. That's it. You're going to wait on the bus."

As she led him back down the driveway, I approached another counselor. "Can I talk with you a minute?"

I learned that Joey had been taken away from a terribly abusive, alcoholic father. Because Joey was so disruptive, he could not even be allowed in a classroom at the facility. He was constantly acting out, starting fights, breaking windows. "We're really sorry we brought him," she said.

I told her that Joey was just the kind of boy who needed the Gentle Barn the most, and I convinced her to let me work with him instead of having him wait on the bus.

Joey was about eleven but was very small for his age and had mousy blond hair. I knelt down beside him, my eyes just about level with his, though he refused to look at me. Although he was thin, almost frail, he held his body rigidly, as though he were wearing a full suit of armor. No one was getting in.

"That spider is so small and helpless. You're huge next to him, huh?"

Joey didn't answer and pretended not to be listening, but I kept talking.

"He's hiding under the rain gutter trying not to be noticed. There's nothing he can do to protect himself from you, and he's hoping you're not going to hurt him." I paused a minute. "Do you know what that feels like?"

Joey was silent for a while, his eyes shifting. He was thinking it over. Slowly his chin started to quiver and his eyes began to glisten. "Yes," he said finally. "I do know what that feels like."

I told Joey the animals were just like him. They needed protection, just as he had needed protection. "Will you do that for me, Joey? Will you help me protect these animals?"

When we rejoined the group around the picnic tables, Joey stood at the back but was attentive to my every word. Once we were in the barnyard, I saw him watching the other kids with the animals. If someone ran after a hen, he said, "Hey, don't chase that chicken. Remember what Farmer Ellie said. The chicken's saying no." If someone yelled, he asked them to talk more quietly so they wouldn't make the animals uncomfortable. I kept tabs on him through the whole visit, watching him and interacting with him. At one point, Joey and I walked into the barn, and I spotted a mouse in the corner. I pointed the mouse out to Joey, then sat down and patted the ground next to me. Joey sat down by my side, and together we watched the little mouse foraging in the straw for food. He told everyone who entered to talk softly so they didn't scare the mouse. Joey had turned from aggressor to protector in an afternoon.

As I worked with group after group of children and teens, I began to find my rhythm and to see what worked and what didn't. I was eager to teach the kids everything I knew about animals. One of my favorite things to talk with them about was how animals communicated. I would start off many of my groups by talking about body language. I'd frown and hang my head and then ask the kids what emotion that was. "Sad!" they'd shout. I'd move through the different emotions, and the kids would guess each one.

"I didn't say a word, did I?"

"No," the kids would say.

"But you guessed what I was feeling. Well, animals speak like that all the time."

We'd talk about how each species has their own vocabulary. A dog wags his tail when he's happy, but when a cat "wags" her tail, she's annoyed. Cows and sheep swing their heads when they say no or want you to leave them alone. Goats lower their horns to say no. Baby horses smack their lips, like chewing, to show submission to another horse. And Katie, of course, was our ever-present example of saying "Back off" with her ears.

I also taught the kids that communication had to go both ways between humans and animals. We not only had to listen for what they were telling us, but *we* had to talk to *them*. With one group of at-risk girls, I asked, "Would it be OK for me to come up to one of you and start brushing your hair without asking you?"

The girls laughed and shook their heads.

"Right. So why would it be OK for me to go up to a horse or a goat and start brushing her without asking, or at least telling her what I'm going to do?"

Then I told them how I'd learned this about animals.

Both Zena the goat and her baby, Amy, had arrived at the Gentle Barn pregnant. "We didn't know for the first month," I said, "especially with Amy. She was just a baby herself. We never suspected she was going to *have* a baby."

Amazingly, little Amy gave birth without any complications to a tiny black goat that we named Zoe. Unfortunately, Zena's labor and delivery did not go so smoothly. The usual birth for a goat was a single kid—just like humans—with the occasional twin birth. But two months after her arrival in our barnyard Zena gave birth to four tiny goats. Two of them were stillborn and the other two were very weak. It became clear very quickly that the two surviving babies were not going to make it either unless there was some intervention, so I placed them carefully in a towel-lined carrier in preparation for a trip to the hospital, then tried to coax Zena into a larger crate. But Zena was not interested in being in a box. I put a harness on her and tried to lead her into the crate. I got behind her and pushed from the rear. But nothing I did worked.

"So, what do you think I did?" I asked the girls.

"You put food in the crate," one of them said.

"Good guess. I thought that was a good idea too. But I tried it, and it didn't work either."

I went on to tell them how frustrated and exhausted I was. At my wit's end I finally had blurted to the goat, "Zena, please, please. Your babies are going to die." I explained to her that I was going to take them all to the hospital so we could save her babies, and then when they were better, they were all going to come back home.

"Did she believe you?" one girl asked.

I nodded. "She looked at me with this expression that said, *All you had to do was ask.* And then she walked right into that crate and sat down."

The girls laughed, then one of them asked, "Did the babies make it?"

One more baby died, I told them, but we managed to save one. She was tiny and white like a little fairy, so I named her Tinkerbell. And that baby and Zena came back home, safe and sound. I pointed out Zena and Tinkerbell to the girls. "The important part," I said to them, "was that I learned that animals understand a lot more than we think they do. Now I always ask permission or explain before I do anything to my animals." During the rest of the visit I heard the girls saying to the goats and pigs, "Can I pet you?" or to Shy, "I'm going to brush you now, OK?"

———

In the early weeks and months of working with groups, my eagerness to teach the kids that animals were not so different from humans sometimes led me a little bit overboard, and I'd end up saying something the accompanying adults did not think appropriate. I sometimes found the parameters of what I could and couldn't say by walking straight into a wall.

Right after I got my first turkey, Tommy—rescued from his fate on the Thanksgiving table—I had a group of twenty very bright kindergartners. Their teacher had told them the animals had been rescued, so the kids asked about each and every animal. "Why did you save that one?" Or "Where did this one come from?" When we came to the turkey, they asked, "Why did you save this one?"

I had learned by this point that I needed to be subtle—especially with young children—so I chose my words carefully. "Well, we rescued him from a place that wasn't going to take care of him, and so we brought him here."

"Why?" the kids wanted to know. "How come they weren't going to take care of him?"

"He just wasn't safe there," I said, "so we brought him to the Gentle Barn, where he could be safe."

"But why wasn't he safe there?" the kids asked.

I was running out of euphemisms. These kids were too bright and too curious to keep at bay. "Umm," I said, and shot the teacher a helpless look. "You know Thanksgiving is in one week, right?"

"Right," the kids said.

"What are you going to eat?"

"Turkey!" the kids sang.

"Well," I said, "that's a turkey."

In unison, twenty five-year-olds said, "Ewwww."

A week later I received calls from twenty furious parents. Twenty five-year-olds had refused to eat the turkey on their plates at Thanksgiving. All I'd told them was the truth, and the kids had made their own decisions.

———

With grace and that absence of judgment unique to nonhuman species, the animals in my barnyard ushered me through my first few months of working with kids. A child's history of acting out or their special needs did not make any difference to the animals. The animals accepted hugs and tummy rubs and treats from all. I was not always as graceful as the animals were. I clung to my "script," afraid to drift too far into improvisation. I fumbled and learned and tried again, and slowly I found my footing and became a little less nervous and riddled with doubt.

The animals' stories were at the core of the healing I witnessed in the children. The animals had been to hell and back, and so had most of these kids. With each new group, I watched the kids closely from the moment they walked in through the gate. Their behavior told me everything about their histories. If they couldn't make eye contact, I knew they'd been made to feel ashamed. If they bad-mouthed or bullied other kids, they'd likely been bullied at home. I picked out the animal's story that best fit each particular group. That way I could talk to the kids about the issues they faced without putting them on the spot. Then I learned more about the kids by watching how they responded to the story. In these animals' histories the kids recognized themselves and could relate to the animals as peers, confidants, witnesses, and models of the healing that was possible. And week after week, group after group, the courage and growth I saw in these children took my breath away.

The difference the animals and I were making was profound, and it propelled me onward in my work. Word was starting to spread, and new agencies were knocking on my door, asking to bring their kids. The kids never did laugh at me; they never did seem bored; and it never took longer than twenty minutes to win over the most resistant of teenagers. The animals spun that kind of magic over all the groups that visited.

All I had dreamed of seemed to be coming true; I was healing animals and then working with those animals to heal kids. I was aligned with my purpose—doing what I had come into this life to do—and everything just seemed to be falling into place. The only thing that was missing was Scott's presence at my side. We lived together in relative peace, but I was alone with the Gentle Barn. Scott had no desire to hear about what was going on in the barnyard—not with the animals, not with the kids.

My true partner in this endeavor, from the very beginning—even before I knew what I was up to—was my sweet Mary, the goat. In early spring, however, I noticed that she was beginning to slow down. On one particular morning, as I filled the goats' hay bins, Mary did not get up. She just stayed where she was on the straw in the barn and watched me from there.

"Aren't you hungry, sweetheart?" I asked her. I went over and sat by her side and stroked her head. Then I went inside and called Dr. Geissen.

"Give it a couple of hours," he said. "Maybe she's just having an off day."

In the afternoon, Mary was still in the same spot, only now she was lying on her side. Looking at her, I felt a sudden surge of panic. *Something is very wrong. I need to get help.* And beneath the panic I felt fear. *I can't do this without her.*

I called the vet again; this time, he said he was dealing with emergencies, but that he'd get over to us as soon as he could.

As I moved around the barnyard and in and out of the house, cleaning and looking after Jesse, I returned over and over to the barn to check on Mary and sit by her side. *Please, please, don't go,* I thought as I stroked her neck. *You're my partner. I need you.*

By nightfall, Dr. Geissen still had not shown, and it became more and more obvious that Mary was leaving me. As soon as Scott came home, I asked him if he'd hang out with Jesse so I could be with Mary. I grabbed a blanket, and as I walked out to the barn, I made a decision. I did not want Mary to feel my panic. I did not want to make this all about me. I wanted her to know how much I appreciated her and that she was to be commended on a life well lived. So I took a deep breath and shoved the panic out of my body as best I could. Then I lay down behind Mary in the straw and spooned my precious girl and covered the two of us with the blanket. I no longer was waiting for the vet; I knew in my bones that it was too late. Instead I focused all of my being on thanking and loving the creature who had made the Gentle Barn possible. And for the next two hours I stroked her neck and kissed her head and sang to her.

"You know you changed my life, right?" I asked her, looking into her magical goat eyes. "You know how lucky I am I found you?" She looked right back at me and, through those secret-message slots, love poured out at me, and in her Eeyore way, she said, *Oh . . . thank you so very much.*

Mary passed away in my arms a half hour later.

CHAPTER 5

At the core of every human being is a resilience that buoys us back to the surface of life. I saw this in my at-risk kids and I saw it in myself. With every painful loss or setback that brings us crashing to our knees, we find some way to keep breathing and move forward. And so it was with losing Mary. I gathered myself up and found a way to move on, but she remained forever in my thoughts and in my heart. Her story would live on in others' hearts too; I told everyone who would listen, especially my at-risk kids, about the animal who'd made the whole thing possible.

I had more kids than ever coming out to visit. The more groups we had, the more the media heard about us and came out to take pictures and write up newspaper stories. That, in turn, brought more people out on Sundays to see what we were all about. As people arrived each Sunday, I had them wait at the picnic tables in the grassy yard until there were about ten people gathered, and then I introduced myself and my philosophy of reverence for all life.

"We may look different on the outside, but we're all the same," I would tell the visitors. "Just because a horse or a goat has four legs instead of two doesn't mean they don't have needs and wants and a voice. We just have to learn how to hear their voice and how to understand their desires. If we walk into their space slowly, quietly, we show our gentle, respectful intent, and hopefully that animal will reciprocate by allowing us to be with them and to pet them. But if they don't, we need to respect that, too."

Before I led people into the barnyard, I taught them about body language—theirs and the animals'—and made sure they understood when an animal was asking to be left alone. The result was a very different experience—for the people and for the animals. At that terrible petting zoo, the animals had been constantly on their guard. There'd been no supervision or intervention; no staff had been on hand to keep children from chasing the animals down, dragging them by their horns, or pulling on their fur.

Sundays at the Gentle Barn were the perfect environment to facilitate emotional healing in these goats and sheep and horses. They were surrounded by humans, especially children—the very culprits who had abused them—and yet no one pulled on them, no one chased them or cornered them, and people respected them when they said no. In this environment they could begin slowly to trust humans and to shed their trauma.

In the early days of opening to the public I personally gave every tour—for four hours straight. Needless to say, I was exhausted! I couldn't keep doing it all on my own. Some of the kids who had volunteered at the grand opening continued to come around, so I began teaching them how to give these tours and to educate people about the animals in our barnyard. Slowly others—kids and adults—started asking about volunteering. They were inspired by what they were witnessing and wanted to be a part of it. I accepted all offers with open arms, and by the end of my first year I had a small handful of regular volunteers. Mostly they came to help on Sundays, but neighbor kids sometimes helped out during the week, too. I requested that each volunteer talk to the animals before they did anything to them, such as grooming a horse or picking up a chicken. The volunteers, in turn, taught the Sunday visitors the same. It was by watching my volunteers that I learned how to better train them. I'd listen to how they talked to the visitors and then make suggestions for something they might add to their repertoire . . . or something they might cut out. I had one volunteer named Marcus who was an animal-rights activist. When Marcus gave his first tour, he took people over to Duncan, our big farm pig, and slapped him on the behind, saying, "This right here. This is your bacon." I had to sit Marcus down and have a discussion about subtlety.

––––––

In May 2000 someone told me about a website advertising miniature cows. Spurred on by curiosity, I went online to visit the site. There were pictures of miniature cows standing next to normal cows, to show that the miniatures were less than half the size of regular cattle. There was also an image of a tiny calf being cradled in someone's arms. Under the pictures was the statement: "If you like what you see and want to add some colorful miniatures to your front pasture, call us today!" There was a block of text beneath that explaining that miniature cows often became the family pet and could live inside your house, but that "miniatures also serve as terrific multipurpose cattle."

Multipurpose cattle? Still pretty new to the realm of farm animals, I didn't know for sure what that meant. But I had a hunch it had something to do with human consumption. I decided I had to call the place and find out.

"They're so easy to raise and easy to kill," the guy on the other end of the line said. "Their half size makes for half the work!" He had a faint Southern accent, even though I was calling Washington State. "They're perfect for single-family consumption. You can raise 'em right in your little backyard and have meat for a year. Or you can have one as a milk cow." He continued extolling the virtues of the miniature cow, hardly taking a breath. "We have this one little cow that our grandkids give bubble baths to. She's so docile they walk her around like a pet dog, and it's just too bad she can't get pregnant; we have to slaughter her tomorrow."

"Wait," I said. "What did you say?"

"They're just so easy and cheaper to raise."

"No, I mean after that."

"About our grandkids giving bubble baths—"

"Did you say you were going to slaughter her tomorrow?"

"Oh, that. Yeah, she's a breeder, but she can't get pregnant."

An animal who's getting bubble baths today and tomorrow is going to be killed—that was just not a situation I could walk away from. "It just doesn't seem right," I told the man. "I want to help that cow."

"Oh, darlin'," the man said. "That's just how life is."

"Can I buy her?" I asked.

"Well," he said, "that's tomorrow morning she's going to slaughter."

"How much would you ask for her?"

"Let's see, that would be about two thousand dollars, but—"

"I'll call you tomorrow morning. Please, I'm asking you. Give me a chance to get the money together."

"Well, you drive a hard bargain, little lady. I'll give you till nine o'clock tomorrow mornin'. But that's the latest."

I didn't have two thousand extra dollars lying around. And my trust fund was beginning to dwindle because I'd loaned so much of it to the Gentle Barn; I needed to hold on to *something* in case of emergencies. But I wasn't going to let these details stand in my way. I was going to rescue this cow. An idea popped into my head. I didn't know if it would work, but I had to try. There was no time to second-guess. I packed snacks and water in the diaper bag and took along the baby sling just in case Jesse got tired. As I headed out the front door I thought to myself, *We have goats, sheep, horses, pigs, and chickens. This is exactly what we need at the Gentle Barn—a cow!* How I was going to break it to Scott, I had no idea. I would cross that bridge when I got to it. First I had to come up with the money.

I walked all over my neighborhood and beyond, knocking on doors. The first house was the hardest. I had never knocked on a door to ask for anything. In truth I was a little shy about approaching people, and I was certainly uncomfortable intruding on someone and asking them to give money to a perfect stranger. *It's not for me*, I thought. *It's for that poor cow.* When I rang the bell, I held my breath, half hoping no one was home. I was sure I would get a strange look or even a door slammed in my face. But the door opened and a woman stood there smiling at me. "Hi," I said. "I'm Ellie. I'm your neighbor." And I told her about the sweetest little cow that was going to be slaughtered the next day, but that if all the neighbors pitched in just a bit we'd have the funds to save the cow and bring her down to the Gentle Barn. I even told her about the cow getting bubble baths, and I promised that she and all the neighbors could come visit the little cow when she arrived from Washington.

"Give me a minute," the woman said, and when she came back to the door she had a checkbook in hand. She sat right down on her porch and wrote me a check for $100.

I thanked the woman profusely and slid the check into the diaper bag. As I walked to the next house, I gave Jesse a hug and said, "Well, that was easy."

Not everyone gave money, but to my surprise not one person slammed a door.

When I headed for home my feet were killing me and it was already getting dark. I was just feeding Jesse when Scott returned from work; I hadn't even started on our dinner, and Scott was hungry. But I had done it. Not only had I raised the bulk of the $2,000 but my neighbors now felt invested in the Gentle Barn. All who had donated were eager to visit the new cow they had helped save. And I could easily make up the remaining couple hundred dollars.

"What are you so chipper about?" Scott grumbled. "And why are you home so late?"

It wasn't the best time to break the news to him, but I knew I had to say something soon; I was buying a cow in the morning. I decided to wait until after Scott had eaten, so I kept the news to myself as I put Jesse to bed and then hurried around the kitchen throwing dinner together.

I didn't work up the nerve to tell him until he was relaxing in front of the TV. I sat down and waited for a commercial and then blurted out the news.

Scott muted the volume. "Tell me I didn't just hear you say *cow*."

"Just a little cow," I said, and I told him all about miniature cows and how this one was going to be slaughtered in the morning if I didn't save her.

Scott lowered the footrest on the recliner and sat forward. "No," he said. "I'm sorry. This is where I'm going to put my foot down." And he literally put his foot, or rather both feet, down on the floor and stood up. "You are not getting a cow."

All through my childhood I'd been told I could not save animals. Those I did bring home were sent back out into the cold to die. One obstacle after another had been thrown in my path as I'd tried to help the only beings in my world who cared about me. But I wasn't a little girl anymore, and I was no longer willing to forsake the animals who needed my help.

"Here's the problem," I said, and I put my feet down too and stood up. "I *am* getting a cow."

"It's the cow or me," Scott said, and there was a finality to it that I'd never heard in his voice before.

The cow arrived the following week.

The Gentle Barn's new resident was a year old and—not yet full-grown—was about hip-high. She was a miniature Hereford, with a red-and-white coat and a broad face. Having been raised as livestock, she had never been given a name. But as the man had said on the phone, she was as docile as a dog. And she took to the barnyard as easily as if she had lived there her whole young life. I sat down on a bench in the barnyard that first day and watched her grazing the alfalfa and thought, *What do I call you?* As soon as I'd had that thought, the little cow moseyed clear across the barnyard toward me, as though she'd heard me thinking.

Peaches, I thought, looking at her. *You look like a Peaches. It would be perfect for your coloring.* At that moment the cow stopped, very close to me, and stared right at me with her big brown eyes, and I heard something inside my head.

"Buddha."

Ever since childhood I'd heard lots of little whispers from the animal world, but they had never been in actual words. It was just a knowing deep inside me. So I had no reason to think the word "Buddha" had come from anywhere but my own head. And yet, it was not the type of name I would ever come up with. Why on earth would I call a cow Buddha—especially a girl cow? *That's ridiculous,* I told myself. *That's not a name for a cow.*

I let my mind wander over other possible names—*Daisy, Betty*—back to *Peaches.* And again I heard *"Buddha"* inside my head. I tried to dismiss it and return to my naming endeavor, but the name Buddha kept forcing its way back into my thoughts. This went on for quite some time; I was arguing with myself over what to call this cow. And all the while the cow stood right smack in front of me, staring me down, until finally I stared right back at her big cow eyes and said, "Is that *you* telling me that?"

She just kept staring at me, a foot from my face, chewing the alfalfa she'd been grazing.

"Well, if it is," I said, "that is the dumbest cow name I have ever heard. I am not calling you Buddha."

Now I was arguing with a cow.

"Look at you," I said. "You're so pretty. You look like a *Peaches*. You're red; it's a perfect name. *Peaches*."

But once again, with even more force, I heard, *"Buddha!"*

Half of me still doubting that it really was the cow I was arguing with, rather than my own thoughts, and the whole thing finally just wore me down.

"Fine!" I said to her. "I'll call you Buddha!" At which point she licked her lips and walked away.

Buddha settled right in, getting along with everyone in the barnyard, and all the animals accepted her right back. I'd never seen an animal need no adjustment period whatsoever. And it didn't take long before I had the chance to witness just how wise the little cow was. On that first Sunday following Buddha's arrival I got to see how she did when she was surrounded by large groups of people. Each time I adopted an animal, I never knew until the first Sunday after their arrival how they would be with crowds. Some animals who were perfectly fine with me or with a small group would withdraw or retreat behind the barn when there were too many people around.

Buddha not only didn't withdraw, Buddha did something I'd never seen any of our animals do. She held perfectly still. Within ten minutes of opening our doors, all the kids had gravitated to our new little cow. A sea of children surrounded Buddha, and she lay down right in the middle of them and let them pet and brush and hug her, and the entire time Buddha didn't move a muscle. Not one twitch until the children had finished and walked away.

I sat back and watched in awe. This was no ordinary cow. Clearly Buddha was going to be a big celebrity at the Gentle Barn, a true ambassador for the animals, modeling just how intelligent and sensitive farm animals were.

That first Sunday evening after Buddha's visitor-day debut, I went into the barn, where Buddha was lying down. I kneeled beside her and put my arms around her neck. "You were awesome," I said. "Thank you so much." She swung her head around, which made her neck into a *U* shape, and that *U* perfectly embraced my back. I'd never felt anything quite like it. Encircled by her neck, I was captured in a cow hug, and her warmth seeped deep into my body. But there was something else, too, some energy that felt both foreign and as familiar as my own breath. In that moment I felt so at peace, so totally accepted by this animal. It reminded me a lot of being covered in butterflies.

As I left the barn that night, I knew I would be getting one of those hugs every day for the rest of this cow's life. I also knew I had to introduce this hug to others; I was not going to keep all that goodness to myself. I would start with the people who needed it most—my at-risk kids. Many of those kids had never experienced a hug of any kind. Everything in their environment was harsh. They'd learned to survive that environment by never letting their guard down. To be vulnerable for them was to risk abuse or even death. And yet the irony was that the healing they so desperately needed was not ever going to happen within the tough, guarded behavior that had helped them survive. The healing could only happen in the opposite, in vulnerability. There was no way to hug this cow—really hug her—without being vulnerable. Hugging Buddha was soft and warm and slow and still—the antithesis of any touch they'd ever received.

"That's not a real hug," I said playfully when the very first boy attempted to embrace Buddha. He'd barely touched her with his hands, his arms floating a foot above her fur, his face nowhere near her neck. "Like this," I said, and I laid my face down on Buddha's neck, closed my eyes, and inhaled her sweet, warm scent.

He tried again, but still it was more of a *hover* than a hug. The other boys did a little better, but not by much. I wasn't going to give up, though. From that point forward, every group of kids was going to start off their visit by hugging Buddha. It would be my one rule at the Gentle Barn from then on. It was in this hug—I was sure of it—that they would begin to shed their survival armor and start to heal.

My next group of at-risk girls did better. One of the girls lingered for a long while with her face nuzzled into Buddha's soft fur, and Buddha swung her head around and encircled the girl in her cow hug. I saw the glint of tears in the girl's eyes afterward, and I knew she got it. I made sure to tell her before she left that day how proud I was of her. If these kids could start there, by accepting love from a cow, maybe they then could accept love from other human beings, and just maybe one day learn to love themselves.

Most of my sessions with the kids left me elated and overflowing with joy, as though I'd just fallen in love. Unfortunately, this was not an energy reflected in my own home. When I'd stood my ground about getting the cow, I had hoped Scott's ultimatum was a bluff. But the day after Buddha arrived, Scott moved out of our bedroom and into the guest room. He was only staying under the same roof, he said, because he wanted to be there for our son. We both tried to put on a happy front for Jesse, who—still so young—didn't seem to be bothered by his parents' new sleeping arrangements.

A full month had passed and Scott and I were still in separate bedrooms, and there was an awkwardness and heaviness to our minimal interactions. Some days I blamed him, feeling frustrated with what felt to me like a silent temper tantrum, and I wanted him to just get over it and come back to me already. Just as Scott hadn't believed I would ever really start the Gentle Barn, I hadn't believed he would ever really stay away. But I was also beginning to get fleeting glimpses into what I had done to contribute to our separation. I knew I could be headstrong and single-minded in my pursuit of righting a wrong. I often didn't get how others could miss the injustice of a situation, or why they wouldn't want to help change it. I expected others to see the world the way I saw it, and I guess I thought Scott would come around when he saw that what I was doing was right and necessary.

But Scott didn't seem to be coming around. And it was too late to change the course of what was unfolding in the barnyard. I simply turned my gaze away from the disaster of my personal life, as one would when passing an accident on the freeway, and I buried myself in my work with the animals and the at-risk kids. This was what I was destined to do, and if that scared men off, then so be it. I knew how to make my own way. I'd done it most of my life. So I tucked away my loneliness and my feelings of rejection and failure and pressed forward with the Gentle Barn. What I couldn't see at the time was that this very behavior—this air of self-sufficiency—was pushing Scott further and further out of my life.

As I failed at love in my home, I learned daily about love from the animals. The interspecies family that was growing in the barnyard was like a net that caught me as I fell through the holes torn in my marriage. These animals loved me as much as I loved them, and they cared for and supported one another, as well. I saw one story after another unfold in my own backyard, stories that told of a love so much bigger than the box we usually try to put it in.

Many stories reached across the species divide, such as the one about Katie the horse and the baby black goat, Zoe. Katie whinnied for an hour one morning, starting at six a.m. I ignored her, thinking she was asking for food a good hour earlier than her usual breakfast time, but when I finally got out to the barnyard, I was surprised to find Katie nowhere near her hay bin. Instead she was standing next to the pigs' mud hole, and in the mud hole was Zoe. The tiny goat was up to her chest in muddy water and every time she attempted to step up and out of the mud hole, she slid back down into the brown water. Katie, the once-irascible horse, had been calling for help for a baby goat.

There was also Olaf the rooster, who insisted on sleeping atop our huge pig, Duncan, every night (despite my urging otherwise for his own safety). And there was Daisy the hen, who chased after me when I took her eggs (I wanted to rescue lives, not create new ones). She so desperately wanted to be a mother, she hid one of her eggs until it hatched, bringing her son Owl into the world as a new member of our barnyard. When I first glimpsed the little chick, Daisy held her head high, and looked at me dead-on. *"Ha!"* I could just imagine the triumphant hen saying.

"Good for you, Daisy," I said. "Good for you."

But the love story that moved me the most—filling me with awe and perhaps a bit of envy—was that of Grandpa Goat and young Emily. Grandpa, who had been crippled when he'd arrived, had regained his ability to walk, thanks to an expert in animal massage. During this period, a young goat named Emily joined our barnyard. Vibrant and fit as a fiddle, she took a shine to the elderly Grandpa. This was not simple camaraderie; it was absolute devotion. She would sit by Grandpa's side and groom him and nibble on him, and when he got up and made his way slowly around the barnyard, she followed his every step. She was completely and madly in love.

Unfortunately, as Grandpa Goat went from old to older, he began to slip back into the crippled state in which he'd arrived. I made a big, fluffy bed of straw for him, and he stayed in that bed nearly all of the time. Emily, of course, stayed right by his side. One night, at two in the morning, I heard a terrible bleating coming from the barnyard. I had learned my lesson from Katie and Zoe, and so threw off the covers and went immediately to check on the animals. Grandpa had fallen from his bed and could not get up, and Emily—unable to help him—was beside herself, baaing frantically.

Grandpa could no longer even get up to go to the bathroom. I cleaned his bed throughout the day and added more straw to keep it soft for his achy body. But finally, one day, I knew the time had come. I couldn't in good conscience let him go on living like he was. I explained to Emily that it wasn't fair to keep him there in this condition, and I told Grandpa that I was going to help him out of this body that no longer worked. Emily was young and fit, and I figured she would find another goat to befriend, but after the difficult morning when the vet and I helped Grandpa out of his misery, Emily took to Grandpa's bed and wouldn't get up.

For a week she stayed in that bed, and there was nothing I could do to cheer her up. One morning when I came into the barn I froze at the door and stared at Emily, holding my breath. She was not moving. I went to her and laid my hand on her side. There was no life in her body. "Emily," I said, as though I could call her back to this life. But Emily had already gone.

I called the vet out and he did an exam and found nothing; there had been nothing medically wrong with this young goat. She had simply died of a broken heart.

In addition to the grief I felt, I was struck through with awe at having witnessed a love so deep that a young girl had laid down her life for it. I had never loved like that—at least, not another adult human—and I wondered what it took to love someone that much.

———

That summer, Scott and I decided to give it another shot. Perhaps it was because—with the summer break from working with the at-risk kids—I had a lighter schedule and thus was a bit more available, not constantly on a mission. Or maybe it was simply that each of us, in our separate thoughts, always had hoped to make things work. Whatever the reason, it was nice to have my husband back, nice to be a normal family again.

It was a few months into this period of harmony in my household that a new volunteer named Chantelle came to the Gentle Barn. She had a fiery red mane and bright blue eyes and fancied herself a witch, but she assured me she was the good kind. We clicked right away and began spending a bit of time together outside the Gentle Barn. One day Chantelle invited me to her place for tea. Her bookshelves were lined with rocks and crystals and dusty old books, and there was a spicy-sweet smell in the air. As she poured me a steaming cup of tea she named all the herbs in it, some of which I'd never heard of. She brought Jesse some apple juice and I lifted him onto my lap.

When she sat down opposite us she said, "You know I have psychic abilities, right?"

"No, I don't think you told me that."

"Well, I want to do a reading for you."

After only the shortest hesitation, I said, "OK, sure. That sounds fun."

She reached for my hand and I thought she was going to read my palm but she just held my hand across the table and closed her eyes. After a long time just sitting there, she said, "I'm sorry you felt so alone during your childhood. No one really got you. No one understood except the animals."

She was definitely telling my story, but I always spoke quite freely about my childhood. Perhaps I'd even told her.

"Simon was especially there for you," she said.

Now, *that* got my attention. I was sure I'd never mentioned my childhood dog to her.

"The Gentle Barn," she said, and I sat up in my chair, waiting for what would come next, but she didn't say anything for a long moment.

Jesse squirmed on my lap and I set him down on the floor, hoping he wouldn't pull anything off the shelves. "It's OK," she said, and she took my hand again, "there's nothing breakable." At this point Chantelle opened her eyes and fixed her blue gaze on me. "You don't believe anyone will ever *really* understand what you're doing with the Gentle Barn. But all that's going to change one day. Lots of people are going to understand; more than you can even imagine."

I felt a welling-up in my chest, sadness and hope all mixed together.

"In fact," she said, and again she sat silently for a moment. Then: "Oh! There's going to be a man."

"A man?"

"Yes, in seven months. A man who will love animals right alongside you. He'll share the Gentle Barn with you. A true soul mate."

"What are you talking about?" I said. "I'm married."

———

I wanted so desperately to share my world with Scott. After Chantelle's reading, I began asking him to please, just this once, come and spend a little time with me in the barnyard. Scott got annoyed, and I didn't take the cue to back off; I pushed and he went over the edge, and in the early spring he moved back into the guest room. I ran out to Buddha for her soothing hug. Embraced in her warmth I spoke to her of my grief and despair and my sense of failure.

"Why on earth do I even try?" I said to her. I could feel the tears making tracks down my barnyard-dusted face. I pressed my cheek against her neck, letting the tears soak into her soft fur. "I hope you don't mind," I said to her. "I hope it's not too much of a burden for me to come to you like this."

Buddha stuck out her long, sandpapery tongue and licked my elbow.

This would not be Scott's final good-bye, not yet. He would stay under one roof with me for another year or more, and we would try more than once to reconcile—to fit our mismatched dreams together. We both wanted to make it work for Jesse, and we each wanted to make this life match what we had envisioned when we'd gotten married, but it was as though our dreams were from two different jigsaw puzzles, and there would never be a true fit.

CHAPTER 6

Shortly after Jesse turned two, Scott's parents—who didn't know yet about our off-again, on-again separation—suggested we put our son in preschool so he could learn to socialize with other children. In my opinion he seemed too young to be away from home like that, even if only for part of the day. But I relented, figuring they knew more about child-rearing than I did. Still, it was heart-wrenching to leave him crying in the arms of the caregiver.

"He only cries for a few minutes," the woman would assure me. "Five minutes after you leave, he's playing with the other kids."

"OK," I would say, trying to feel reassured. But it never got easier to hand him off and drive away.

We did, eventually, fall into a daily rhythm. After I dropped Jesse off at preschool, I came back and fed the animals and cleaned up the barnyard. My groups arrived at eleven or one. After the group was over, I addressed any medical issues with a vet. Then, bursting to see my son, I'd rush off to pick him up and spend the rest of the afternoon giving him my undivided attention. When Scott came home, he took over with Jesse so I could feed the animals dinner.

As organized as this sounds, I am not, and never have been, a left-brain person. I have only a loose grasp on linear time, dwelling more naturally in the fluid world of the heart and the present moment. I still often got caught up in the heavenly atmosphere of the barnyard, waking with a start as though from a dream to greet my arriving group or run inside to give Jesse a bath. The business aspect of the Gentle Barn was also beyond my grasp; my nonlinear brain shied away from numbers in general, whether attached to a clock or a dollar sign. It never occurred to me to create a business plan; I didn't even know what was supposed to be in one. Neither had it ever entered my mind to consult with someone who did have business savvy. Although I had formed a board of directors when I'd established the Gentle Barn as a nonprofit, and although the board members loved the Gentle Barn and wanted to see it succeed, none of them had a solid business background.

For the most part, the Gentle Barn and I traveled forward flying blind, relying purely on instinct to guide us. And somehow everything kept falling into place. That didn't mean I didn't worry. There were only small trickles of money coming in from various different sources and I never knew if there would be enough. We only asked a $5 donation per person at the door on Sundays and the same for field trips. Although I had a set price for a ten-month period for the probation camps and foster-care facilities that visited, most didn't have the money, so I opened my doors to them for free. Because the Gentle Barn had begun appearing in the media, we did start receiving occasional donations from people who had read about us or seen us on the news, but I had no idea how to make more of that happen. With my trust fund just about gone, Scott and my parents came in to pick up the slack with loans and gifts, but I wanted the Gentle Barn to be self-supporting.

So when I learned that one of my new volunteers had a background in corporate America, I started asking questions. Jay had first come to the Gentle Barn to bring his eleven-year-old stepdaughter to volunteer. They came every Friday, and before long he was working right along-side her, helping with whatever tasks or projects needed doing. Eventually he began showing up on other days too, to offer more help with feeding and cleanup or with fixing things. I was surprised at how good Jay was with tools. He looked like he'd never held a hammer. He had manicured fingernails and no calluses, and every hair on his head was in its perfect place. I found out that he'd been a vice president of marketing and had been laid off when his company had taken a nosedive. He was spending his time volunteering as he searched for a new job.

After Jay saw that I fed the animals fruits and vegetables to supplement their diet, he showed up the next time with a big box full of fresh produce. "All organic," he said as he set the box on the kitchen counter.

"Wow, thank you!"

"Thank Whole Foods," he said. "It's all donated."

It had never occurred to me to ask for donations from food markets. I had always paid for the produce I fed my animals. Apparently supermarkets over-ordered produce as a matter of course and had to throw good stuff out daily.

Jay began to make the rounds to five Whole Foods Markets and filled his van with organic produce that was only a day or two old and still looked beautiful. We'd sort and prep the produce, putting out the greens and grapes for all the animals in the barnyard, and then fill big bowls with the rest of the produce for the pigs. As we worked I'd ask him all kinds of questions about running a business and promotion and marketing.

"Do you have a website?" Jay asked one day as he was washing potatoes and carrots in the sink.

"Sure we do," I said, proud that at least I'd known enough to have a website made. I took him to my computer and brought up the site.

"May I?" he asked, pointing to my desk chair.

"Of course."

He was a big guy and he dwarfed my little chair. He had to lower the seat to see the monitor properly. "Hmm," he said as he scrolled around the site. "I don't see a Donate button."

"There isn't one," I said, and I could feel myself blushing. I hadn't even realized I could receive donations through my website.

He clicked on some links and poked around the site, then said, "I could make this website a lot more dynamic." He turned to me and added, "If you'd like me to."

Wow, free fruits and veggies and now free tech support? "I'd be incredibly grateful," I said, and I was surprised by the tears that sprang into my eyes.

Over the next few weeks, Jay worked to bring our website up to a whole new level. He also designed a brochure for us to put out in vegan restaurants and health-food markets, and to hand out at playgrounds. It was a full-color tri-fold that invited people to come meet the animals on Sundays, visit our website to learn more about us, or to make a donation.

Sometimes Jay came to the Gentle Barn straight from picking up his younger daughter, Molli, from preschool. Molli looked like the girl on the poster for *Les Misérables*. She had huge eyes that took in everything around her, but she never said a word, not one peep. Although she was a year older than Jesse (who was two and a half at the time), she was smaller than he was, with the tiniest little fingers and the most delicate features. While Jay worked at the computer I would take the two kids out to the barnyard to play. But as hard as I tried I couldn't get Molli to speak or even to laugh. Sometimes, when Jay had a date night with his wife, I would babysit Molli, and although she didn't talk she let me brush her hair and she would lean into me when we watched TV.

By fall of our second year, I had groups of kids coming out three to five days a week. I had a handful and a half of volunteers, and more inquiring every Sunday. And I had the press coming out every couple of months. And yet, even surrounded by all these people, I was filled with a profound sense of loneliness. I felt it only in the rare moments when I wasn't up to my armpits in the responsibilities of raising a growing child and the duties of running a growing organization. But it was always there in the background. I was all alone in this expanding endeavor. And even while the numbers of visitors increased, I saw people in my intimate circle falling away. Girlfriends I'd gone out with for drinks or a movie, other moms I'd done playdates with at the park or at each other's houses. I'd said "Sorry, I can't" so many times, they had simply stopped calling.

At least it was a consolation prize to have such a gung-ho volunteer as Jay. His enthusiasm for the Gentle Barn gave me hope.

"What would you think about coming to our next board meeting?" I asked him one day as he helped me fill water buckets in the barn. It had occurred to me that, with his corporate background, Jay might have some insight or suggestions to offer. He came to the next meeting and listened attentively to everything that was said, and then he proposed some thoughts of his own—half a dozen great fundraising ideas. He even offered to write grants for us. By the end of the meeting he was advising us in business matters none of us had even considered. It wasn't long before we asked him to join the board, and I moved forward feeling a little bit lighter.

Like everyone who spent any time at the Gentle Barn, Jay developed a fondness for particular animals. The first was Olaf the rooster. Olaf and his brother Elvis were Polish Bantam chickens someone had rescued from a little shop in Chinatown and brought to the Gentle Barn.

Olaf and Elvis offered constant comic relief, though they seemed to take themselves very seriously. They were white and smaller than the average rooster and their heads were topped with fluffy pom-poms. Always together, they strutted around the barnyard as if they were leading a massive parade. They'd lift their feather-adorned feet high, as though stepping in time to music. Perhaps in their fluffy white heads, they were even seeing fireworks and large, adoring crowds. Yet, despite this seeming self-importance, the Chinatown brothers were very affectionate with humans. Kids could pet their soft feathers, kiss them, and carry them around. The brothers adored the attention and were a fan favorite from the moment they walked into the barnyard on their red carpet.

I was never quite sure why Jay fell for Olaf over Elvis. To be honest, I found it difficult to tell the two apart. True, Olaf's pom-pom was a tad larger, making him look like a Russian tsar with one of those huge fuzzy hats. Sometimes when he walked he even looked like he was doing that squatting Russian dance with arms crossed and legs kicking out in front of him. Elvis had more of a *cool* thing going on, with his particularly wide "bellbottoms." But these were subtle differences. I'm sure Jay had his reasons; love wasn't always logical. What drew someone to a particular animal was as mysterious as the chemistry between humans.

Jay's other barnyard love affair was with Kaylee the dog. Kaylee was one of my eight and was a smooth-coated Australian cattle dog, with white-and-fawn mottled fur. She was a very gentle soul, still a bit skittish from her rough start of neglect and surviving being hit by a car. Jay always visited Kaylee first when he arrived, and if he got to the Barn early in the day he would help me walk the eight dogs, always making sure Kaylee was in his set of four.

During these walks, Jay and I talked about fund-raising ideas and how to attract more people. But over time, our talks turned to more personal topics—his concerns about his marriage, and my guilty feelings about putting Jesse into day care. We enjoyed each other's company, and the more we talked the more we realized we had in common. I was amazed to find out that his sister had been in my class in high school and one of my brothers had been in Jay's class in elementary school. Our families had belonged to the same congregation, and yet the two of us had never met.

Just like me, Jay had grown up in a household that had hardly noticed his existence. His bedroom had been in the basement, which afforded him the opportunity to sneak out whenever he wanted and to smuggle stray dogs back in. The only regular attention he got was beatings and bloody noses from his stepfather, until one day after he'd turned eighteen and he'd simply had enough and started fighting back.

Throughout his childhood, animals had been the only ones he'd truly trusted. Just like me he spoke better Animal than Human; his human relationships suffered for it, and his marriage was disintegrating fast. In many ways, it seemed, we had lived parallel lives, and I was grateful for this new friend—a true brother.

One day, after we'd returned from walking the dogs he said, "I'm going to take Kaylee home, OK?"

What? Sure, we'd all taken a liking to this man, and clearly he was feeling quite comfortable at the Gentle Barn. But take my dog? "Um," I said. "You're going to what?"

"Just for the day. I want to take her home and give her a bath."

"You can give her a bath here," I suggested.

"I miss having a dog at home," he said. "And I want her to hang out with my kids."

Kaylee was my dog; she belonged with me at the Gentle Barn. But Jay had a way of presenting ideas that was so full of confidence and so full of charisma that I couldn't figure out how, or even why, to say no. "Uh," I said, stalling. "Well, if Kaylee wants to go . . ." But I knew Kaylee wouldn't want to go. She'd come a long way, but she still got nervous around cars. "Do you want to go, Kaylee?" I asked her as Jay walked to his van. He opened the door and Kaylee jumped right in.

I stood there in front of the house as they drove off, feeling like I'd just been jilted.

Two hours passed and I hadn't heard from Jay, so I called to see what was happening. When he picked up the phone, I heard kids laughing in the background.

"I think it's time for Kaylee to come home now," I said. I sounded like the mom of a teenage girl.

"We're just blow-drying her," Jay said. "We'll bring her home ooon."

When they got back, Kaylee jumped out of the car, clean and fluffy and wagging from nose to stumpy little tail. Kaylee didn't walk; she pranced—all around the living room—swinging her head from side to side, which in Kaylee-speak was a big, huge smile.

I had to admit, I was touched by how much Jay loved my dog. And Kaylee obviously loved him right back.

———

Fall arrived, but in the San Fernando Valley, that didn't necessarily put an end to summer. With shorts weather as the backdrop, I began to plan the second annual Thanksgiving celebration. I had come up with the idea the year before when someone had brought a turkey to the Gentle Barn. Tommy the turkey had been raised for the Thanksgiving table, but the man who had raised him could not bring himself to slaughter the bird and brought him to me instead. With Tommy as the guest of honor, I had invited bunches of people to participate in a potluck feast, asking people to bring only vegan dishes so no animals would be harmed in the making of the celebration. Two hundred people had shown up, and I'd decided that this would be a yearly tradition—*rescuing* a turkey rather than feasting on one.

When Jay heard about this tradition, he jumped on board to help put on the second annual celebration.

"We won't do a potluck this time," he said with his trademark self-confidence. "We'll cook instead and ask Whole Foods to donate all the ingredients."

"Who's going to cook all that food?" I said. Jay didn't know yet that I was not a good candidate for the chef crew; I had a repertoire of about two dishes, and one of them was halfway decent.

"I'll head the team. We can get volunteers to help."

Jay rolled out the rest of his plan. We would hire acrobats to entertain, as well as get someone to sing, maybe jazz—with a good sound system. We'd have table linens in fall colors and real china—none of those cheap paper products; that wasn't environmentally friendly. And on each table, we'd have a cornucopia as a centerpiece. I was gaining more understanding every day as to why Jay had been a vice president of marketing.

Preparing the barnyard would be my domain, as well as rounding up the contact info for our guest list. Jay and I worked together for the next few weeks in preparation for our gala event. We also went to rescue our honored guest from a place that sold live turkeys for Thanksgiving. I was surprised and delighted when Scott said he'd help out the day of the event, not only by watching Jesse but with whatever else needed to be done.

We were expecting about 250 people, 50 more than the previous year, and our kitchen crew had prepared a little extra, just in case. We had finished putting up the last of the decorations and had begun laying out the food on the long tables at the side of the yard when the first guests arrived. We had a volunteer at a table at the gate, taking the suggested donation of $25 and making sure we had everyone's e-mail address. I couldn't believe how well this whole thing was set up. I'd never had such a high-class, well-organized event at the Gentle Barn.

When the food was all laid out, we thanked everyone for coming and announced that the buffet was open. People lined up at the long tables with their plates. It looked like just about everyone had arrived; there were at least as many guests as the previous year. But as the line of guests moved along the buffet, more people kept arriving through the gate. And the line at the buffet kept getting longer.

I made my way through the crowd to Jay. "How many people do you think are here?"

Jay was scanning the crowd, his eyes wide—a crack in his self-confidence. "A lot," he said.

"Do we have enough food?"

"I don't think so," he whispered, as though trying to keep a secret. He looked around, searching. "Help me round up some volunteers. We'll go buy more food."

Scott decided to go along, but I could see he wasn't happy. "There must be five hundred people here," he said to me before they went out the gate. Scott did not like big crowds, especially when they were crammed into our own backyard.

The first wave of diners had settled in at the tables. All the chairs seemed to be taken, but many more people were still in line for food. I ran into the house with a couple of volunteers and we grabbed every available chair or stool we could find, including the two tiny chairs from Jesse's play table.

The guys got back with the groceries and hurried into the kitchen to start cooking up more food. A few minutes later, I peeked in to see how it was coming. There was a flurry of knives and spatulas and big stirring spoons; I decided I was more comfortable outside with the guests, who knew nothing of the chaos in the kitchen.

Soon more dishes of steaming food appeared on the buffet table, and they kept coming in waves, barely keeping up with the influx of people in the line. This went on for quite some time, until finally everyone seemed to have gotten their dinner.

I had barely caught my breath when it was time for me to address our guests. Standing in front of a crowd with a microphone was not my favorite place to be. It didn't matter that I'd taken acting classes. I'd been nervous about this moment ever since I'd planned out what I wanted to say. I'd practiced over and over in front of the mirror, trying to organize my speech in an order that made sense.

"Hi," I said into the mike, and I couldn't tell if my voice was loud enough. "Thank you so much for coming," I said a bit louder. "I'm Ellie, and I started the Gentle Barn."

Everyone clapped and smiled. They didn't seem to mind that they were scrunched in around tables meant for half as many people. Seeing all of the warm, kind faces, I relaxed a little. I told the story of how the Gentle Barn had started with one little goat named Mary. Then I introduced everyone to our two honored guests, who were wandering freely around the tables—the turkeys we'd rescued this year and last. I told each turkey's story and I also talked about the kids who came to work with our animals and the miracles I witnessed daily in the barnyard. I finished by saying, "It's because of the generosity of all of you that we can do this work."

Relieved that my speech was over, I introduced our singer. We'd found an eleven-year-old boy who sang like Louis Armstrong. The crowd was as blown away as we had been and gave him a standing ovation. Then the acrobats came on. They wore colorful bodysuits and face paint and made a human pyramid by standing on one another's shoulders. Then one man held a pole and others climbed up it and sprang off into the air, doing flips and pirouettes. They tossed and caught one another and twisted their bodies into impossible shapes. The crowd was thrilled.

All through the performances, I kept circulating, making sure everything was going well. At one point I spotted Scott sitting near the back door to the house. His jaw was clenched and he practically winced every time a guest went into the house to use the bathroom. I also noticed that Jay kept running back and forth from the kitchen to the table where his wife and daughters sat. I found out later that his wife was cold sitting outside and not happy that he wasn't sitting with her throughout the whole event.

As the entertainment came to a close we laid out the desserts on the buffet table. As people again lined up, I saw Scott storm out of the house. It was a silent storm, but I could read his body language perfectly; he was pissed. He fumed his way across the yard and through the tables to the utility shed and then fumed his way back across the yard and back through the tables, a plunger in his fist. Before he entered the house, he glared at me for a hard, cold three seconds.

I looked from the back door, where Scott had disappeared with the plunger, to Jay. Jay had seen the whole thing, and the two of us burst into laughter. Perhaps it was just a needed release, but, boy, did it feel good at that moment to have a partner in crime—someone who was as excited as I was that five hundred people had shown up to support us. A clogged-up toilet seemed a small price to pay.

———

In the end, we didn't raise much money; we had spent too much on entertainment and the extra food and not charged enough at the door. It would be a few years before the art of the fund-raiser would be mastered at the Gentle Barn. We did, however, raise awareness about the organization, and about farm animals and how badly they're treated more often than not. We also added a couple hundred names to our e-mail list. Although it had been a wonderful experience overall, I was relieved that we were not putting on an event for the winter holidays. I planned to lie low and just hang out with Jesse and the animals.

For Christmas Eve, I usually went with Scott and Jesse to my in-laws' home. But the atmosphere in our house was especially tense ever since Thanksgiving and the stopped-up-toilet incident. I was happy to have Scott take Jesse to his parents'; I was going to spend the evening in my favorite place—surrounded by the residents of the barnyard.

That evening a volunteer helped me give the animals extra servings of fresh fruits and veggies as a Christmas present—grapes and greens spread around the yard for everyone, carrots for the horses, and potatoes, beets, and other veggies for the pigs. After the volunteer left, I sat in the fading light, hugging my knees to my chest to keep warm, and watched the animals gobble up their fresh treats. A chicken darted between two goats to nab a grape, then ran off as the other hens chased after her. The pigs ate with their usual noisy exuberance—all together, except for Susie Q, who shared her dinner with Buddha.

Susie Q, a big brown farm pig, and the newest large animal in our barnyard, had arrived terribly depressed a few months back. She had been in line to be slaughtered at a sausage plant and had made a daring escape by crashing through the fence. She'd been found running down the street in a neighborhood near the slaughterhouse, and when the slaughterhouse had denied ownership, she'd been sent to the pound. When she'd arrived in our barnyard, she wouldn't eat, wouldn't drink, and wouldn't get up. She just lay by the fence, the farthest point possible from any of the other animals. Occasionally another pig or a goat would come by and sniff at her, but mostly the other animals ignored her, as though in her despondency the pig had made herself invisible.

Buddha was the only animal who did not ignore her. Instead, she made it her mission to make Susie Q more comfortable. For six days Buddha kept vigil with the new pig, lying by her side at the far end of the barnyard, and slowly Susie Q began to emerge from her despair. Buddha had performed the final stage of Susie Q's rescue. She had given our new pig reason to live.

As I watched the two best friends share their meal on this Christmas Eve, I noticed that Buddha had stopped eating and was making a strange movement, with her head thrusting forward. I'd never seen her do this before.

"Buddha?" I said, and I jumped up and went over to her. Her sides were heaving, and she began making a horrible sound, like a hairball being coughed up. "Buddha, what's wrong?" I stroked her convulsing sides, as though by touching her I would understand what was happening. Then I looked down and there in Susie Q's bowl, the few remaining vegetables were fully intact, not chopped up at all.

"Oh no," I said. "OK, Buddha, I have to try to see what's stuck." I pried open her mouth to look inside but couldn't see a thing, and I kept losing my grip on her jaws because her body kept heaving. "Oh, sweetheart," I said as I pushed up my sleeve, "I'm going to have to reach inside your mouth." But I couldn't get my hand past the back of her tongue. Then I felt along the outside of her neck and in the front, at the base of her throat, was a huge bulge the size of a softball, only oblong. Buddha must have swallowed a whole potato.

I ran inside to call the vet, knowing it was going to be near impossible to reach him on Christmas Eve. There was a message with a phone number for an emergency facility. I called that number, and the woman who answered said they weren't making house calls that evening; I'd have to bring my animal in. I pictured Buddha with her heaving cough and knew there was no way I was going to get her into a trailer on my own. Then I remembered a vet who'd come out once when my usual vet had been out of town. I searched through my purse and finally found the card.

"I'm sorry to bother you on Christmas Eve," I said into the phone, "but I think my cow is dying." I couldn't believe the vet herself had answered the call.

"OK," she said, "hold tight. I'm at a party, but I'll get there as soon as I can."

Dr. Fox arrived forty-five minutes later wearing a gorgeous evening gown and a red Santa Claus hat. She had her husband and both her parents in tow, all dressed to the nines.

"I'm so sorry for interrupting your Christmas Eve," I said as I hurried with the vet and her entourage out to the barnyard.

"No worries," she said. "Let's just see if we can help your cow."

I led Buddha into the barn and turned on the light. As Dr. Fox palpated my cow's neck, she asked if I had any idea what she might have swallowed.

"A potato, I think." And I explained that a volunteer had neglected to cut up the vegetables.

"Vegetables?" the vet said, and when her hand passed over the bulge in Buddha's throat she said, "Oh boy."

This didn't sound encouraging.

"OK," said Dr. Fox. "Let's see if we can't get that potato out," and the next thing I knew the vet was pulling down the straps of her fancy evening gown in my barn. She eased the dress off her shoulders and left it hanging down around her waist. She now stood there in her heels, her bra, and a Santa Claus hat and instructed her tuxedo-clad husband to stand behind Buddha so the cow couldn't back away.

Dr. Fox slid her hand into Buddha's mouth and reached in all the way up to her elbow, then up to her upper arm, then up to her shoulder. Buddha coughed and heaved even harder, trying to expel not only the potato but now also the vet's arm. Dr. Fox looked up to the rafters as she worked, as though trying to picture the inside of my cow in her mind's eye. Then she shook her head lightly and said, "Hmm." She bent her knees and shifted the angle of her arm a bit. I could see the strain on her face as she reached and struggled to grab the tuber. But again she shook her head.

"It's just out of reach," Dr. Fox said. She withdrew her arm and it glistened with saliva and digestive juices. "I can touch it with my fingertips but I can't get hold of it."

"Oh my God," I said quietly, and my knees started to tremble. I felt absolutely helpless.

Buddha's stomach had by now blown up like a balloon, making her look pregnant. The vet explained that because burping was a natural part of ruminant digestion, the stomach bloated if the burping got obstructed. "If they bloat too badly, it can be fatal," she said matter-of-factly.

My own stomach clenched, and I could hardly breathe.

"We have to do an emergency surgery," the vet said.

"Of course," I said. "Whatever it takes."

Dr. Fox asked her husband to go get her surgical kit from the car, then she asked me to bring out some lights, extension cords, and blankets.

As the vet and her family turned my barn into an operating room, Dr. Fox listed all the things that could go wrong with the surgery. She was going to cut my cow's neck, so there was the risk of cutting a major artery and she might bleed to death. There was also a risk that Buddha might not wake from the anesthesia. If she made it through the surgery, an infection could set in, warranting a secondary surgery. If Dr. Fox was trying to scare me, it was working. I was flooded with fear, and also regret. Why hadn't I supervised the volunteers more closely? Why hadn't I spent more time with Buddha that day? If I had known it might be her last day on Earth, I would have stayed by her side every second of that day and looked in her eyes and hand-fed her her dinner. I stroked Buddha's face. "We're going to get you through this, sweetheart. You're going to be all right." And I hoped to God it was the truth.

Dr. Fox injected Buddha with a sedative, and moments later my cow was slumping to the ground as I cradled her head. When the anesthesia took full effect, Buddha finally stopped coughing and heaving. The vet asked me to have a seat and had her parents hold Buddha's head while her husband held a floodlight, and then Dr. Fox did a full-fledged surgery right there on my barn floor, wearing a Santa Claus hat and not much else.

She made one incision on Buddha's neck, large enough for the potato plus her hand to fit through, and another incision over the rumen—the first chamber of a cow's stomach—to release the trapped gases. I, of course, only half-watched, waves of squeamishness forcing me to look away during the bad parts.

"OK," Dr. Fox said finally. "I'm done."

The potato was out, the surgery was over, and Buddha was still breathing. I took my first deep breath in a couple of hours.

As we waited for the anesthesia to wear off, the vet pulled her evening gown back up and listed all the possible postsurgical complications. Then she gave me a lecture on bovine alimentation. "No vegetables," she said. "Ruminants are designed to eat grasses, period."

It took weeks for Buddha to heal. I had to reach inside the incision in her neck twice every day to clean out any accumulated fluids and disinfect the wound. From that day forward I watched her carefully at mealtimes, making sure she didn't eat any of Susie Q's vegetables. And each morning when I went into the barn to hug my cow, I was acutely aware that I had almost lost my precious Buddha. In the blink of an eye, she had nearly vanished from the world. Life, I realized—now more fully than ever—is a fragile thing and can never be promised. It can be here one day and snatched the next from under our nose with no warning.

As I moved forward I committed to live each day as though it were the last day I would see the ones I loved—human and animal alike. If I felt love, I expressed it. If I thought of someone, I told them. I recommitted to living in the moment as a hedge against regret, for I knew in my gut that regret could eat me alive.

CHAPTER 7

Two things happened at the beginning of 2002. The first was that Jay got me a gift. On the morning of my birthday, at the end of January, he showed up in the barnyard and asked me to come out to his van.

"What . . . why?" I asked.

"Just come with me."

I followed him down the driveway and when we got to his van, he pulled open the door. "Happy birthday," he said. Inside the van was a crate, and the crate contained a turkey. She cocked her head and looked at me and made that soft purring sound turkeys make when they're content. Jay had rescued her from the animal shelter and named her Spring.

I looked at Spring and then looked back at Jay. He had a huge grin on his face.

"There is nothing I would have wanted more for my birthday than Spring," I said.

The second thing that happened was that Scott moved out. Not just out of the bedroom this time, but out of the house. From the moment he had unclogged the toilet on Thanksgiving, it was as though he had begun extracting himself from this "crazy life" I led. He had stayed through the holidays and into January, but he had clearly been pushed to his edge.

Finally, one day he said, "I can't do this anymore."

I thought it was just more of his usual disgruntlement, but then he said, "Really. I'm done." He didn't want to be anywhere near the Gentle Barn; he had had it with the animals and the visitors and the press. He said this was not the life he had signed up for. "We'll have to work out how we can both spend time with Jesse, but I'm leaving by the end of the month."

A week and a half later, as Scott loaded his stuff into a moving van, Jesse—now three—finally understood what was happening. He cried for two hours after Scott drove away and nothing I said or did calmed him. He finally cried himself to sleep in my arms, and I realized what an awful job we'd done with this transition. We had not properly prepared him for such a huge upheaval in his young life.

The next morning, after I dropped Jesse off at day care, I sought solace in Buddha's warm hug. "What am I going to do, Buddha?" I had always had a boyfriend or a husband. I didn't know how to do life on my own. And even though Scott and I had not actually been *together* much of the previous year, knowing he was in the house had been a comfort to me.

When Buddha's neck was wet and salty with my tears I leaned back carefully against her, cautious not to press on either of the nearly healed surgical sites, and said, "Where is that man Chantelle promised me, anyway?"

Buddha shifted her weight under me and heaved a big breath.

"I know just what you mean," I said.

Over the next couple of weeks, Jesse began to adjust; Scott had gotten an apartment very close by so Jesse could visit frequently, and our little boy was calmed by the realization that he could see his dad whenever he wanted.

With Scott's move out of the house, it was the end of his financial support for my life. I still had help from my parents, and more donations were coming in all the time, especially now that Jay was writing grants for us, but I didn't trust it yet. I didn't have faith that the universe would support me or that the Gentle Barn would be OK. I felt like I was about to step off an enormous cliff.

In the weeks that followed, however, the cliff never showed up; the dreaded free fall never happened. The Gentle Barn and I just kept moving forward. Every week, we had more people coming to visit—about fifty or sixty each Sunday. More agencies for at-risk and special-needs kids were signing on; more donations were appearing from people who had heard about us. Also, as the media coverage grew, we started receiving more animals from people who had rescued a pig or a horse or a bunch of chickens but didn't know what to do with them.

In late February we received eighteen rabbits from a rescue agency, who assured us all the rabbits were male, so none of them had to be neutered. Since we'd never had rabbits at the Gentle Barn, we had to build them appropriate accommodations. Jay and I went to work on an outdoor pen under the biggest shade tree—a fruitless mulberry in the corner of the barnyard—enclosing a large area over and around the roots of the tree. The rabbits would have dappled light, piles of straw, and little cubbies to nest in between the enormous roots. On the day the pen was finally finished, Jay and I were excited to transfer the rabbits from their temporary housing in the barn to their beautiful new atrium. When I entered the rabbits' stall, all the bunnies flew into a frenzy—squealing, hopping in circles, and thumping the ground to warn the others of danger.

"It's OK, guys. This is the big day," I said. "You're moving into your new atrium. You're going to love it." But this didn't seem to calm them. I tried getting down on my knees, and they all just ran into the corners, as far from me as they could get. I tried approaching them slowly, cooing to them, but they still thumped and squealed and hopped in crazy circles.

"Oh my gosh," I said to Jay, "you'd think we were the angel of death." I could just imagine them yelling, *Run! Run for your lives!*

When I managed to corner and catch one of the rabbits, all the others again ran frantically around, squealing and thumping. *Oh no!* they must have been yelling. *They got Bobby! Bobby, we're so sorry they got you!*

I carried "Bobby" out to the atrium and set him down inside, where he sniffed the straw-covered ground and hopped gently through the dappled sunlight.

"Not so bad, huh?" I said to him.

Jay caught the next rabbit, and that bunny's compatriots again squealed and hopped frantically around the stall. *Oh my God, oh my God, they got Fred!*

This went on with each and every one of the rabbits—the rest of the bunnies in the barn stall squealing and thumping and mourning the loss of the comrade who'd just been nabbed—until all eighteen rabbits were peacefully exploring their spacious new home under the mulberry tree.

"I wonder if that's what death is like," I said to Jay as we stood outside the pen and watched the rabbits hop contentedly through the straw and over and around the tree roots. "Everyone sobs and mourns for the dearly departed, and yet here's the dearly departed in bliss over on the other side. But he can't tell his friends how beautiful it is here in paradise."

Jay laughed. "So they just freak out over and over every time some-one dies."

"Exactly," I said.

Jay's marriage had been falling apart for some time. When I next saw him, he told me it was finally over; he had left. He began spending more and more time at the Gentle Barn, stopping by nearly every day, working us in around his job interviews. Molli spent the week with Jay and lived with her mom and half-sister only on weekends. So Molli was at the Gentle Barn a lot too. Jesse was thrilled; he thought Molli hung the moon. He was eager to share toys and snacks with her and would follow her around and do anything she asked of him in her quiet little voice. And Molli was as at home in the barnyard as I was. She would watch me when I did my chores and mimic my every move. If I fed the chickens, she fed the chickens. If I raked up manure, she'd go looking for a rake. And just like me she was not afraid to get dirty. She'd sit her dainty self right down on the ground, dusting her pretty pink and yellow dresses with barnyard dirt.

One early evening toward the end of March, I was sitting in the rabbit pen when Jay arrived, this time without Molli. He came through the gate in the pen and settled into the straw with me. "Where's Jesse?"

"He's with his dad."

We sat quietly for a moment, then Jay said, "How are the rabbits doing?"

"Great," I said. "Look how elaborate their warrens have gotten. There are holes over on this side now too." For days after we'd built the pen, I'd been spending an hour or more every day sitting with the rabbits in their little paradise. Slowly they came to trust me, hopping across my legs and sometimes even resting for a while in my lap. As I'd hoped, the crevices formed by the tree roots made for perfect nesting spots, but some of the rabbits also dug holes in the dirt, hollowing out warrens under the network of roots.

"It's amazing how their natural instincts kick in once they have the right environment," he said.

And just at that moment something caught my attention out of the corner of my eye—something small and white popping up from one of the holes. I turned to look just in time to see a little white puff disappear back into the warren. "Look," I whispered and pointed in the direction where the white fluff had disappeared. Jay and I inched closer and then sat quietly waiting for the apparition to recur. After fifteen minutes one of our big rabbits popped his head out of the hole, and I wondered if that was all I'd seen, the head of one of our big bunnies. But then the rabbit slid entirely up out of the hole and was followed by the little white puff that had caught my eye. A tiny white bunny. "He had a baby," I said.

"He?" Jay said. Of course he was right. I wondered how many of our "all-male" rabbits were female.

Another white puff popped up then. Two baby bunnies! And Jay and I both started laughing.

"Definitely not all male," he said.

As we sat there giggling in delight, one white puff after another came flopping out of the hole. Now there were four baby bunnies. Then another puff appeared. Five babies. And another. Six. And each time another little ball of fluff appeared we laughed harder until our eyes started to tear. I watched Jay through the tears in my eyes—this huge guy sitting in a pen full of bunny rabbits laughing to the point of crying.

When we had counted ten babies, the parade finally was over. "Congratulations," I said to the new bunny mama. Then I turned to Jay and said, "Thank you."

He raised his eyebrows, a quizzical look on his face.

"It means so much to me to have a friend to share this with," I said. Scott would not have sat with me in a bunny pen and laughed at a parade of new babies. Scott would have said, *Great, now we have ten more mouths to feed.* "Thank you for enjoying this as much as I do."

Jay scooted closer to me in the straw and took my hand in his. Then he looked directly into my eyes and got very serious. "That's why I'm here," he said, and goose bumps spread over my entire body. Suddenly Jay seemed like a whole different person from the man I'd known since the previous fall.

———

As soon as Jay left, I headed straight for the phone.

"Chantelle," I said, "I need you to do a reading for me."

"Sure," she said. "I have time Thursday."

"Is there any way you can do it sooner?"

"This sounds serious," she said. "Can you come by tomorrow evening?"

The next evening, when I got to Chantelle's house, I'd barely made it through the door before I'd blurted it out: "I need you to tell me if Jay's the guy."

"The guy?"

"Yeah, the soul mate you said would come in seven months. The man who was going to run the Gentle Barn with me." How could she have forgotten such a prediction? Then it hit me. I stood right there in Chantelle's kitchen and counted forward on my fingers from February 2001, the month Chantelle had done the reading. *March, April, May, June, July, August, September.* "Seven!" I said. "Jay first showed up in September, I'm pretty sure."

"But you're not really into him, are you?" she asked.

"I *wasn't.*" It was true I had never thought of him that way. But in that moment in the bunny pen something had changed.

Chantelle took out a deck of tarot cards and said, "OK, sit down."

There at Chantelle's kitchen table, the cards confirmed what I felt now in my bones.

Before I left Chantelle's house I called Jay and told him I needed to talk to him. He was out with some friends not far from where I was. "Can you meet me at Coco's?" I asked.

Twenty minutes later, I was sitting in the passenger seat of Jay's car in the Coco's parking lot. I was nervous and didn't know how to begin. Here was this person I had come to rely on for help with the animals and in the office and with fund-raising. He'd also become a good friend. If he didn't feel the same way I now felt, he might pick up and leave and I'd never see him again. I could lose the best support I'd ever had with the Gentle Barn. But something told me I had to take that risk.

I took a deep breath and said, "I have this crazy story to tell you." And I told him about Chantelle's prediction and how I hadn't believed it, but that sometimes, when things were bad with Scott, I had wondered where that prophesied soul mate was. "Do you know what month you first arrived at the Gentle Barn?" I said.

Jay nodded. "September."

A flutter of adrenaline shot upward in my chest. "Well, that was seven months after Chantelle's prediction." Then I told him about the tarot card reading she'd just done for me. And most important, I told him that the day before, as we'd sat together in the bunny pen, I had started to feel feelings for him that I'd never felt before. "My heart just kind of opened up," I said. Then I stopped and held my breath and half looked at him, and half not—with no idea whatsoever how he might respond.

Jay's gaze was steady on me. "Come here," he said, his voice smooth as silk.

I scooted closer to him, and he touched my face with those large, soft hands of his. Then he drew me to him, and when he kissed me, my whole body felt electric.

We were like teenagers sitting in that car, after-hours in a restaurant parking lot. I ended up squeezed into the spot between the two front seats so we could sit as close to each other as possible. And just like teenagers, for the next three hours we hardly came up for air.

I had always wanted to know a man first as a friend, to slowly learn all about him and have him slowly learn all about me, before getting into a relationship with him. But it had never worked that way; my relationships had always started with a spark and turned quickly to romance. Finally with Jay I got to follow my plan. We'd come to know each other well, and I had liked him more and more as time went on. But the waiting had nothing to do with willpower. I'd just never seen him as anything other than a friend.

Now that the veil had been lifted we were making up for lost time. When we took the dogs for walks, we held hands. We made each other laugh, and I marveled at the beautiful sound of his laughter; I told jokes just so I could hear it. We walked the horses, too; we'd take them to a nearby field and sit in the tall grasses and talk for hours while the horses grazed. Everything in my world seemed to have suddenly come more alive. Colors were more vibrant. Flowers smelled sweeter. The air seemed fresher. And when we would come back to the house, we'd turn on the music, and Jay would sweep me up onto my feet and start dancing with me. If I could have dreamed up my perfect fantasy life, this would be it.

Just a short time after our night in Coco's parking lot, Jay and I decided he and Molli should move into my house. By then, Jay was spending every night with me anyway, and was at the Gentle Barn constantly.

We sat Molli down to tell her the news.

"Molli," Jay said to her, "Ellie and I have decided something."

Molli nodded, her eyes unblinking. Sitting on the dining room chair, her hands were folded on her knees like a little lady, but her feet didn't touch the floor.

"I'm not sure how you're going to feel about this . . ." I said, "but you and your dad are going to move in here with me and Jesse."

Molli jumped to the floor, abandoning her ladylike pose, and threw her arms up in the air. "Yes!" she shouted. "I knew it. I just knew it."

She jumped up and down. "I knew we were going to move in here, and I knew you were going to be my mommy!"

I could see we weren't going to need much of an adjustment period.

It was just as easy for Jesse. On the surface nothing really had changed; his pal Jay and his best friend Molli were always around anyway. We'd just made it official. And for me it was heaven. Living with Jay felt so comfortable it was as though we'd been doing this our whole adult lives.

Jay not only tolerated my fixation on animals, he joined me in it. I taught him how to trim hooves, bottle-feed newly rescued babies, and test for dehydration. When an animal was sick he'd be right there in the barn next to me, taking temperatures and administering supplements. When the barnyard overflowed with visitors on Sundays, he worked beside me to greet people and tell the animals' stories. He even began watching me lead groups of at-risk and special-needs kids so he could take over some of the sessions.

That June, Jay and I did our first rescue together. We took in an eight-week-old calf who had started out his life on a beef ranch in New Mexico. Lucky for this little calf, the farmer's wife had taken pity on him because he'd been born blind. She'd bottle-fed him and fallen in love with him, but her husband did not believe in having a cow as a pet and gave her one week to get rid of the calf. When we received her desperate e-mail, we said, "Absolutely, we'll take him in." She then made the three-day trip to bring him to us. Because he'd been raised by a human, and was clearly loved by her, he was sweet and trusting with us right from the beginning. He happened to arrive on World Vegan Day, so we named him Vegan (the irony being that he was the only species who was *supposed* to drink cow's milk).

Knowing he'd been separated from his cow mother at birth, we couldn't wait to introduce him to Buddha. Now full grown and weighing about six hundred pounds, she'd become the matriarch of the barnyard, nurturing all who came anywhere near her, no matter the species.

But she'd never had a calf of her own. We led Vegan into the barnyard and walked him over to where Buddha was lying in the shade. She got one look at him and jumped to her feet, her tongue at the ready, prepared to give him his first proper bath. She got one lick in, and the little red calf jumped in the air and ran from her, pulling the lead straight out of my hand.

I looked at Jay; he was as surprised as I was. We'd expected the calf to be thrilled to have a mother. But apparently he'd forgotten what a cow was. Buddha was not one to give up easily, so she followed after him and tried again to groom him, and again he fled from the enormous, frightening animal with the huge sandpaper tongue. We saw we were going to have to keep them apart until Vegan became less afraid. We kept him in the grassy yard next to the house, separated from Buddha by a chain-link fence. Each day we led him into the barnyard to try again, leaving him with Buddha for longer and longer periods. It took five days for Vegan to finally submit to whatever it was this strange animal wanted from him. When I came out to feed everyone on that fifth evening, I found Vegan sopping wet, head to toe, and a triumphant Buddha hovering nearby.

After that Vegan submitted to daily tongue baths and Buddha held her head just a bit higher, a proud new mama. If she could have nursed him, I'm sure she would have.

———

Two months after Jay and Molli had moved in, we heard the sound of hammers and power tools coming from next door. That property had sat vacant for the last three years, so the noise was unexpected. Someone must have bought the place and was renovating before moving in.

Uh-oh, I thought, *my rabbits.* By then the rabbits' warrens were so elaborate they not only had dug under the chicken-wire fence—and were now hopping freely around the barnyard—they also had dug their way under the wooden fence that separated the barnyard from the property next door. The bunnies loved hanging out in that overgrown yard, and sometimes even the chickens followed them over there. Since the property had been vacant, I'd never bothered with filling the holes.

I hurried over to the house to explain, and a tall woman answered the door and smiled at me.

"Hi, I'm Ellie," I said. "I'm your neighbor." And I pointed to my house. "I'm so sorry that my rabbits and chickens are in your yard. I didn't know someone had bought this place. It's been vacant for so long."

Her name was Paige, and she in turn apologized for all the noise.

"No problem," I said. Then I told her I could come right over and round up the chickens and rabbits if she didn't mind my coming into her yard. "Then I'll get right on it and fill those holes so the animals don't bother you."

"Oh, please don't," she said. "I'd love to have their company. I don't have other plans for the yard, so if they want to come visit, that's great."

"OK," I said. "Fantastic. But if you get tired of them, please just give me a holler."

"They won't bother me," Paige said. "I'm a big fan of the work you're doing. I love the Gentle Barn."

As it turned out, Paige had been following the Gentle Barn since the beginning. She'd bought the house *because* it was right next door to us. I couldn't believe how lucky we were to have someone like her as our new neighbor.

Once Paige had moved in, if we saw each other we always said hi. She sometimes came over, not just to see me and the kids but to spend time with the animals. If she had friends visiting, especially if they had children, she would call to me over the fence to see if she could bring them over for a tour of the barnyard. "Sure," I would say each time, happy they were all so interested in what we were doing.

With Jay now in my life, and a great new neighbor, that summer I felt surrounded by a love and support unlike anything I had ever experienced. It seemed like the universe was saying yes—finally yes—to my dream, and the Gentle Barn came into its own in a whole new way. We were now thriving, not just surviving on crumbs. The Gentle Barn was beginning to make a name for itself, and people were now seeking *us* out in order to bring their groups of kids or give us donations or have us host a birthday party.

Late that summer I hosted a moms' club, who brought their young children to the Barn for a playdate. After a tour of the barnyard, everyone sat down at the picnic tables in the smaller grassy yard to have lunch. When the children finished eating, we moved down onto the patio to make chalk drawings on the concrete. As the kids and I covered the patio with pink cows and purple goats, Paige came in through the side gate, which I always left open when I hosted a group.

She walked right up to me and said, "Hi, Ellie. Listen, I really want to put up a brand-new fence between our properties."

I looked around at the kids drawing and the moms sitting and talking at the picnic tables. Didn't Paige see I was hosting a group?

"I'm doing some remodeling," she continued, "and I want to make some changes to the backyard."

"Um," I said, and held my chalk-covered hands out in front of me as though they provided the evidence that I was in the middle of something. "Could we talk about this later?"

"Oh, I'll just be quick," she said. "See, this fence won't look good with my remodel plans; I want to replace it with a brand-new one."

I stood up and wiped my chalky hands on my jeans, glancing at the mothers who had started to look in our direction. "Well, I see what you're saying, Paige. Um, but the thing is I just put in a brand-new fence seven years ago, and I've kept up the stain every year so it's in really good shape."

"But it's not pretty," Paige said.

All the mothers were staring at us now, and even the kids had stopped their chalk drawings.

I had never seen Paige this insistent. If I just agreed, maybe she'd go away and let me continue with my group. What did I care if the fence had a different look—as long as it functioned to contain my yard and keep the animals safe? "Sure," I said, "I guess that would be OK."

"Great, so why don't we just go halvsies on it."

"Halvsies?"

"Yeah, since it's between our two properties, I figure the fair thing to do is split the cost."

I had spent over ten thousand dollars on that fence just seven years earlier. There was no way the Gentle Barn or I could pay thousands of dollars now for a superfluous new fence. "I get that you want to have a fence that you think looks nicer and that you're excited about your remodel," I said, treading carefully. "But I run a nonprofit. I don't have that kind of money just lying around."

"I'll tell you what," she said. "I'll go ahead and put it in and you can just owe me the money."

I could feel the heat rising into my cheeks. "Paige," I said, "it looks like we need to have a longer conversation about this. Why don't you come back in an hour, and we can sit down and talk about it."

"No, I want to get this settled now."

"Look," I said, "I'm so sorry, but I'm sure you understand. This is a very young, struggling nonprofit and I just can't go into that kind of debt right now. This is just not something I can do." I glanced at the open gate, wishing she would leave, but she was nowhere near ready to go.

Her face was bright red and she started to scream, making the veins in her neck pop out. "You just don't understand! I've had this ugly fence along my yard all this time, and I want a brand-new one. And it's just right for you to pay half of that!" She stomped her feet and hollered and looked like a two-year-old having a temper tantrum. Spit was flying with her words and she hardly stopped to take a breath. I tried to say, *We're neighbors. We're friends. I'm sure there's a win-win solution.* But I couldn't get a word in edgewise. I glanced around at the horrified mothers and the cowering children and could see there was no interrupting this woman. I realized that the only way to get her to stop screaming was to remove the target of her attack—me. I turned and quietly walked into the house and locked the door.

I stayed inside until she finally stopped yelling and left through the gate, at which point I returned to the backyard and apologized profusely to my guests.

———

"It was like she was possessed," I told Jay later that evening. "I've never seen her act like that, not a hint of it."

"And she just kept going?" he said. "In front of all the people?"

"She's crazy, Jay. And I didn't even see it."

"Why don't I just go talk to her," he said. "I'll smooth things out and we'll start fresh. I'll go over first thing in the morning."

But the next morning, when Jay rang her bell, there was no answer. An hour later, after Jay had left for an appointment, there was a knock on our door. Thinking it was Paige, I took a deep breath and braced myself, but when I opened the door, there on our porch were two officers from Animal Control.

"Oh, hi," I said. I'd seen these guys plenty in my line of work. They even asked me sometimes to take in abused animals they found.

The taller of the two spoke first, an odd look on his face. He was almost cringing. "Um, we got a complaint," he said. He looked at the ground. "Someone filed a complaint that there are abused animals on your property."

"On *my* property?" I wasn't sure I'd heard him right.

The officer nodded, then the other one chimed in: "Also dead animals."

"Abused and dead animals on *my* property?" Then I got it. I stepped out onto the porch and looked over at Paige's house. "She's the one who called, isn't she?" But I knew they weren't supposed to answer that.

The first officer gave a barely perceptible nod. Then he lowered his voice. "Look," he said, "we know you. We're huge fans. I'm sure this is a bogus call, but we have to check it out. So, if you could just let us in, we'll have a look and then we'll be out of your hair."

"Sure," I said, "come on in." I glanced again at Paige's house but I didn't see any sign of her lurking.

The officers took a look around the house and the barnyard. "Everything looks great," the officer said. "I'm not at all surprised. We're just really sorry to have bothered you." The second officer tipped his hat, and they both left.

I decided it was time to fill the holes the rabbits had dug under the fence, so after the bunnies and chickens returned to our yard that evening for their dinner, Jay and I filled the holes and poured cement along the perimeter of the fence. "No more digging," I said to the rabbits. "Next door is off limits now." Then Jay went next door again to see if he could smooth things out with Paige, and this time she answered the door. I could hear her screaming at the top of her lungs about the ugly fence and how selfish she thought we were. She screamed for ten minutes without stopping. It sounded like she never even took a breath. Finally Jay abandoned ship and came back home. He stood there in front of me, just shaking his head.

"Oh my God," he said finally.

"I know," I said.

A few days later there was another knock on our door. It was the Health Department. "Oh, hi," I said, and for a moment I thought I must have forgotten our appointment. We got an inspection every six months; we passed with flying colors every time and were on good terms with the inspector. But hadn't they come just three months earlier?

The guy stood there and started apologizing. "I'm so sorry to bother you," he said. "I'm sure you're busy. I mean, the work you do is really amazing. We totally support you. In fact, you're the cleanest facility we regulate." He paused. "But we got this complaint . . . so we have to do an inspection."

"Of course," I said, "come on in." *Wow,* I thought, *she's just not going to let this go, is she?*

The inspector took a look around, then said, "Oh my God, this is ridiculous. The place is spotless. I'm sorry to have wasted your time."

"You're kidding," Jay said that evening when I told him about the second surprise inspection. "We've got to stop her."

"I don't think there's any way to stop her," I said. "That's the thing about crazy people."

Jay was pacing the floor now, his fists balled up. "I'm going over there," he said.

I was worried about him going next door when he was so angry. "Sweetheart, just wait a minute, OK? You know, there's really no harm. We haven't done anything wrong. The agencies came out and they saw that. Besides, there's not really anyone else she could call."

I was wrong about this last point. The next week Building and Safety showed up.

"I came to your grand opening," the man said as he stood on our front porch. "I didn't see any problems then, but a neighbor called . . ."

I ushered him inside and then out to the barn.

After he looked around the property, he said, "Everything still looks tip-top. I'm going to get this case closed out." He walked out the front door, then turned around. "You know, I just want to personally thank you for the work you're doing."

All three agencies closed out the cases.

Although we heard Paige moving around her backyard now and again and saw her lights on in the evening, we had no further interaction with her and no more visits from the authorities. Jay and I crossed our fingers, hoping that was the end of that nonsense.

CHAPTER 8

There are three kinds of animals who come to the Gentle Barn. The first are those we nurse back to health so they can live a full, vibrant life. The second are those who come to us in the final stage of their life to die a dignified death surrounded by love. And the third are the animals who find their way to us to learn a life lesson; once that lesson is truly attained, they can then transcend their body and move on.

Katie had arrived at the Gentle Barn furious at the world. She'd been used and abused for so many years as a pony-ride horse and had simply had enough and decided she hated humans. In her first weeks and months at the Gentle Barn she'd reminded me of a wrinkled old lady with a cigarette hanging from her mouth who screamed expletives at anyone who passed. (In Horse, this translated as biting or baring her teeth.) What she didn't know was that a life lesson awaited her; she was going to learn that not all humans were abusive and that there was love for her in this world.

Three years after her arrival, the transformation was complete. Katie had not just become a sweet, humble pony who approached *us* for love and attention, letting little girls braid her tail and tie bows in her mane, she'd also become an incredible assistant to me in the barnyard. Katie was kind of like the barnyard's "hall monitor"; she never hurt any of the other animals, but I could call on her if somebody was being stubborn or interfering with my workday. Our big white farm pig, Duncan—who was not always the most cooperative member of the team—would often choose a nice spot for a nap right in front of the tack room or some other door to the barn. When I needed to open the blocked door I would plead with Duncan to move. But when a twelve-hundred-pound napping rock does not want to move, he simply does not. "Katie," I would call, "I need your help." And she'd trot right over and back up toward the napping pig. As her hind legs neared him, Duncan would whine, apparently not asleep after all. Then she'd cock one back leg, as though ready to kick, and Duncan would hop up and run. She never actually kicked him; just the prospect of it would stir him to action.

But at the beginning of the summer I had noticed a nodule on Katie's neck. In the space of two weeks it had spread to both sides of her neck and up under her chin. When Dr. Geissen examined her, he said the tumor was entwined with Katie's trachea and jugular veins and thus was inoperable. Besides, Katie was by this point so ancient she wouldn't likely make it through a surgery.

"My recommendation," he said, "is that you just love her as much as possible until the point where she starts having difficulty swallowing."

Katie had become a crowd favorite; I knew I had to let people know, so that all who had been touched by this pony would have a chance to spend some time with her before she left us. Throughout the summer people came by to hug and kiss Katie and tell her how much they loved her, and I stood back and watched them fuss over her. *Mission accomplished*, I thought. It wasn't only *my* mission of rescuing and rehabilitating an old, angry horse. It was Katie's mission here on Earth—as though she had come here to accomplish this transformation, and now that the transformation was complete, she was done and could move on.

By the end of the summer, Katie was starting to lose weight; it looked like she was having trouble swallowing. I did not want her to suffer at all; I knew it was time. My heart heavy, I let all of Katie's fans know I would be calling the vet out to help her leave her body. People came and actually waited in line to say good-bye. If I hadn't been so incredibly sad, I might have laughed with joy to see how much love surrounded her.

Before the vet arrived, Jay and I went to the peach tree in the front yard and chose the ripest, juiciest peach. I held it under Katie's nose, and although she hadn't been able to eat all day, I believe she knew this was a love offering. She closed her eyes and bit into the peach, and as she slowly chewed, with juice dripping from her mouth, we told her— yet again—how proud we were of her for her amazing transformation and for helping soften and transform countless teenagers. Jay stroked her face and I kissed her forehead, and we thanked her for all we'd been through together.

Katie had been horribly treated and yet, given the time, she had forgiven the hurts and healed 100 percent. Animals just seemed to heal emotionally much more quickly and completely than humans did. Their process was streamlined because they didn't assign meaning to their hurts, thus dragging those emotional injuries along with them through time. We humans are not as adept at this process.

Paige was a perfect example. When fall arrived, Jay and I were disappointed to see that our once-wonderful neighbor had not laid her anger to rest after all. The break she had taken in calling out the authorities had apparently just been a time of research—digging through city code books.

The barrage of complaints was back on, and the authorities started calling us and knocking on our door again. Only this time Paige had apparently found loopholes to back her up. Building and Safety sent someone out to check on the distance of our barn from the fence that divided our property from Paige's.

How on earth had she measured the distance between the fence and my barn? She would have had to hop the fence in the middle of the night with a measuring tape.

"Unfortunately," the inspector said, standing next to the barn, his measuring tape in hand, "she's right. The barn is almost twelve inches closer than it should be to the fence."

The infamous fence was fine, but the barn was too close to her property.

Jay and I walked the guy to the door, my head spinning with questions.

On the porch, the inspector stopped and said, "I'm so sorry you're going through this."

But sorry or not, two weeks later we got the official notice in the mail. We were being ordered to tear down our barn. If we tore down the barn, our animals would have no shelter. Rebuilding a perfectly sound barn a foot farther from the fence seemed absurd, not to mention very expensive.

We hardly had a chance to figure out what to do about the barn before another complaint came in. It was a Sunday morning and we'd done our usual preparations for our visitors' day. One of the last things Jay did before we opened each Sunday was to pressure-wash the fence. Our pigs' favorite spa treatment was to soak in the mud hole and then, still wet and muddy, give themselves a good massage against the wood. The fence bore the evidence of their daily rubdowns. That Sunday, as Jay put away the pressure-washer, the front doorbell rang. Sometimes this happened. People would miss the hand-lettered sign telling them to go around to the side gate. Prepared to redirect our first visitors of the day, I opened the door and I froze. Standing there in front of me were two policemen. Black uniforms, silver badges. This was a first.

"Mrs. Laks?"

"Yes," I said, and quickly did a mental headcount of all my family members. Two kids in the house. Jay out back. Talked to my mom last night. My brothers? My dad? "Is everybody OK?" I said.

"We got a report from your neighbor that you sprayed her in the face with a pressurized hose."

"Oh my God," I said, and I closed my eyes and shook my head. "Come on in." I took the officers through the house to the backyard, and when Jay saw them I could see concern on his face. I pointed at Paige's house, and I saw his concern turn to anger. "Apparently there's been a report that we sprayed Paige in the face."

We showed the officers the fence and explained about our muddy pigs. Jay wheeled the pressure-washer back out from the tack room and pushed it over to the fence. The pressure-washer was a big, heavy machine with a four-foot-long hose. The fence was six feet high, the same height as Jay. We stood back and let the officers imagine the scenario; it would have taken some impressive gymnastics to spray our neighbor in the face. We also explained that this neighbor had been calling out the authorities for anything she could come up with.

The two uniformed men looked at the pressure-washer and the fence, then at us, then at each other. One of them shook his head and the other said, "OK, we'll make a note of our visit. You folks have a good day."

The complaints kept coming, some easily resolved, others not. But the one that hurt us the most, the one that really landed its blow squarely at the core of the Gentle Barn, was the second complaint Paige made to Animal Control.

When I answered the front door and saw the Animal Control officer standing on my porch, I must have made an audible sigh because he said, "I know. I'm sorry. I was hoping I wouldn't be back either."

"She called again?" I said.

The officer nodded.

I was baffled. *What on earth could she have dug up now?*

"It's about your pigs," he said.

"My pigs?"

"We know you have pigs," the officer said. "You've gotten some of them from us, and we totally support you. . . . But technically you're not zoned for pigs."

Not zoned for pigs? "There must be twenty-five pet pigs in the neighborhood," I said.

Jay joined me at the front door. "Even Paige has a potbellied pig now," he said.

"Would you like to report her?" the officer asked.

Jay and I looked at each other. As angry as I was at the mess Paige was making for us, it wasn't her pig I wanted to see behind bars. "No," I said.

The officer looked over at Paige's house and shook his head. "You know she badgered us for days, threatened to have us all fired if we didn't serve you notice. I'm so sorry to have to do this." And he handed us a slip of paper.

On the slip it said we had one week to get rid of our pigs. It also said we had to keep our roosters seventy feet away from any neighbors' houses. The only spot that was seventy feet from all neighbors was behind the barn, and we'd have to cage them to keep them in that spot.

I had promised all of our animals they could live the rest of their lives with us in peace, that we'd never hurt them or cage them and we'd never give them away. Not only was my promise in danger of being compromised, my whole mission was being threatened again. I couldn't believe I had come this far, helping so many animals and so many kids, and one person was about to pull the rug out from under us.

"What are we going to do?" Jay said.

"I don't know. I was hoping you had the answer."

The Animal Control officer had hinted that the seven days on the notice was just for official purposes, that they were going to give us leeway on the deadline. Building and Safety had indicated the same about our barn. At least that gave us time to figure this out. But over the next few days, we made no headway in coming up with a solution. I tried to picture finding homes for our pigs, maybe at another rescue or with a family who would love them—with lots of space and a great mud hole. But each and every time, I ended up in tears. I kept running out to the pigs to reassure them that we were not going to send them away, or to the roosters to promise we would not put them in cages. Each and every day I ended up leaning into Buddha's solid frame to let her fur sop up my sadness.

I began to wonder what the universe was trying to tell me. Was it time to wrap up this whole endeavor? How could that be, after all I'd put into it? I had felt so guided as I'd built up the Gentle Barn; was that same force now guiding me to dismantle it all? Or did the Gentle Barn have a life span that had reached its end, just like Mary and Katie and the others who had died of old age?

In between my bouts of tears and uncertainty, I was flooded with anger. I didn't understand why Paige was doing this. Didn't she understand how many people and animals she was hurting? How could one person be so selfish?

In the midst of all the upheaval I would go out to the barn and stand there looking at the animals, trying to remind myself of why I was doing this work in the first place. Sometimes I couldn't see past the fear and grief. I felt targeted, victimized, hopeless. Other times, especially when I worked with the groups of kids or sat with Buddha, I connected with a sense of hope, a glimmer of my old sense of purpose. "I have to keep on going, right?" I'd say to Buddha. "This is my path."

We tried to carry on as though everything were normal, especially with the at-risk kids and with our Sunday visitors. We'd pull it together when people arrived, and sometimes I even did forget for an hour or two about the whole mess we were in. But as soon as the group was over or the visitors had left, reality came flooding back in. I felt trapped in a horrible situation and my old childhood feeling of despair returned. *Nobody understands. What's the point? It's not even worth it to continue.*

Each Saturday night I was filled with dread. We used to have fun preparing for visitor Sundays—making the place spotless, prepping for special activities, guessing at how many visitors we'd get this time. Now it was a tension-filled day or two, as we tiptoed around hoping that Paige would not strike while we had a barnyard full of visitors.

After one particularly tension-filled Sunday, Jay had finally had enough. "We're taking that woman to court," he said.

With what money? I thought.

"She's ruining the Gentle Barn," he said. "She's destroying our business. Our kids are upset. We're going to stop her."

The next day we started calling around in search of legal guidance, and the following days were filled with research and meetings and phone consultations. Could we fight this in court? Did we have a case that would hold up? How much would it cost?

Notices continued to arrive from Animal Control and also from Building and Safety, and the language was growing stronger with each letter. Get rid of your pigs and tear down your barn, or else. I started to wonder if we should even be trying to fight this at all or if it was simply time to give up. Maybe we needed to place the pigs in a good home, keep as many animals as we could privately, and shut down the Gentle Barn so we'd no longer be a target for those who wanted to hurt us.

We were still sorting through this tangle of questions, trying to get a foothold and find a path out, when the winter holidays arrived, bringing everything to a lull. The lawyers had gone out of town; the consultants took days to return our calls; even Paige seemed to be taking a break. So when a horse rescue called and invited us to have a look around their place, we decided to jump on the opportunity to take a vacation from our troubles and get out of town for the day with our kids.

I'd heard a lot about this horse rescue but had never done the hour-long trip up to Ojai to see it. We drove on out of the city and through the rolling hills that were lush and green this time of year. An hour later we headed through the gate and onto a property covered with ancient oak trees, and I could feel my body begin to relax. Our host, Liz, greeted us with a huge smile and then took us out to the stalls housing the rescued horses. We had packed along some carrots and apples for them and walked from stall to stall giving them treats. There was the tiny pony who served as their mascot, then a gorgeous chestnut mare trained in dressage, a tall black quarter horse who was terrific at trail riding, and several other horses eager to say hello and accept our offerings. These particular horses were in great shape and had mostly ended up here because their owners had moved away or lost a job and could no longer afford the upkeep.

Then I came to the stall of a gray mare. Unlike the other horses, she didn't come get a treat but instead stood way at the back of her stall. I climbed over the rail and walked slowly to her. "Hey there, girl," I cooed to her as I approached. "What's going on? Don't you want a treat?" I held a carrot out to her, but there was no response. Then I took out a piece of apple and held it right under her nose. Still no response.

"What's going on with that gray mare?" I asked Liz.

"That's Blue," she said. Blue had lived for many years at a home with another horse. When the family's kids had grown up and gone off to college, the two horses had been dumped at the rescue. "The other horse, Sasha, got adopted out. Blue didn't. She's been like this ever since."

"What's going to happen with her?"

"Well, just like Sasha, Blue's a kid pony, so she'll probably be adopted by another kid. When that kid outgrows her, she'll go to another kid."

I looked at Blue, head down at the back of her stall. "What if we were to take her?" I asked, just trying the idea on. "Maybe we could try to cheer her up."

"Well, you're certainly welcome to try," Liz said.

On the drive home, the kids conked out in the backseat, and Jay and I talked in the fading light about Blue.

"There's just so much going on in our life," Jay said. "Do we really have the right to bring another animal into this mess?"

"But if we don't, she's just going to go from kid to kid to kid. We could save her from that."

"I don't know," he said.

"It would remind us of who we are. We were born to save animals, and we can't let anything, or anyone, get in the way of that. And besides, no matter what happens, we're never going to just abandon any of our animals. If Blue joins us, she won't be abandoned either." As I talked about this new potential project—taking on a new horse and trying to raise her spirits—I could feel my own despondency lifting. In fact, just being out of our usual environment had done me a lot of good. I realized as we drove home that I'd been drowning not in an ocean but in a tiny little pond. All I needed to do was step out of it. There was a whole world out there.

The next morning Jay had come around, and we called Liz to tell her we wanted to come get Blue the following weekend. On Saturday, we took a trailer back out to the horse rescue and brought Blue home, and I began her emotional rehabilitation. But after a few weeks of concentrated effort, Blue was staying true to her name. Nothing I did seemed to lift her spirits. I even tried equine massage, which had been a miracle cure for our horse Shy when she'd arrived depressed. Not knowing what else to try, I called Liz at the horse rescue. "We've got to get that other horse back," I said.

"But we adopted Sasha out," Liz said.

"Blue is dying of heartbreak. I think seeing Sasha is the only thing that will bring her back."

"I'm sorry, Ellie. We placed her. I can't just yank her out of the home without cause." Liz told me she'd let me know if Sasha ever got returned. But she said she doubted that would happen, at least not anytime soon.

I had hoped that taking on a horse rehabilitation project would lift both the horse's spirits and ours, but the project had not solved a thing. Now we not only had a neighbor who was making our life hell but also an inconsolable horse. It seemed like a collection of failures was racking up, and I secretly began to wonder if the magic I had felt in my barnyard since the start of the Gentle Barn was beginning to wear off.

When the winter holidays were over, my sessions with the at-risk kids picked up again. I even had a new group sign on. Before each session I had to pack away all my doubts and grief, push aside the mess with Paige, and quell my worries about Blue. I would take several deep breaths to steady myself. *Be present for the kids*, I would remind myself. *Blue will be fine, just like all the animals end up being fine. And don't let one angry neighbor rob these kids of your attention. They deserve better than that.*

The group that had just signed on would turn out to be not just another new group; working with them would ultimately be the experience I needed to remind me—really remind me—of why I did this work. They were from a foster-care facility. Among them were a few older teenagers who looked almost too old to be in foster care. My guess was that they were "transitional," just about to age out of the program. Whereas an eighteen-year-old with a solid family structure generally has his parents' support through the transition to college or a job, a kid in foster care gets dropped the moment he turns eighteen—dumped from the program and stripped of government support, with very few systems in place to pick up the slack. Many end up on the street or in a homeless shelter, or even in jail. Some don't make it to adulthood. Understandably these kids develop well-honed attitudes of indifference as a defense, and the teenagers in this group walked into the barnyard with their strut and their tough-kid masks.

One of the older boys stood outside the far edge of the group, like a satellite held in orbit just beyond my grasp. He was tall and kept his arms crossed over his chest and his eyes focused on the ground. Nothing I did or said got his attention, though I kept trying. "Hey, come on over," I called. Or: "Do you want to give this pig a tummy rub?" Never a response. I kept looking up to see if he'd uncrossed his arms, let down his guard, but there was no change in him even as the rest of the group softened and began to engage more wholly with the animals. He was the most resolute teenager I'd ever had in the barnyard. I could feel all the pain that was balled up inside him under that false front of apathy.

But the other kids needed my attention too, so finally I had to just let it go and focus on the rest of the group. *I guess you can't win them all,* I thought. I hated feeling like I was giving up on him—just like the system was about to do.

I sat down with some kids who were petting the chickens and rabbits, and we talked about how to tell if the animals wanted to be picked up or not. Then I showed them how the goats liked to be scratched right between their horns because it was a spot they couldn't get to themselves. Eventually it was time to wrap up, and as I watched the kids navigate their way through the barnyard, saying good-bye to the animals, I heard a deep, quiet voice behind me.

"Can I pet that chicken?"

Could it be? I whirled around to see the tall, quiet boy standing there, his arms still crossed and his gaze still on the ground. But he had spoken to me and he wanted to pet a chicken.

"Of course," I said. "That hen there?"

He nodded, and I practically ran to where the hen was pecking at the dirt. "May I pick you up, Strawberry?" She stopped pecking and cocked her head. "Thank you," I said, and I brought her over to the boy and held her out to him.

He allowed me to set the hen in his arms. For a second he seemed frozen, just staring down at Strawberry. But then very gently he began to pet her head with two fingers. He opened his hand and stroked her from head to tail feathers with the tenderest touch. I gestured to one of the counselors who'd accompanied the group to give us a few more minutes, and the boy stood there petting Strawberry as though in a trance. After a while he looked off into space, and his eyes were glistening. "I used to have a chicken when I was a little kid," he said. "I came home from school one day and she was gone. No one would tell me where she was."

"I'm so sorry that happened to you," I told him. "That happened to me too when I was little, and I know how much that hurts."

"She was the only one who understood me," he said.

"Mm-hm." I held him in my gaze, even though he was looking down again.

Slowly, as he talked and as I let him know I understood, his gaze traveled higher and higher, until finally he was looking right into my eyes. "I miss my parents," he said.

I nodded.

He told me he hadn't seen them in a very long time, that he'd been put into a foster home, and then another and another. He told me his name was Andre, and he gently petted the hen the whole time he talked.

This was a different person from the tough, apathetic teenager who'd walked in two hours earlier. Locked so deeply within his pain and isolation, he'd been unable to give anyone a chance to get inside. He'd built a fortress to keep out the hurt, but those thick walls had also kept out the love. Andre's walls came down that day because of a little hen named Strawberry; she'd opened him up wide and allowed him to feel my empathy.

As I waved good-bye to the group, I felt a fire ignite inside me. I was not going to let Paige stop this boy and others like him from getting the love and healing they needed. Hell if I was going to give up on my dream! I didn't know yet which path would lead us out of this insanity, but we had to find a way. The Gentle Barn was not going to shut its doors because of one selfish person.

The path became visible one cold evening in the barn. I have no idea how it materialized, but I think maybe Buddha had something to do with it. I was leaning into her warmth when inspiration struck. I'd been sorting through the questions we'd been facing for weeks, trying to figure out what our next step should be, tears washing down my cheeks—which was a frequent state for me ever since Paige had let the fence literally come between us.

"What should we do?" I said to Buddha.

Move, something inside me said. I stopped crying. That thought had never even occurred to me. I looked at Buddha and listened. *Get off your ass and move.* I wiped at the tears and sat up taller, and I felt it suddenly in my whole body. *You've been dreaming for ages about a huge property with room for lots of animals. Now is the time.*

But I liked my house; I was comfortable here, and it was fully paid off. Besides, moving all these animals would be an enormous task. "This is my place," I said out loud. "This is the place I always wanted."

Truth was, this was not what I had envisioned. It was a step in the right direction, but my vision had always been on a much grander scale. More acreage, more shade trees, room for more animals, space to heal more kids.

"Oh my God," I said. "Is this really what's supposed to happen now?"

Move, I heard (or felt) again. I jumped up, my heart beating faster. I had to tell Jay.

CHAPTER 9

We were standing in the living room of a beautiful house with a gabled roof and exposed rafters. The place had been kept up impeccably, white and sealed wood on the inside and a cheery yellow exterior. We wouldn't have to do a thing to move in; it was in tip-top shape. The problem was the rest of the property. The hill fell away from the house on a steep grade. Mountain goats would be the only animals who could live on this land.

Next.

Jay and I were on a hunt for a new home for our human and animal family. At first Jay had not agreed that moving was the answer to our problems.

"I think we should hold our ground," he had said when I'd told him about my epiphany. "I don't think Paige should get away with this."

"But don't you see?" I said. "This is what I'm always talking about. How everything happens for a reason, and for the highest good. Maybe she's not victimizing us; maybe she's helping us. I've meditated and visualized forever, trying to manifest a huge haven for the animals, but I've never done anything about it. I think this might be the opportunity to do something about it."

"But you've created all of *this*," Jay said, gesturing to the whole of the Gentle Barn. I loved Jay for his belief in me and his appreciation of all I had worked for.

"Why don't we just look around," I said. "Just to see what's out there."

I owned the house free and clear. We could sell the property and have plenty for the down payment on a new, larger place and something left over to get a fresh start.

It only took Jay a few days to come around. It became clear to him that fighting Paige was taking too much of a toll on our family. Removing ourselves from the situation would preserve our energies and allow the Gentle Barn to continue on with its positive growth.

That's when we had called Larry, a real estate agent, and so there we were, being driven to the ends of the earth and back, looking for a new place. The kids—who were now four and five—came along with us to see most of the properties and they each got to add their vote to the mix. To them it was a grand adventure.

After showing us a slew of properties—including one with horrible drainage in a flood zone and another with a falling-down barn and a house much too small for our family—Larry called us up with genuine excitement in his voice.

"I can't believe how little they're asking," he said. "And I can't imagine a better fit. This place has your name written all over it."

This property was in Ojai, not far from the horse rescue where we'd gotten Blue. Larry drove us and the kids on out of the city, back to those beautiful rolling hills. As we drove through the gate and onto the property, I grabbed Jay's arm. We were all looking wide-eyed through the window, and Jesse had his nose pressed up against the glass. To the left of the long dirt driveway there were tall sycamore trees next to a creek bed, and on the right was a gently sloping hill dotted with enormous oak trees. Some of the oaks must have been two hundred years old the way their branches stretched out over the chaparral, creating huge disks of deep shadow.

"You wanted shade trees, right?" Jay said.

I nodded, my mouth hanging open.

"We could have a swing!" Molli said.

We drove and drove and yet still we were on the driveway.

"How many acres did you say this was?" Jay asked Larry.

"Seventy."

"And how many barns?"

"Four. Here's one, just up ahead." Larry pointed to an old but solid-looking barn big enough to house all our animals and more. And this was only one of them.

Fourteen times the acreage we'd requested. A hundred and forty times more than we currently had. Four times the amount of shelter for the animals. It didn't seem possible this was in our price range.

When we got to the house, we saw why.

The structure would be better described as a shack, with windows that were barely visible behind all the wood that had been used to board them up. The stairs up to the high front porch were missing footboards every other rung (they'd probably been used to board up the windows). There was no paint visible on the shingles, which had turned a dark, warped gray and were starting to rot. Yellow tape was strung across the front stairs.

If it had been just Jay and me, we would have snapped up this dream of a property in two seconds. We could have camped out in one of the barns while we slowly raised the money to build a house. But it wasn't just Jay and me. We had two children to consider. Two children who needed hot meals and running water.

Reluctantly we drove off that property and returned to square one.

"We're never going to find anything," I said to Jay. We were lying in our bed in the dark.

"Sure we are," he said, and he wrapped me in his big bear arms. After hours on the road, a promising buildup, and a shiny new dream yanked away, I didn't have the energy to be a visionary. It was his turn to play optimist.

Limbo is not my favorite place to be. My heart was no longer completely there on our half-acre but it had nowhere new to land. I continued to work with Blue, who remained inconsolable. I continued to lead my groups and have visitors come on Sundays. I continued to be a mom to two kids and sixty animals. But I was restless and distracted. It didn't help that notices kept arriving on our doorstep with words like "final warning" and "pending legal action."

Doubts and a sense of urgency began clouding my perspective, and Jay and I returned to our talks about whether to fight Paige in court or just give up on the dream entirely and get day jobs.

Larry kept calling, but now I was asking loads of questions over the phone before I got back on the emotional roller coaster of visiting places that were *almost* right. *What shape is the barn in? How is the house? Would you live in it? When you say a "hill" do you mean a sheer drop into an abyss?*

One time he called to say, "I've got the perfect place. The house is beautiful. The barn is brand-new. There are ten acres with a very, *very* gentle incline. . . . It's just a little outside your budget."

Oh, just a *million and a half* outside our budget? Sure, I'd love to drive forty miles to go see how amazing our life could be if only we were rich.

Larry's calls no longer held promise, only frustration and a chunk of my day stolen. So when Jay told me one Saturday that Larry had called and that he sounded more excited than he'd heard him in a while, I said, "Oh God, please don't make me see any more properties."

"But what if this is the one?" Jay said. "Larry sounded really amped. Besides, what's our alternative—shut down the Gentle Barn?"

I succumbed and called the agent back.

"I'm asking you, please," Larry said, "just come see this property. I think this might be the one meant for you."

This was not the first time I'd heard him say this.

"I just can't do it," I told him. "I think I'm done. It's running me ragged."

"If you see this place and you don't like it, I promise I'll stop calling."

Larry drove Jay and the kids and me from Highway 101 south to the 405 north to the 5 north to the 14 north, and I thought, *Where in the world is he taking us now?* As we followed the signs for Santa Clarita, the terrain went from dry to dryer to parched and scarred—land so arid the weeds were clinging by a thread to their life force. *Hell if I'm bringing my animals and kids to live out here,* I thought. As we headed down a steep road called Sand Canyon, I looked over at Jay. He was frowning and squinting hard at the sun-scorched hillside, and I was glad we both seemed to be on the same page.

"I don't see any houses," Molli said.

"Me either," said Jesse.

"I promise there's a house," Larry said.

We turned onto another highway and about two minutes later the car slowed and we pulled off the road onto the sandy shoulder and up to a gate. As we drove in through the gate onto a gravel driveway I felt just a bit less disgruntled. I can't explain why; there were still no trees and the land looked just as barren. But my mood lightened and I found myself smiling.

"Hey, this looks like really good drainage," Jay said.

He was right. The land sloped in a very gentle grade. And yet, I doubted drainage was necessary; it looked like it never rained.

There were no barns whatsoever. There weren't even any fences dividing the land into corrals or pastures. The whole of the place was covered with dried-out weeds. Larry stopped the car and we all got out, and the kids ran ahead of us into the dry grass. As we walked across the land I began seeing perfect spots for corrals and barns. The place was six acres, plenty of space to put in shelters and fence off a barnyard and a corral, plant shade trees, maybe even a grassy area for the kids.

"Look," Jay said as we arrived at a level spot. "This would be a perfect place for the barnyard."

"We could plant shade trees right along here," I said.

Each step of the way we were designing a habitat—corrals, barns, maybe even an infirmary.

"A house!" Jesse yelled.

When we caught up with him at the high end of the property, we got a better view of the house.

"It's a princess palace," Molli said.

And sure enough the two-story, gray-blue Victorian—with red, green, pink, and blue trim—looked like it had come straight from Disneyland, or off the top of a wedding cake.

Larry opened the low gate and led us up the front steps. The living room was large and airy, with shiny hardwood floors that extended into the dining room as well as a breakfast nook. There was also an additional family room and a bathroom just off the kitchen. Upstairs there were three bedrooms and two more bathrooms.

"We'll take it," I said.

"Ellie," Jay said, "wait a minute. Don't you want to talk about this first?"

I turned to face him. "Well, what do you think?"

A smile spread slowly over his face; then he nodded. Molli beamed and Jesse gave me a thumbs-up.

"We'll take it," I said.

Over the next days and weeks, the energy in our home and barnyard was completely different. I sang as I fed the animals each morning. I practically danced as I mucked out the barn. Another notice arrived from Building and Safety, and I threw it on the coffee table unopened. My stomach no longer tied itself in a knot when I heard Paige in her backyard. We were outta there and on to bigger and better things.

We had plenty of work ahead of us. We were going to have to put in all the fencing to create the corrals and barnyards. We would have to build barns and stalls and we'd have to run electricity and water down to them. And with all the money we were about to spend on the property, it looked like we'd be doing all the work ourselves. But we were up to it. Our excitement would carry us through.

A few days before escrow was to close I got a call from Liz at the horse rescue in Ojai.

"Ellie, you're not going to believe this," she said. "Sasha has been returned." Blue's friend, Sasha.

The little girl who'd received Sasha as a gift had been doing great with her . . . until her mother decided to get in the saddle to "fine-tune" the horse's manners. Apparently she had tried to beat the poor horse into submission, at which point Sasha had begun bucking and behaving badly. They'd brought Sasha back to the rescue, returned for defective behavior.

"Liz, that's amazing. Oh my gosh, we're going to be able to reunite them." But where? Any moment we were about to move to a property that had no horse corral, no fences, no shelter. We were hoping to get onto our new land as quickly as possible and start building the corral and barnyard, but we had no idea how long that would take. And yet I didn't want to put off Blue and Sasha's reunion. They had waited long enough.

"I'll tell you what," Liz said. "Why don't I arrange for a temporary foster home for the two of them."

Liz took Sasha to the foster home, and later that same day we loaded Blue into the horse trailer and drove her north on Highway 5. We arrived an hour later, and as I was leading Blue out of the trailer, a horse whinnied just around the corner from where we'd parked. The moment Blue heard this, she whinnied back and tossed her head and snorted, then rose up on her hind legs, straining against the lead. I had never seen her so full of life.

When we had rounded the corner, Sasha—a black mare taller and younger than Blue—came into sight. I let go of Blue's lead and she headed straight through the open gate into the pasture. The two horses ran at each other, whinnying. They circled around each other, found each other's faces and inhaled each other in a horse greeting. They reared up, side by side, then circled again and rubbed their bodies together, then groomed each other with their mouths. Suddenly Blue withdrew and stomped her feet and bellowed. I could just imagine her saying, *Where have you been, Sasha? You had me worried sick! How dare you leave me like that!* Sasha stood patiently until Blue was done scolding her. Then Blue approached again and the two went back to rubbing against each other and grooming each other. They went on like this, loving and nibbling and grooming, for a good hour. Jay, the foster family, and I watched and wept. We couldn't tear ourselves away until the two horses had finally settled down and gone off side by side to eat and drink.

Before we left that day, we went to Blue and Sasha and promised them they would never be separated again. But the two would have to wait to come to their permanent home until we could get onto the new land and build a corral and shelter for them.

—————

Escrow closed on both properties on the same day, which was both exciting and nerve-wracking. We had sixty animals to move thirty miles, and we had to do it *immediately*. We'd had no time to build enclosures, so we phoned a company called Fence Factory, who came out to our new place and, in one day, installed temporary fencing and shelters for all of our animals. It looked like a little refugee village, but it would keep the animals safe until we got the permanent structures in place.

Our first project would be to put in the corral so we could bring Blue and Sasha home.

We began with a trip to Home Depot to rent a weed whacker. As the kids ran around the property and rode their bikes and collected rocks, Jay and I got our first taste of the work that lay ahead. I had seen—and heard—people using weed whackers for years. It looked easy enough. You just hold a little stick in the weeds and let the machine do all the work. I was excited . . . for about the first fifteen minutes. But there were a lot of weeds on our new six acres. After the first hour of Jay and me trading off, my arms were shaking and my shoulders ached. By the end of the day, I had a new respect for gardeners everywhere.

The next day we went back to Home Depot to rent a posthole digger, which, as I found out, is a contraption that could double as a torture device—rattling the poor victim's bones and jangling their nerves until they confess. It takes two people to operate this machine, so it can even be used to torture two people at once. We started it like a lawn mower, by pulling a cord, and the thing set off to vibrating like a dentist's drill for a dinosaur. For hours on our second day, Jay held two handles on one side, I held two handles on the other, and together we pushed downward with all our might, drilling a large hole in the ground for the future fence post. It was so jarring and noisy that it was impossible to see while we were using it or hear anything the other person said.

I had expected this to be a two-day procedure: day 1—dig the holes; day 2—put up the fence. Until we were a few hours in, I had no idea how naïve that was. We found out in the process of drilling that although the soil was sandy it was also very compact and was filled with enormous rocks that we kept hitting with the machine. We'd have to stop the motor and manually dig out the boulders. Between the corral and the upper barnyard, we had about 125 postholes to dig. By the end of the day, we had dug ten. But my entire body ached like it had been hit by a truck. I couldn't even open my hands without it hurting.

And digging was only the first stage.

As we rounded the bend from spring into summer, we got to experience firsthand the reason for the arid land out here. In Tarzana
we had had one mountain range between us and the ocean. Now we
were two mountain ranges removed, with no hint whatsoever of coastal
moisture or onshore breezes. This heat and the distance from civiliza-
tion scared off most of our prior collection of volunteers. Aside from
the occasional drop-in volunteer or day laborer from the Bible Tab-
ernacle down the road from us—as well as one delightful visit from a
couple from Hawaii, who lent us a hand for a full week—most days,
Jay and I worked alone under the blazing sun, developing strong backs,
sunburned arms, and lots of calluses.

It took us the entire summer to finish the expansive horse corral.
We still had to put in stalls, but we had temporary roofs to shelter
the horses from sun and rain. It was finally time to bring Blue and
Sasha home. We hooked up the trailer to my truck and, with great
excitement, went to bring the horses to the last home they would
ever need.

Once back, we led Sasha and Blue into their beautiful new corral.
We had not cut down the weeds in the center, leaving the long grasses
for the horses to graze on. The reunited friends ran through the pasture and rolled in the dirt, and finally settled in to graze together. It
seemed to me they understood the words we'd spoken to them. "You'll
never have to move again. You're safe here, together, for the rest of your
lives." That night we double-checked that their water troughs were
clean and topped off and that they had plenty of food to graze on. As
we kissed them good night, I was filled with a deep sense of peace—an
important mission brought to a close.

———

Our bedroom window looked out from the second floor over the full
expanse of our land. The next morning I went straight to the window

so I could see the horses in their pasture. There was Sasha, standing tall, but Blue was lying on the ground. *Maybe she's just resting,* I thought, but I felt uneasy. "Jay, I'm going down to feed and check on the horses," I said.

When I got to the pasture, I saw that Blue was definitely not resting. Clearly in distress, she was now rolling on the ground and trying to bite at her sides, and her eyes were filled with fear. "No," I said, and I tried to push the dreaded word from my mind, but it wouldn't budge. *Colic.* In horses, colic could be anything from a tummy ache to a fatal twist in the intestines. My mind flitted to Jesse; it was his first day of kindergarten. I called up to the house from my cell phone, and until I spoke, I didn't know which words would come tumbling out of my mouth. *Will you take Jesse to kindergarten?* Or: *You're going to have to call the vet for Blue; I'm taking Jesse.* I was torn, as I'd always been torn ever since I'd brought my beautiful son into this world. I knew he needed me, but so did my animals. "Jay," I said, "call the vet. I think Blue's colicking. We're going to have to tag team. . . . I have to be there for Jesse's first day."

As I ran up to the house, Jay ran down to the horses. I stayed with Jesse and Molli as Jay called the vet out. I got the kids dressed and got their hair and teeth brushed. Then Jay called me from the pasture. The vet had come and told him to get Blue to the hospital immediately; the closest equine hospital was an hour away. "You have to take Sasha too," I said. "We promised never to separate them." As I made the kids breakfast and packed special lunches, I had to rein my mind in, to pull myself away from Blue and whether Jay was having trouble getting her up and into the trailer; I had to focus on these children, on my son, who would have one and only one first day of kindergarten. *Listen to Jesse,* I told myself. *You made a choice; commit to it with all your being.* As the kids ate breakfast, Jesse told me how excited he was to go to school. I marveled at how brave he was and how big and handsome he'd become. Before we went out the door, I slid Jesse's brand-new backpack over his shoulder, and I buckled the kids into the backseat. Again, as I drove, my mind tried to pull away from me, and I had to use every ounce of my willpower to bring myself back to the car and the present moment. *You can think about Blue later. Now is Jesse's time.* I took Molli to her first-grade class and then met Jesse's new teacher. I walked him to his desk and then hugged and kissed him over and over. "I'm so proud of you, Jess." I didn't leave until the teacher finally kicked all the parents out of the classroom.

Outside in the fresh air, my heart started to pound and adrenaline shot up through my solar plexus. It was now, finally, time to switch gears. I punched Jay's number into my phone, but he didn't pick up. I tried again from my car. No answer. Five minutes later, he called me as I was pulling onto the highway.

"What's happening?" I said.

"Are you driving?"

"Yes."

"Pull over."

When I'd pulled back off the highway and parked the car, Jay said, "She didn't make it."

"What do you mean she didn't make it?" She'd been reunited with her best friend and was ecstatically happy. It didn't compute.

"I'm so sorry, Ellie. They opened her up and there was a tumor wrapped around her intestines. They said they knew right away they couldn't save her." Many feet of intestine had already died off because of the constriction. Sasha had gone along to the hospital and was in a stall down the hall from the operating room. Before they had led Blue in to surgery, Blue had visited Sasha and they'd rubbed noses and breathed each other in. Now, with Blue gone, Sasha had gone off the deep end, bucking and rearing and banging her head against the ceiling. They'd had to sedate her to keep her from hurting herself. I felt just like Sasha as I sat sobbing uncontrollably, unable to drive my car.

For the next three weeks we had to keep Sasha sedated to keep her safe, and we asked our neighbors if we could board her with their horses. Because they're herd animals, horses are much more comfortable around others of their species than alone. Right away we began looking for another rescue horse to keep Sasha company.

I puzzled daily over Blue's death. I had thought the whole purpose of finding Sasha was to heal Blue from her sadness. But here was Sasha now alone, and it was becoming clear that Sasha needed more healing than Blue had. Even once Sasha had calmed down and we'd found another horse to keep her company, we noticed that she was uneasy if anyone got too close to her without warning; and if a saddle came into view even ten feet away, she would rear up and grind her teeth, showing an extreme level of anxiety.

I hired a trainer and the two of us worked daily with Sasha. Horses tell their stories by how they respond to being handled and ridden. If they were abused under saddle, they need to be lovingly saddled and ridden in order to give them a chance to express and free their body of the emotion, as well as to be convinced that the abuse is finally over. If you skip this part and simply set them free to retire in a pasture, the unhealed trauma will be held in their bodies and cause stress and behavioral issues and even cancer. They have to be taken gently back to the "scene of the crime" in order to have a new experience and to heal, so that when they are turned loose in the pasture, they can truly be free. This type of work gives a whole new meaning to the phrase "Get back on the horse."

Sasha slowly told us everything. Her extreme reaction to simply *seeing* a saddle told us she'd been terribly damaged by an impatient and abusive owner—maybe more than one—and it took us days to get anywhere near her with the saddle. Each day I'd bring it a couple of feet closer. At the first sign of anxiety I'd put the saddle away and we were done for that day. After a couple of weeks, I was able to bring the saddle close enough for her to sniff it. Ears would go back, teeth would grind, saddle removed from the premises. By the end of October, I could hold the saddle up over her back before the anxiety would kick in. Each and every time, the moment any sign of anxiety arose, I'd remove the item or stop the activity that had triggered the fear, proving to Sasha little by little that nothing bad was going to happen to her. Working in this way, in incremental phases over many weeks, I finally got the saddle onto Sasha's back, and then even got myself up into the saddle—first for a minute, then three, then five. Sitting on her back, I would simply gather my energy together, shift my weight forward ever so slightly, bring aliveness into my hips, and wait for her to respond. When she finally stepped forward, I'd say, "That's it, Sasha. Good girl."

Once we got forward movement down, the trainer stopped coming, and on my own I advanced to asking Sasha to turn. After she'd taken a few steps forward, I shifted my attention and my shoulders slightly to the left, and then—with the rein collected in my left hand—I gently turned my pinky outward, drawing the tiniest bit of tautness into the left rein. Sasha's immediate reaction was to throw her body into a defensive stance, splaying her front legs as though bracing herself, her whole body saying, *Oh no, don't hurt me!*

"I'm not going to hit you, girl," I cooed to her, and I simply sat there calmly in the saddle, maintaining the slight tautness in the left rein and giving her plenty of time to figure it out. Eventually she turned her head and took a step to the left, and I said, "Good girl. That's it."

A couple of sessions later, I asked her to turn in the other direction, and she braced again for the expected beating.

"It's OK, sweetheart," I told her. "You have all the time in the world to figure it out." And eventually she took a step in the other direction. "That's it, Sasha."

We always ended the session on a triumph. In this way we began to heal the trauma in her body, but it was a slow process and would take hours and hours over the course of the next two years to completely heal her.

As Sasha showed signs of improvement, hints that she might make a full recovery, I found myself thinking, *See, Blue, we're taking good care of your Sasha.* And it finally dawned on me that Blue's life was not a tragedy at all. In fact, it was the most beautiful love story I could ever imagine. With a tumor steadily growing inside her, Blue had clung to life until she'd seen her Sasha again and brought her to a safe and loving home to be healed. What courage and stamina. What hugeness of heart.

I had been caught in my limited human perception, unable to see the miracle right before me. Once I settled into this shift in paradigm, I began to see everything in a different light—even the fiasco with Paige. If we had lived in harmony with our Tarzana neighbor, we would still be on that small property, limited to a couple of handfuls of animals and small groups of kids. Now we had space to rescue hundreds more animals and bring in hundreds more at-risk kids.

One morning, after I'd fed all the animals breakfast and taken Jesse and Molli to school and done my day's session with Sasha, I sat down at my desk before the picture window that looked out over our beautiful new paradise with newly planted trees, and I took out a small notecard with flowers on the front. In the card I wrote: "Dear Paige, thank you for being our angel in disguise."

CHAPTER 10

I was not the only one who was beginning to see the world differently. After coming into this life blind, our steer, Vegan—who was now just over a year old—was going to get a shot at sight. With a gift from a family foundation in hand, we drove Vegan the two and half hours to San Diego for his surgery.

It had turned out that Vegan's blindness was due to congenital cataracts, but it had been quite a search to find a vet who could remove cataracts on a steer. (Bovine vets generally do not have the skills required because such surgeries are not performed on animals headed for the dinner table.)

The surgery went well, and Vegan's vision was restored to about 70 percent of what a normal cow had. A blind spot remained in the center of each eye, but if he turned his head a bit, he could see clear as day. I sat and watched him for hours as he explored this new, visible world. Whereas he had stopped bumping into things as a blind cow, suddenly he was bumping into everything. Just because he could see the tree in front of him didn't mean he understood that he would bonk his head on it if he walked straight into it. Sight was not yet connected for him to the physical world as his other senses were. He knew how hay smelled and tasted and felt in his mouth, but he didn't yet know what it looked like, so he spent hours staring at it, then sniffing and licking it and nudging it around, then staring at it again. With each object or animal he encountered, he was slowly wiring his sense of sight to his other four, established senses.

As Vegan continued to explore and understand the world anew, he discovered that the beautiful vinyl fencing we'd installed—which wrapped around the metal fence posts in all of the new enclosures and had a lifetime warranty—was not as sturdy as we'd been promised. At about 1,500 pounds, and on his way to an eventual 2,000, Vegan had found that he not only could bonk into the fence, but he could begin to bend it out of shape.

One day, as Jay and I drove down the long driveway on our new property, I saw Buddha watching me from the cow pasture, her eyes following the truck.

"Look how Buddha's staring at me," I said. "I think she's trying to tell me something."

"She's probably just saying good-bye," Jay said. "Just wave to her."

"No, she's definitely trying to tell me something, Jay. Stop the truck."

"Ellie, we're late." But he sighed and put on the brakes.

I got out and ran to Buddha. "What is it, girl? What's wrong?" Buddha turned her body 180 degrees, like a weather vane, her nose pointing at the wash below the enclosure where she and Vegan lived.

"What is it?" I asked, and she seemed to stare harder at the wash.

So I headed down the hill, and there was Vegan wandering around, licking the trees and trying to eat them. He had found his way out—or rather *through*—the fence.

In our first year on the new land, Jay and I learned all about fencing—and re-fencing. We learned about building and cementing and installing and adapting, too. And it took us that entire first year to make the land a workable, sheltering haven for both the animals who lived with us and the people who would be invited back to visit once the place was ready.

It was new terrain for us and for the animals. The vistas were grand, with craggy mountains across the road and rolling hills behind the house that turned green after a few rains. And the sky seemed to go on forever. But the terrain also came with wildlife, unfamiliar weather patterns, and a new breed of perils.

We had to make sure our children knew what a rattlesnake looked and sounded like and not to stick their bare hands into a wood pile or walk through the high brush. I so wanted to let them run wild the way I had as a kid, and yet my fear for their safety won out. The rule became: *Play where I can see you and you can see me.*

In addition to rattlesnakes, there were black widows, tarantulas, coyotes, bobcats, and mountain lions. These last were a threat to our smaller animals, so we'd had to make the fences around the upper barnyard six feet tall. The backup security was our pack of dogs, who barked whenever strangers came onto our land—whether human or animal.

In our first couple of weeks on the property, our neighbors had stopped by to welcome us to the area. When I'd gotten the dogs to stop their barking, the neighbors filled us in on some other things we needed to be cautious about.

"I know you all are city folk," the man said. I was surprised it was that obvious. "Since you don't know the terrain around here, let me tell you what you're up against. First of all, this is fire territory. You got to be careful with cigarettes and matches."

"If you see smoke," the man's wife said, "you have to take it seriously."

"Second," the man said, "we don't have that city water you're used to, where you never run out. You got your well, and that's it."

"So take quick showers, and turn off the water while you're soaping up," the woman said. "You don't want that horrible feeling when you turn on the faucet and nothing comes out."

"And forget about that lawn." We had a back lawn that had been green when we'd first seen the place, but it was already turning brown in the heat. "And third," the man said, "we've got these gale winds out here that come up out of nowhere. They're like hurricanes, so don't be surprised if you see stuff blowing away."

"Stuff?" I said, looking around at the beautiful, calm day. I could feel the lightest breeze on my face. "Like papers and trash?"

"Like your shed or your new trees. You've got to really anchor stuff to the ground."

I looked at the pepper tree saplings we had just planted along the driveway. *But they're* in *the ground,* I thought.

"You just can't be too careful," the woman said.

We thanked them for being so nice and stopping by, but privately I thought: *Boy, they exaggerate worse than I do.*

A week later, after we had watered our lawn and then all of us had taken nice hot showers, I was putting the kids to bed, and we heard a horrible grinding sound coming from the garage.

"What the hell is that?" Jay said. He went down to the garage and after fifteen minutes, came back up. "It's the water pump." He turned on the bathroom tap, and not a drop came out. Our well had run dry, and the pump was working overtime to try to dredge up water that wasn't there. We spent the next two days with no water, except for the bottles of water we stocked up on from the store. We even ended up having to replace the pump.

Not long after that, we had our first windy day. I was looking out the window at the young pepper trees swaying wildly and thinking, *Maybe they weren't exaggerating so much,* when our neighbors drove up our driveway in their pickup truck. "Jay! Ellie!" they called out.

We ran out through the wind to their truck.

"Your tool shed just blew down the wash."

Our twelve-by-twelve-foot metal shed had blown fifty feet down the wash. After we dragged it back up, we decided to take seriously everything our wonderful neighbors had warned us about.

The animals, of course, needed some time to adapt to the new environment too. Mostly they loved it. They had so much space, and there was new terrain to explore and fresh grasses to eat. But the first couple of winds blew their dinner away, and we had to install special feeders that would hold on to the hay in any weather. We also bought pool nets to strain the wind-blown leaves out of their water.

The member of our barnyard who took the longest to adapt was our pig Susie Q. From the moment we arrived, she descended into a funk even worse than on her arrival to our first property. This time she wouldn't eat for weeks. We had one vet after another come out to examine her. All agreed on the diagnosis: depression. There was nothing physically wrong with her. We tried giving her special treats and smoothies and desserts. We even tried beer, which one of the vets said would stimulate her appetite. She wanted nothing to do with any of it.

I sat with her; I meditated with her; I showered her with love. "I get it, Susie Q. You thought you were going to that bad place again." It was the first ride she'd had in a trailer since the trip to the slaughterhouse that she'd escaped from. "I'm sorry that scared you, but you're not at that bad place. You're here with me and all your friends, and look how beautiful it is."

Finally one day, when four weeks had passed and Susie Q still was not eating, I sat down right in front of her and said, "Now look here, Susie Q! I know you believe that you're going to slaughter, but you're not. You're here with me and your friends in a home where you're loved. So you need to just cut this shit out!"

Her eyes shifted like she was thinking it over.

"What are you going to do? Just lie there and die? Look around you; your belief was wrong! You're in paradise with me, and I will never let you down. Now, get up and eat something, dammit!"

She lifted her head as though to get a better look at my face. Then she stood up and ate her dinner.

Now that Susie Q was OK and everyone had settled into the barnyard, we slowly began rescuing some new animals. Mostly it was horses; I was just so excited to have all this space, and now a brand-new corral. As usual, I didn't have a laid-out plan, I simply followed the whispers, which led me to one horse that needed to be rescued and then another. Toward the end of our first year on the property, we had the beginnings of a wonderfully mismatched herd.

As with Sasha, some of these horses needed to be healed by revisiting the saddle to rid their bodies of trauma. When the horses graduated from being ridden in the corral, Jay and I added a trail ride to our daily rhythm of building, feeding, and rehabilitating. We took the horses out into the hills behind our house, where the grasses were waist-high after a winter of rains, and purple, pink, and yellow flowers filled the meadows. These rides were a wonderful break from all the manual labor we'd been doing, and we returned home rejuvenated.

With all this focus on building the new Gentle Barn, getting ourselves and our animals adapted to the new terrain, and healing the new horses, we did not have time to do any fund-raising during that first year, and neither was our place in any condition yet to reopen to the public. Thus when our one-year marker arrived, the bottom of the barrel was well in sight, and there were no new funds coming in to replenish it. We decided that we needed to refinance our place in order to loan the Gentle Barn more money. We had put a lot of our own funds into the property with a large down payment; it was time to take some of it back out so we could get up and running again.

We paid the bills with money from the refi, and Jay went back to applying for grants, mainly from private family foundations offering five thousand dollars here, ten thousand dollars there. With the horse barn now in place next to the corral, a shelter next to the cow pasture, four Tuff Sheds serving as a barn and tack room in the upper barnyard, and makeshift running water in each area, we were now ready to invite the at-risk kids back out. We'd been off the radar for more than a year, then reopened a half hour farther from town; I had no idea whether the agencies would still be interested or would want to travel the distance. But the moment we announced our reopening, we had agencies lined up to bring their kids out. That September we had three groups of at-risk kids coming out each week, as well as school field trips. By late fall we were starting to hit our stride again, even if the money was slow in coming. The new herd of horses breathed new life into my sessions with the kids. When we had small groups, each kid could pair up with a horse to groom her, allowing for a deeper bonding between animal and child. And with the more expansive space, there was more to do and explore with the kids, including visiting the three separate barnyards, going on nature hikes, and starting a garden.

I still started off each group by having the kids hug Buddha, but I now had a new way to end each session. Up in front of the house, a decorative, old-fashioned well stood atop the actual underground well that fed our water supply. The moment I'd first caught sight of it, I knew that everyone who came to the Gentle Barn now would have to make a wish before they left. So, with my first group of kids on this new land, I took them up to the well at the end of their session.

As we circled around it, I said, "Remember earlier I told you that this was my dream since I was seven years old?"

The kids nodded, their faces rosy from the heat and wide open from having spent the last two hours with the animals.

"Well, I didn't have a good childhood," I said. "I didn't have anybody's support. And I definitely didn't grow up on a farm. So there was no logical reason for me to have all this . . . other than I'm very stubborn and I refuse to take no for an answer."

A couple of the kids laughed.

"That's why I'm living in paradise now. That's why I wake up each morning and look out that front window there and say to myself, 'Yes! It's another day in my dream.'"

"You have a really nice home," one of the boys said.

"Thank you," I said. "I wish that for you, too." I looked around the circle to be sure all the kids were paying attention. "My dream came true, even though it didn't seem like it possibly could. Now I believe that dreams can come true for *everyone* . . . just as long as we don't give up on them."

Before we ended, I asked the kids to think of something they wanted for their own lives. "It can be as simple as 'I wish to be happy' or 'I wish to have a wish.' Or maybe you already know something big you want for your life. Any wish is OK." I asked them to put their hands on this magic well. "Now, make your wish with every fiber of your being, every inch of your heart and soul. Don't judge it. Don't criticize it. Don't doubt it." Then I asked them to stay there with their hands on the well until their wish filled their entire being. "When that happens, you can clap two times and walk away."

And thus I introduced these kids to the ordinary magic of believing good things are possible.

Working with the kids fulfilled me more deeply than it ever had, and I was thrilled to have them back. I saw myself coming into my own— venturing more often away from my "script," beginning to trust my instincts, taking risks in the moment, and reflecting back to the kids what I saw in them. And I could see my growing confidence reflected back to me—in the animals, in the kids themselves, and by the very fact that the groups who had come to us at our old location were still eager to schedule visits despite the fact that they had to travel twice as far to get to us.

Over time my work with the at-risk kids evolved to include a horse walk, where each child or teen was paired with a horse of their own to lead on the trails that headed off the property and into the surrounding grasslands. We never had the kids ride, but instead kept their feet on the ground, where they could be shoulder to shoulder with the horses. These children and teens had spent their life being shut down and tough and arrogant, trying to dominate others as a response to having been dominated. It made no sense at all to teach them to dominate still another being by putting them on a horse's back. Instead, we wanted to give them the opportunity to be humbled, to allow them to surrender and bond. We wanted to open them up in a way that traditional therapy had failed at; it was in this vulnerability that they would find their healing. And there was no better path to this than to integrate them with the herd.

In a herd, no two horses are equal. There's always a leader and there's always a follower, and every horse knows her rank in relation to every other horse. It's the same if a human pairs up with a horse; that horse will know immediately whether she's the leader or the follower. Horses are a wonderful mirror, reflecting back each kid's issues, which allows me to see what's going on with them. If a teen is acting fake or cool, a horse will not tolerate it; horses want your heart available and open or they have no interest in being around you. Especially sensitive to inauthentic or shady behavior was Addison, our donkey. When Addison refused to follow a kid's lead, I would say to the kid, "Addison has been severely abused. He's sizing you up, trying to see if you can be trusted or not. Can you?"

Usually the kid would answer yes.

"OK, good," I'd say, "but you're going to have to show him that. This cool, tough, kind of fake way you're being is making him believe he *can't* trust you. He needs you to be real and safe for him. Can you do that?"

Time and again, I have seen a "tough" kid get quiet and still and gentle when approached with this request. And sure enough, Addison's behavior would change accordingly and he would follow that kid's lead all the way through the horse walk. It was a vivid way to prove to these young people that love and fidelity come to those who are real.

Similarly, if a kid lacks leadership skills and appears weak to the horse, that horse will take advantage of it, stopping to eat grass or pulling away to go where she wants to go, and the kid will have no control. So whenever I saw a horse rank herself above a kid, pulling the kid all over the place, I would walk beside that kid and coach him on how to be a leader. "Look up, ahead, not at the ground. Look where you're going. Pull your shoulders back, head high. Walk with intention. Walk with purpose. That's it." And by the end of the walk, the horse would be at the kid's hip, walking in line, following his requests. And that child would be beaming with triumph—instantly rewarded for strength and confidence and a clear sense of direction.

Before I took a group of kids on a horse walk, I told them the horses' stories. Sasha and her fear of the saddle, Mama Dear and Cinnamon who'd been ridden into the ground, Bonsai and Addison who had suffered extreme abuse. And Caesar, the movie star, with a long list of film credits, who had been fired from the studios when he'd finally shut down—afraid to make the dreaded mistake and suffer the consequences—and stopped performing on command. I told the kids about these horses' hurts, and—more important—about the horses' healing and recovery. I also told them about Sasha's instant crush on Caesar and how the two had become a duo, mated for life.

One day, when I was relaying all these stories, a boy named Ethan, who was angry and defiant, stood at the back of the group, kicking at the dirt. He had refused Jay's and my invitations to come closer. Then I got to Bonsai's story.

"He's our miniature horse who was abused by an alcoholic owner until he was seven years old," I said. "By the time I met him, he was so angry and hurt he'd decided never to trust anyone ever again."

Ethan perked up, his eyes on me, and he began hanging on my every word.

"We worked for a year to be able to touch him. I could see him just fighting with himself whenever I was nearby—one step forward, one step back. He really wanted to trust, but another part of him had learned so well not to." I finished the story with Bonsai's triumph. "He decided to trust one more time and he ended up with the best possible life. He taught us that it's not about *whether* to trust, but about *who* to trust."

Ethan pushed his way to the front of the group and pulled on my arm. "Please tell me that story again."

I told it again, and when I'd finished, he asked me to repeat it once more. After I'd told the story a few times through, Ethan went to Jay and asked *him* to tell the story. When he'd heard the story many times over, Ethan asked us to please take him to meet the little horse. Ethan approached Bonsai slowly, then wrapped his arms around the horse's neck, and with tears streaming down his face, whispered into Bonsai's ear, "It's gonna be all right; you're gonna be OK."

Bonsai's story was not the only one we'd told over and over that day; we had also told Ethan's.

This work was not only life-changing for the children and teens; it was fulfilling for the horses and served as an important part of their continued healing. It gave them a sense of purpose. In most work that horses do with humans, the horses are asked to suppress their sense of self and behave like machines, following the same commands no matter what's going on with the humans or the environment around them. The horse walks were a success *because* our horses were asked to be themselves and express their own voice. And our herd thrived on this freedom and took their work seriously by choice.

After every session with the kids, I felt more centered than ever, more connected to the source of all life. Even this wide-open land and expansive sky somehow pulled me to a new level in my work, drawing the creativity out from the depths of me. I was doing what I was designed to do, and I felt like I could fly.

It was after a wonderful session one day with a group of foster children that Jay came and found me down in the horse barn, his hand on his hat so it wouldn't blow away. We were having wicked winds—where dust and debris were whirling in eddies along the walkways and the grasses were blown flat. I hadn't dared to take any of the horses out that day; the kids and I had simply groomed them in their stalls.

"Saddle up, Ellie," Jay said. "We're going for a ride."

We'd been taking Sasha and Caesar out on regular trail rides. Jay and I joked that it was a daily double date. But there was no way he was getting me on a horse in that wind. "A ride?" I said. "There's a tornado out there."

"Come on," he said, hoisting a saddle onto Caesar's back, "go get Sasha's saddle."

A gust of wind blew through the horse barn, nearly knocking my hat off. "You're out of your mind," I said.

"Ellie, please. Come on." He sounded a little desperate.

"I'll tell you what," I said. "I'm hungry. I'm going to go up and make a sandwich, and then maybe the wind will die down by afternoon."

But Jay persisted. He wanted to go *now*. And somehow he managed to win me over and get me to agree to his crazy idea.

We mounted the horses, and five minutes out, we rounded a bend in the trail and Jay reached for my hand, as he did sometimes when we rode together. "I want to look in your eyes," he said.

I wanted to turn my gaze to him, but when I rode I needed to see where I was going. I glanced at him briefly, but then turned back to the trail.

Jay stopped the horses. "Look at me now," he said.

His face looked serious and he gazed at me for a long moment with those deep blue eyes of his. Then finally he spoke. "Will you marry me?"

"Yeah," I said. But I thought he was just being sentimental, feeling the emotion of the moment.

Then he pulled out a small black box, and I thought, *Wow, is this for real?* I searched his face, looking for the beginning of one of his huge grins. But he stayed serious and vulnerable and tender. He flipped open the box, and there sat the most beautiful ring, with a white diamond on either side and in the center a yellow diamond—my favorite color. I looked up at Jay, my eyes filling with tears, and saw tears in his eyes too. "Oh my God," I said. "Yes. I'll marry you!"

He got off his horse, and then helped me down off mine. He took me in his arms and kissed me, and then slid the ring onto my finger. We stood in the middle of the path for a long time, wrapped in each other's arms and drinking each other in.

Finally, he took my hand and said, "I want to show you something." He led me and the horses off the trail and into a meadow, then pushed aside the tall grasses to uncover a picnic basket he had hidden there. He opened the basket and spread out a red-and-white checked tablecloth, then sat down and patted the spot next to him. Inside the basket were beautiful salads and sandwiches and red wine, with real wineglasses. And for the next hour, it was as though we were inside our own little bubble while time stopped and the wind stopped and the horses grazed nearby.

When we finished eating, Jay gathered up our picnic. As we mounted our horses, I became aware of the wind again, which hadn't stopped at all. Then Jay turned Caesar in the direction of home.

"Aren't we going for a ride?" I said.

"Hell no," Jay said. "It's windy out here. It's too dangerous."

CHAPTER 11

By the beginning of 2004, all our animals had fully adjusted to their new environment. And by the end of that year, the horse herd was thriving, and our at-risk youth program was flourishing along with it. Although our new collection of volunteers was only a tiny handful, I was grateful to have them and trusted that more would sign on in time. Jesse and Molli—now six and seven—were finally both in school a full day, giving Jay and me uninterrupted time to run the Gentle Barn. I was sinking my teeth into working full-time, being completely present for the animals and the at-risk kids. At the end of the day, when our own children came home from school, I happily changed gears and entered their world, being present for them. Jay and I were a great team both for the Gentle Barn and in our parenting. If one of us was taking the kids to school, the other was feeding the animals. Our days had a lovely flow to them, and I had the sense that the Gentle Barn was setting its roots firmly into this new soil.

Added to this daily rhythm was an extra sparkle of magic ever since Jay and I had gotten engaged—as though each day shimmered around the edges. The magic was not only for the two of us, but for our kids. They felt as if we were all getting married to one another, unifying us into one true family.

As lovely and magical as my days felt, I was exhausted by the end of each and every one of them. I didn't get one second of downtime from the moment I set my feet on the floor in the morning until I lay myself down in bed at night. There was always someone needing me or pulling on me or asking me questions. Not that I minded being there so fully for all these gorgeous beings—animal and human alike—filling them up, helping them know how beautiful and loved they were; but after I poured myself into my children and animals and Jay and the at-risk kids, I sometimes felt as though I'd poured all of myself out, neglecting to reserve just a little bit for me.

I certainly never would have imagined that I could add another element to the list, another being who might need me not only throughout the day, but also through the night. A small, helpless person who depended on me for their very life, who took sustenance quite literally from my body.

In February 2005, just a few months after Jay had proposed, I felt off for a couple of days. More than off. Tired, nauseous, awful. I had a fleeting thought that perhaps I had the stomach flu, but deep down I knew it wasn't the flu. I had only felt this particular type of nausea once before, when I'd been pregnant with Jesse.

I slipped out and bought a home pregnancy test, and an hour later I was sitting on the side of the tub, staring at the pink plus sign on the plastic wand, half expecting it to change any moment to a minus sign. Although I'd already known it in my gut, I still couldn't believe it. I hadn't thought I could get pregnant again.

The first wave of emotion was excitement. *Oh my God, Jay and I are going to have a baby!* Talk about unifying our family. And I would get to relive that amazing experience of holding my own newborn, another tiny human I was inextricably connected to. When I told Jay, he was as excited as a little boy. His whole face lit up; his whole *being* lit up. He practically jumped in the air. Then he took me in his arms and kissed me for a long, tender moment.

But by that night, tiny tendrils of fear were creeping their way into my thoughts. How on earth were we going to manage? I was maintaining a very delicate balance between my many roles—mother, wife-to-be, rescuer, educator, one-woman cheerleading support team. It was a virtual high-wire act, with spinning plates and all. I worked hard not to lean too far this way or too far that way and have it all come crashing down. Where was a brand-new baby going to fit into this picture? How could I be there for a new, fully dependent life and still give myself to everything and everyone else I cared about? I was in a panic.

Jay, however, was as ecstatic as the moment I'd told him, and he stayed that way. Adding another child to the mix would be "easy," "piece of cake." *Naïve,* is what I thought.

Over the next couple of weeks, I felt every emotion on the spectrum. I was still concerned about how we would manage logistically and financially, but I also felt the excitement slowly returning. I was going to have a new baby to hold and kiss and coo over. There was joy and awe and wonder, and within a short time I grew attached to the new life growing inside me. Each passing day gave me more certainty that it would all work itself out.

We waited to tell Jesse and Molli until we had confirmation from the doctor. Sure enough, I was pregnant, as pregnant as anyone can be. I was throwing up, trying not to throw up, and fighting exhaustion all day long. Some mornings I couldn't even get out of bed.

"What's wrong, Mom?" Jesse said. It was one of *those* mornings, and he was standing by my bedside staring at me.

Then Jay and Molli came in. Jay had gotten the kids ready instead of me.

"How come you're still in bed?" Molli asked. It was an unusual sight for all of them.

Jay sat down. "Well," he said, "your mom is going to have another baby."

Both kids looked doubtful. They didn't believe it for a second. Another one of Jay's jokes.

"But what's wrong with Mom?" Jesse said.

It took some explaining to clarify why I was feeling so sick. *I* still didn't understand why bringing a new life into the world had to make me feel so miserable for the first three months.

When the kids finally realized it was true, they got very excited. *A new little sister or brother!* But just like me, their first few days were filled with mixed emotion. Would they still get to be special? How was I going to play with them if I was holding this little baby all the time? Jay and I did a lot of assuring and reassuring, explaining and including. The kids sometimes came along to my appointments at the birthing center. They saw the ultrasounds and heard the midwife talk about what was happening. And we included them in our discussions about possible names for the baby.

At the beginning, we shared the news only with family, friends, and the volunteers who had become close. Others would know soon enough, when I started showing. We had done the same with the news of our engagement, figuring our wider circles would know when it was time to start inviting people to the wedding. It was a good thing we'd waited on that one because it didn't look like a wedding was going to be happening right away. If I was too sick some days to get out of bed, I certainly wasn't going to be walking down the aisle. I knew the nausea would pass in a couple of months, but then I didn't want to walk down the aisle with a big belly poofing out my wedding gown. Once the baby was born, I wasn't going to walk down the aisle nursing a baby. And there was no way we would take a new baby on a honeymoon. No, the wedding would not happen for a while, and I was OK with that. Together Jay and I were paying a mortgage, running a nonprofit, and raising children; that was enough of a commitment for me. No one was going anywhere.

Finally I entered the glorious second trimester. The nausea disappeared, my energy came back, and I could return to my old self—or at least pretend I was my old self. I got back in the saddle and we resumed our trail rides, and I fed the animals breakfast without feeling like I was going to lose my own.

In my third trimester, I continued to feel great. There was just this big belly in the way, making everything a little more awkward. But I still had a barnyard to run, so I chugged right along, acting like I wasn't pregnant at all. I did all my chores, including shoveling horse and cow poop and toting heavy wheelbarrows across the uneven turf. Jay would catch sight of me moving a picnic table, and he'd rush over, calling, "Ellie, wait, let me do that." Or he'd see me out the window as I lifted a large dog into the back of the SUV and he'd say, "You shouldn't be doing that."

"Oh, I'm fine," I would say, and I'd hoist another dog in beside the first one.

———

All this time, as my belly grew, there were some other things brewing inside me too. I was attending a parenting class and was learning all about parent-child attachment. I was now seeing that some of the choices I'd made with Jesse had not been the best ones. Between the Mommy's Helpers and preschool, Jesse had been handed off to a rotating collection of caregivers at such a tender age, and I had worried over the years about the toll it might have taken on him. I had seen our relationship shift over time, with a distance growing between us.

He seemed to get angry easily, for no apparent reason, and he had a harder and harder time looking me in the eye. Suddenly I understood why, and my heart ached to realize it had been my own actions that had hurt him. I had always been a firm believer that a woman could be both a mom and a career woman. This view was starting to change; I understood how critical it was that I be home with my child for the first few years of his or her life. I began working hard to make up for it with Jesse, learning how to be a better mom to him. And as the pregnancy progressed, my commitment to do things differently this time deepened. I had the chance with this new baby to do it right from the very beginning. But I knew that meant things were going to look different at the Gentle Barn for a while, and I did my best to prepare Jay for the shift—Jay, who was expecting "piece of cake."

In late November, the day finally came. I went into labor—or so I thought. After examining me, our midwife told us these were false contractions; I was not dilated at all. We went home, but the contractions did not subside; neither did they build into true labor. They just dragged on . . . for a full week. We went back to the birthing center; I was still not dilated, and the baby had not dropped. The midwife suggested we go check things out with our backup doctor just to be safe.

"This duration and intensity of contractions can rupture your previous C-section," the doctor said, "and if that happens, you could lose the baby."

Two hours later I was being wheeled into the operating room for my second C-section. The midwife came to the hospital to support us through it, and she stuck around to make sure the baby was not taken away from us—which was the usual protocol at a C-section birth. Jay got to hold our beautiful new daughter, Cheyanne, while the surgeon sewed me up.

When we were all settled in our room, Molli and Jesse—who had been staying with my mom—got to meet their new little sister for the first time. They even got to help the midwife give Cheyanne her first bath.

When we brought Cheyanne home from the hospital, I said to Jay, "The Gentle Barn is yours now."

As much joy as Jay took in working by my side, he had always felt that it was *my* dream, that he was just my sidekick. No amount of reassurance had convinced him that the Gentle Barn was his, too.

"I'm serious," I said. "Cheyanne is my priority now." I was going to gaze into my daughter's eyes for hours every day. I was not going to leave her with strangers, and her needs would come first before anything else—including the animals—as much as that decision would sometimes tear me apart. Jay was going to see how much this rescue operation was his because he was going to be running it more or less without me for a while. For the first couple of years of Cheyanne's life, I would be staying in the background while Jay took the helm.

I would, of course, come down to visit the animals with Cheyanne, and if she was asleep, I would carry her in the baby sling on my hip as I fed the animals or led a tour. From the time she was a few months old, we'd sit in the barnyard for hours every day and watch the animals, listening to the chickens making their stream-of-consciousness peeping. *Oh, that was a good bit of grain. How about this one? No, that was a rock.* Cheyanne was as at home in the barnyard as she was in the house, and she was giving tummy rubs to the pigs before she could walk.

Jay learned fast that adding a new baby to the mix was not a piece of cake after all. My commitment to be there first and foremost for Cheyanne had landed him with a whole set of responsibilities that had always been shared by the two of us. It was a lot for one person to handle on his own—running all the groups, managing the office, doing all the fund-raising, and taking care of the animals. Before long, it became clear that Jay needed to hire someone to assist him in the office, and that we needed some additional help in the barnyard, too. As the Gentle Barn moved forward, finances became tighter than ever, especially with a new baby in the house and hired help at the Barn. Although we were open on Sundays again—which was bringing in a trickle of money—and donations were slowly coming in, it wasn't anywhere near enough yet. We were having trouble getting financial traction.

We'd refinanced our home twice already to keep the Gentle Barn going, and together we decided to do it one more time. This would tide us over until I was fully back on the job and we had built up our corps of volunteers—or so we thought. Before Cheyanne was a year old, we had to do yet another refi—four in all. Slowly we were draining all the equity out of our home. But our accountant assured us that once the Gentle Barn was back on its feet, our organization would be able to pay all the money back to us. Yet, with all these refis, we still couldn't get a leg up on either our personal finances or those of the Gentle Barn. The mortgage company began threatening to take our house and our land. Every letter was a bill, and every phone call was a creditor.

One night at the end of summer, when Cheyanne was not quite a year old and still sleeping in our bed, my eyes snapped open in the dark. It was the sound of dogs barking that woke me, but then I heard something else, out on the gravel driveway. *Wheels,* I thought, and pulled Cheyanne close. "Jay?" I said. "Somebody's here."

"Huh?" he grunted, but he didn't move. He was a heavy sleeper.

I grabbed his shoulder. "Jay, honey, wake up."

He rolled over, and I could see the faint glint of his eyes in the dark.

"Do you hear that?"

"Dogs," he said.

"No, but listen. There's a car."

Jay sat up. "Oh shit!" Now he was awake.

In less than a minute he had his pants on and was running down the stairs. I made sure Cheyanne was still sound asleep, turned on the baby monitor, and took the speaker with me as I followed after Jay.

Outside in the dark, Jay was pleading with a huge guy dressed in black. "We have three kids," he was saying. "We run a nonprofit. Please, just give us a little more time."

Then I saw there was another guy, sitting behind the wheel of a truck. A tow truck.

"I've got to drive my kids to school in the morning," Jay pleaded. "We have to go buy food." I glanced up at Jesse's and Molli's bedroom windows, hoping they wouldn't be woken by this.

"Sorry," the guy said. "I gotta take it. It's my job."

We were going to be stranded, with three children and eighty animals. I joined Jay in pleading with the man, tears now streaking down my cheeks.

The big guy shook his head. "Sorry, man." Then he motioned to the other guy to back up the truck.

Jay stepped in front of our car and planted his feet in the ground, as though he could stop a moving tow truck with his body, and I opened the car door and frantically began gathering our things—my purse, the car seat, toys, and sweaters. The truck was making that *beep beep beep* sound of backing up. And then I heard Jay yell, "Just stop a minute!" To my amazement and relief the beeping stopped. I pulled my head out of the car and saw Jay dig into the pocket of his pants. He held something out in the direction of the guy in black and said, "Just give us one more day. Please."

The guy hesitated, but then stepped forward and took Jay's offering. He pocketed it without a word and got in the truck.

Jay wrapped his arm around me. I was still crying and I could feel Jay's body shaking. He guided me back inside and said, "Well, that's this week's groceries."

He had bought us a day from the repo men for $300.

———

Was it possible our parents had been right all along, that we were being irresponsible and throwing our money—and some of theirs—

into a sinking ship? Were we being selfish putting our kids through all this uncertainty? Had that deep, inner guidance I'd gotten to move to a larger property been false—my own willful thinking, and not the universe talking to me after all? I couldn't believe that tossing away my dream could possibly be the right decision when it would cause so many animals and kids to lose out on the healing they needed. And yet we couldn't keep doing what we were doing. The strain was too much. Something had to give.

Jay and I went over and over the choices—every one of which felt like a dead end. After much discussion and soul searching, we finally knew we had to face the truth; despite all we had poured into this endeavor and our very best efforts to make it work, we had simply failed. As excruciating as it was, it was time to say uncle.

We agreed that we would not give up the animals we'd already rescued, but the Gentle Barn would have to shut its doors. No more rescues, no more at-risk youth programs, no more Sundays open to the public. We would both get jobs and find a smaller property in a cheaper area and sell our piece of paradise.

We hired a real estate agent who specialized in ranches and equine properties in the area to see if she could find us something inexpensive with a habitable house and enough land for our animals. After three weeks of seeing condemned shacks on ragged, desolate land, we finally found a five-acre, fenced lot in Lancaster—about thirty miles from our current place. There was space for all of our animals, and at the front of the plot sat a small modular home with wall-to-wall green shag carpet. But it wasn't boarded up and it had indoor toilets. We'd make do.

The agent, Maurine, came to us in Santa Clarita to have us sign the paperwork. She was a warm, lovely woman in her late fifties with flaming-red hair, and she always said hello to our kids. When she finished oohing and aahing over Cheyanne, she set the papers on the dining-room table.

"What you're signing here is simply permission for me to sell this property. I'll be handling both the sale of your place and the purchase of the one you're buying."

She handed me a pen, and I tried to focus on the papers in front of me, but I felt like someone had just punched me in the stomach and I couldn't see the words because my eyes were filling with tears. I blinked and tried not to cry, but it didn't work. Tears streamed down my face and I started snuffling and tried to take a deep breath, but my chest felt tight. Jay brought me some tissues and put a hand on my shoulder, and that sent me over the edge and I started sobbing.

Maurine cleared her throat and said, "Um, can I ask what's wrong?"

"Oh . . . don't mind me," I managed to get out through the tears. "I'm OK." But clearly I wasn't OK. I was bawling and blowing my nose into the damp tissue I was holding, and I could feel Maurine's eyes on me. "It's just, this was my dream since I was seven," I said, and I told her how hard we had worked, with our own hands and our own backs. How we'd planted every tree and dug every posthole and made this place so beautiful. How we were helping so many animals and so many kids, and that it just seemed wrong to come this far just to fail. At which point I began sobbing so hard I was hyperventilating and couldn't get another word out.

Three tissues later I finally calmed down enough to pick up the pen. But as I lowered my shaky hand to the paper, Maurine grabbed my wrist, and my breath caught in my throat.

"Don't sign that paper!" she practically yelled, my wrist still in her hand.

"What?" I said.

"I'm not selling this property."

"What do you mean?" I said. Her stern tone had startled the sobbing right out of me.

"I'm not selling your dream out from under you."

"We've thought long and hard about this," Jay said.

"We can't pay the mortgage," I explained, "and they tried to take our car—"

"Don't you dare give up on this!" Maurine said. "This is your dream!" She shook my wrist for emphasis, and then released me. "Don't you ever give up." She grabbed her coat and headed for the door and we followed after her.

"Where are you going?" Jay said.

"What do you mean you won't sell our house?" I asked.

She walked quickly down the front steps and out the gate to her car, then said, "I won't be involved in your failure. This is what you're meant to do. You can make it work. You keep trying! You just keep trying!" She paused there for a moment, then went to her trunk and opened it. She reached in and pulled out a DVD. As she handed it to me, she said, "You watch this movie every single day for thirty days." Before she shut her door she said, "And don't call me again!"

As Maurine drove off, Jay and I simply stood there staring at each other, mouths open, not quite sure what had just happened.

Finally Jay broke our silence. "Well," he said, "we might as well go inside and watch the movie."

And we did. We watched *The Secret* every single, solitary day. Each time I watched, I felt things shifting and changing inside me, like old layers were sloughing off—layers of hopelessness, fear, false beliefs. In place of all that, something new and fresh was growing, tiny and delicate. A sense of hope and wonder. A burgeoning faith that maybe I would get to keep my dream after all. I'd worked and fought for it, but at the very root of my efforts had been the belief that in the end it would all be taken away, it would all fall apart because I wasn't really supposed to have it in the first place. It was one thing to tell the at-risk kids they could have *their* dreams; it was another thing entirely to believe it for myself. Now this movie was telling me—each and every night—what I had always told the kids. *Well, of course you can have your dream. You just have to believe it.* A whole reorganization was taking place inside me. I started watching my thoughts and words. I started making new choices, speaking and acting in new ways, coming to understand that my very attitude could create my world.

But it wasn't only the movie. The movie was reinforcing again and again the gift Maurine had given me—Maurine, our angelic real estate agent. I'd never had an adult tell me "This is what you're supposed to do. Don't you dare give up on it." I'd been commanded by an angel to believe in myself.

We called the bank that had given us the car loan and we called the mortgage company. Instead of begging, we were simply finding out what steps we had to take to make this work, because now we understood we were supposed to make things work. The Gentle Barn was supposed to exist, was supposed to thrive.

We ironed things out with the bank on the car loan. But the mortgage company said they wouldn't even talk with us until we'd made a $5,000 payment. Five thousand dollars all in one chunk. We worked hard to keep our positive attitude, doubling up on screenings of *The Secret,* but we couldn't see where the money was going to come from. Every single penny we could scrape up went to feeding our children and our animals. There was nothing left on top of that. Where were we going to get $5,000?

Two weeks later, Jay and I were sitting in the office, answering e-mails, searching for new grants, and trying to figure out how to make ends meet. We were also attempting to hold on to our fledgling attitude of positivity, but it was challenging from behind such a tall stack of bills. We'd watched *The Secret* sixteen times, but we still had not come up with the $5,000.

I put one more bill on top of the stack, and the phone rang, a number I didn't recognize.

"Gentle Barn," I answered. "This is Ellie."

It was a woman's voice on the other end. "Hi, my husband and I found out about you from a friend," she said. "We've heard so many good things. Is there any possibility we can come by and see your place?"

I hesitated for half a second, thinking I should tell her about Sundays, when we were open to the public, but something told me just to say yes. "Sure, when did you want to come?"

"We have time now," she said.

I didn't have any groups scheduled that day, and it would be another few hours before Molli and Jesse were home from school. It would do me some good to get out from under this pile of bills and into the barnyard. Besides, I could use a good hug from Buddha.

Forty-five minutes later, two people arrived at our gate, a young couple with that L.A. sheen—fit, attractive, and well put-together, making casual look elegant. I glanced at the woman's clean, cream-colored pumps and hoped her shoes would survive the terrain.

With Cheyanne on my hip, I took them first to meet the cows.

When we were inside the cow barn, the woman said, "I've never been this close to a cow."

I set Cheyanne down and wrapped my arms around Buddha's neck. Cheyanne toddled over and laid her tiny hand on Buddha's nose.

"Oh, that's so cute," said the woman.

"Obviously you trust this cow," the man said.

"With my life," I said. "Here, come give Buddha a hug." Both of them hugged my cow and took my encouragement to lay their faces against her neck and really take a moment with it. Their faces melted into that easy, open smile I'd seen on so many people as they hugged Buddha.

We went next to the horses, and I showed how to feed them carrots, with a flat, open palm. All along the way, I told the animals' stories, and I explained our at-risk youth program, saying that the shared histories of abuse were part of the healing. The couple was warm and receptive and seemed genuinely moved by each and every story I told.

When we got to the upper barnyard, Jay came down from the office to say hello.

"This place is amazing," the man told Jay.

We were standing outside the barn, where our pig Bodhi was asleep in the straw with a goat resting near his head and a handful of chickens popping in and out of the open doorway. "I didn't know they could all live together like this," the woman said. "The different animals get along so well."

"Actually, they get along better than humans do. They're more forgiving and live more in the moment." Then I added, "Besides, they know better than to expend energy trying to be right." At this both the husband and wife chuckled.

When the tour was finished, I glanced down at the woman's pumps. Not one scuff. It was like she had a fashion shield.

"Well, this has been wonderful," she said.

"It's always nice to see people are interested in what we do," I told the two of them. I felt rejuvenated by their visit, touched by how affected they were by the animals and their stories. Here in the barnyard was where the magic was. Sharing the Gentle Barn with others felt like a better way to solve our problems than toiling and figuring from behind a computer and a stack of papers. "Thank you so much for stopping by," I said.

"No, thank *you*," the woman said. "You do awesome work here."

"We'd like to make a contribution," the man said, and he took a pen out of his breast pocket, then a checkbook, and he began writing. When he handed me the check I burst into tears. I handed the check to Jay, and his eyes filled with tears too.

On the check were the words "five thousand dollars."

CHAPTER 12

The generosity of strangers blew a gust of relief into our lives and stoked my burgeoning faith. We handed the $5,000 over to the mortgage company and, as promised, they entered into discussions with us about how we could keep our property. Jay redoubled his fund-raising efforts and—working around our toddler's needs—I did whatever I could to help out. But despite all these efforts, for a good year we continued to struggle financially. My faith—still new and fragile—wavered as we approached the end of each month, racing against time to scrape together our mortgage and our car payment—only to start all over again the following month. It was like slogging up a muddy hill and slipping back to the bottom again and again. And no matter how many times we got to the top, the bottom always reignited our fear. The belief and trust that had been commanded by our angel seemed to slip from our grasp when we were faced all over again with the possibility of losing the Gentle Barn.

I made sure not to show my concern in front of our kids or even the animals. Frightening our children would not help our cause, and the animals—who'd already been through so much hardship in their lives—did not need any of my burden on top of their own. The only exception was Buddha; I knew in my bones she could handle it. In fact, it felt to me as though she were asking to hear all about it, as a good mother would want to listen to her child's fears so that she could quell them. And this was exactly what Buddha did for me, each and every time I spoke to her about my troubles.

Despite our struggles and the monthly press to pay our bills, deep down inside me things *were* still shifting and changing. With Buddha's help, and with the help of *The Secret,* which we returned to again and again, I began to recognize a pattern. Every time we had reached the end of our rope, something miraculous had landed at our feet . . . even if we didn't recognize it at the time as a miracle. Before long, when the fear would hit, I wouldn't get stuck in it quite as long, for I had a new paradigm to anchor me, a new roost to fly back to. I had been given permission to have my dream; the Gentle Barn was supposed to be.

Finally, about a year after Maurine had refused to sell our property, my faith hit critical mass. It made no logical sense from the outside. Money was even tighter than usual, and we were behind a month on the mortgage. But I peered down that path to fear that I'd trod so many times before, and it just didn't beckon to me this time.

"Ellie, I just don't see it," Jay said. "I see no way out of it this time. I have no idea where the money's going to come from."

"I don't know, either, Jay. But I'm tired of being afraid. I think at this point . . . I believe in miracles."

"Have you seen our stack of bills?" he asked me. "I've been trying all day to figure out how we're going pay them. We're worse off than we've ever been."

"I'm just going to have faith," I said. "A miracle's going to find us."

That was a Saturday in October 2007. The next day, Sunday, we went to the park in the morning with Cheyanne, who was almost two. It was just the three of us that weekend; Molli and Jesse were having a sleepover at my mom's in the city. As we were driving home from the park, just topping the rise of the Sand Canyon hill, Jay said, "Ellie, look at that smoke."

Sure enough, there was a plume of black smoke off in the distance. It didn't look that close, but ever since our neighbors had warned us about the fire hazard out here, we had kept our eyes open and taken smoke seriously.

"We better go check it out," Jay said.

When we reached our gates, we passed them and instead drove north up the road for about twenty minutes until we found the origin of the smoke. It was a reasonably small fire and looked well contained, surrounded by fire trucks.

"They got it," Jay said. "They're right on it." And he turned the car around and headed back home.

We were having one of our windy days, and as we drove up our long driveway, our young pepper trees were swaying and the dust and hay were whipping all around. We had guests coming over to our house a bit later, a family we'd invited for a playdate—Stacy, Logan, and their toddler—and by the time they arrived, the wind had picked up even more and Jay thought the smoke in the distance looked thicker and blacker.

When Stacy came in she said, "Ellie, where's a box? I'm packing you up."

"What?" I said. "Why? The firefighters had it under control, we saw them. And the fire's so far away." I set Cheyanne down on the carpet next to her little friend, and I went to make lunch for the kids. As I cut carrot sticks, Jay came into the kitchen, visibly agitated. "I thought they were going to put this fire out. But it seems worse to me."

He headed for the back door. "I'm going to hike up the hill to see if I can tell how close it is."

"I'm going with him," Logan said, and he headed out the back door after Jay.

Meanwhile Stacy was in the living room filling boxes and suitcases with our stuff—photographs of our family, jewelry, clothes—anything that looked important.

"We haven't even gotten an evacuation warning," I said. "Wouldn't they tell us?"

Stacy shook her head. She had grown up in the Hollywood hills and had been through several fires. To her, the air tasted way too familiar. "You don't want to wait for them to warn you," she said. "Not if you want to take anything with you."

Take anything with us? I sat down on the carpet and pulled Cheyanne into my lap. My mind went to our animals—ten horses, eight goats, six pigs, two cows, lots of chickens and turkeys, all our dogs and cats, and a cockatoo—eighty animals in all. What on earth would we do with our animals if the fire came any closer? We'd never really thought this one through; we were city folks.

Five minutes later Jay called. "The fire is here. Start grabbing animals and let's get out!"

"What?" I said.

"There's no time for denial," he said. "We have to move now! Logan and I will meet you in the barnyard."

"Oh my God." I stood up with my daughter in my arms. I hesitated for a moment; Cheyanne had never been away from me for longer than a few minutes. *She's two now,* I told myself. *She'll be OK.* And I handed her to Stacy. "Take the kids and go," I said.

"What about you?" Stacy asked.

"We've got to get our animals out." I kissed Cheyanne's cheek and looked her in the eye. "I'll see you very soon," I told her, and Stacy took the two kids and the boxes and suitcases and loaded them all into her car. As she drove off, I rounded up our dogs and cats and the bird. The dogs went into my car, the cats and bird into the car of our employee Randi, who happened to have come in to the office that day. As Randi headed back to the office to pull out computers and important files, I ran down to the upper barnyard, the wind whipping hard across my face and my eyes tearing. By the time I was inside the barnyard, I could taste the ash in the air, and I could see thick, black smoke billowing up behind our house. I worked as fast as I could, gathering all the crates I could find for the chickens, turkeys, and potbellied pigs. I had no idea how we'd get all our animals out in time; we only had our one small hitch trailer and would have to make several trips. But there was no time for thinking. We'd figure it out when we got to that part. Now it was time for action: Grab a chicken, put her in a crate; grab a pot-bellied pig, put him in a crate. . . .

Jay and Logan made it down from the back hill and helped me crate the animals. Jay looked up at one point and yelled, "They're here!"

"Who?" I said, coughing on the thickening smoke. Jay answered, but the wind had grown so intense, the fire whipping it into a frenzy, that I couldn't make out what he'd said. Out of the corner of my eye, however, I saw a flock of people—volunteers!—headed our way through the smoke. A huge stock trailer—for transporting "livestock"—was pulling in behind them. My ever-resourceful Jay; he had called a sister rescue organization just north of the fire. We grabbed the crates that held the smaller animals and started loading up the stock trailer, which went quickly now that we had the help of the volunteers. Then we carried the goats to the trailer one by one. By this point the smoke was so thick, I could barely see and my eyes were stinging. And we were all coughing and choking as we worked.

Finally the upper barnyard was all cleared, except our three farm pigs—Susie Q, Bodhi, and Biscuit (the last of whom we'd gotten after Duncan had passed away). Because of their sheer weight, I knew we would need their cooperation if we were going to move them to safety; there was no way we would be able to carry these enormous pigs.

"OK, guys," I said to the three pigs, calling out above the

screaming wind. "There's a fire, and we're in danger! We need you to move quickly to the trailer. It's going to take you to safety." Susie Q and Bodhi stood up from the hay, as though they had understood every word, and we guided them from behind to the awaiting trailer. Biscuit, however, decided this was a good time for a strike. He sat down in the hay and would not budge. Volunteers gathered and pushed, pulled, urged, begged . . . but Biscuit was not interested in moving. The fire had taken over the hill behind our house and was headed in our direction. It was my first view of actual flames, and my heart started pounding in my ears.

"Come on, Biscuit," I pleaded. "It's time to go now!"

"We have to get out!" shouted one of the volunteers. "Forget him. We can't save them all; we've got to get the others to safety."

"No!" I yelled above the wind. "If he stays, I stay. I won't leave any of my babies behind!"

One of the other volunteers took out a rope and started tying it around Biscuit's snout.

"What are you doing?" I said, alarmed. "That's not how we treat our animals."

"Do you want to get this pig out?" he said. "'Cause we have about five seconds."

"OK, OK, you're right." As the guy tied the rope around my pig's upper jaw and snout, I said, "I'm sorry, Biscuit, but I'm just not going to let you die."

Jay and the volunteer pulled on the rope tied to Biscuit's snout while two more volunteers and I pushed from behind, and after much heaving and grunting on our parts, we got Biscuit up into the trailer. We were soaked in sweat, but my stubborn, thousand-pound baby was headed to safety. By the time the trailer left with these animals, the fire had traveled down the hill alongside the house and the upper barnyard. In every direction, just fifty feet away, there were flames. Luckily the gravel driveway was between us and the fire, giving us an escape route. Now it was time to get the horses and cows out.

Randi and I drove our cars full of animals down the hill and parked them out on the main road, away from the fire. Then I ran as fast as I could to the horse barn and the second, enormous stock trailer, my eyes and lungs burning. Jay and Logan met me there and had brought down our own small trailer. The horses, just fifty yards down the hill from the flames, were panicked and were whinnying and banging the metal feeders with their hooves. We were racing against wind-stoked flames, but I knew we'd get the best results if we let the horses know what we needed from them. "You're going to be led one by one to the trailers," I called out, trying to keep my voice even and hoping they could hear me above the screaming wind and fire. "Please trust us. We're going to take you to safety!" Jay, Logan, the volunteers, and I began leading our horses into the trailers, trying our best to move slowly, talk calmly, and reassure the horses that they were safe and could trust us.

I could see the fire leaping down the hill toward us, eating up the trees and fences in its path. Luckily there was a wash that was stalling the flames between the upper and lower barnyard, but I knew the fire would leap the wash soon. It was hard to see anything through the thick black smoke, yet we continued to move the horses as calmly as we could into the trailers. Huge gales of wind were blowing, forcing the fire closer, kicking up branches and dust in our faces. The horses had every reason in the world to spook and try to run, but instead every one of them walked calmly by our side and into the trailers, even though some of them hadn't been in a trailer for years.

We had room for nearly all the animals, but there were a few we just couldn't fit: our newest members of the herd—two young Belgian draft horses, Zoe and Lazar—and also Buddha and our steer, Vegan, who now weighed two thousand pounds.

There was no way I was going to abandon our four remaining animals. I would stay behind while Jay and the volunteers drove the rest of the animals to the other rescue, which was north of the fire zone. Jay didn't want to leave me there, but we both knew they had to get as many animals out of there as they could while I figured out what to do with the ones left behind.

"I'll be fine," I insisted. "And Randi's staying to help."

Jay nodded, though he didn't look reassured. "I'll be back as fast as I can to get you guys!" he said. "As soon as they're all unloaded." And he slid behind the wheel of the truck.

The flames had now leapt the wash and were consuming the brush and trees on the lower end of our acreage. It was getting dark out—it must have been nearing six o'clock—and this added to the darkness of the smoke. The wind, dust, and heat of the flames were making it almost impossible to see or think straight. We stood and watched as the fire surrounded the empty horse and cow barns. I knew that Jay and Logan and the others were not going to make it back in time to get us.

"Let's at least walk them out to the road!" I yelled to Randi through the howling wind. I had wanted to keep the remaining animals on our land to keep them contained, but the fire was just too close, so Randi took the two draft horses and I took the two cows, and we led them out the gate to Sierra Highway. Being that close to a deafening, hot fire was more than a mature horse usually could tolerate, and Zoe and Lazar— young and inexperienced—were edgy and jumpy. But I just kept asking for their trust and, amazingly, they gave it to us. As for the cows, Buddha was easy—she would have followed me to the moon—but Vegan was even more opinionated than our pig Biscuit and was twice his weight. Vegan felt that there, in the middle of a firestorm, would be a good time to eat sweet grass and lick the trees. Outweighing me by a couple thousand pounds, he pulled me like a kite behind him. Finally I managed to plant my feet and wrap his lead rope around a tree to get him to stand still.

So there we were, two humans, two cows, and two giant horses, waiting at the side of the road as a wall of fire advanced our way and debris whipped all around us. What exactly we were waiting for I wasn't sure; I was certain Jay and the trailers would not get back before the fire took over everything. And I was quite sure there was no bus that was going to come by and let us all on board. But still we waited; there was nothing else we could do. I was working very hard to stay calm in order to pacify the horses, yet a sense of panic was finally getting me in its grip when I saw what I was sure was a mirage. Just like an oasis in the desert appears to those dying of thirst, here was a truck in a fire-storm, heading down the road toward us. A truck pulling a trailer. On impulse I jumped in front of the truck, my hand out like a traffic cop, and yelled, "Stop!"

The truck turned out to be real, and amazingly, it didn't hit me.

"Can you take our horses to safety?" I yelled.

"Yes!" the driver said, just like that, no questions asked.

We ran the two horses into the trailer, and away they went. I had just given our gorgeous horses to a total stranger, yet I had no choice; I had to believe that everything would be fine. When you're pushed up against the wall by a life-threatening force of nature, suddenly trust is all you've got left. Trust and a belief in angels sent to save you.

One more miracle, I thought. *One more miracle for our cows.* And sure enough, another truck pulling a trailer appeared on the horizon. "This is way too good to be true," I said as I stepped out into the road and prepared to stop our second truck of the day.

Buddha walked into the trailer elegantly and easily. But Vegan was still on a mission to eat and explore. Slowly I reined him in, but he wouldn't walk into the step-up trailer. The fire was beating down on us, and there was no way I was going to take no for an answer from our last animal to be rescued from the inferno. I cajoled, I pushed, I pulled. Finally I lifted one of his front feet and *put* it into the trailer, then the other, and by the grace of God and everything holy, Vegan went into the trailer. We slammed the door shut and the truck raced away.

"OK, get yourself out of here!" I yelled to Randi, and we ran to our cars—hers filled with the cats and the bird—and off she went.

With the animals headed safely out of the blaze, I turned around to see what the fire looked like. Everything was aglow, the once khaki-colored landscape now entirely ember-orange. From where I stood I couldn't see our house at all; the flames had engulfed the whole of it—our house, our office, the barns, everything. *We got everyone out*, I thought. *That's what matters most.*

Before I ducked into my car, packed with eight dogs who were very happy to see me, a lone fire truck pulled to a stop outside our gates.

"It's too late!" I called out over the roar of the fire, but he turned up our drive and disappeared into the flames.

———

My pores were filled with soot, as were my nostrils and mouth. I felt completely black, inside and out. My hair had been whipped into a rat's nest, my ears were still ringing, and my whole body was trembling. This was my state as I leaned against my car in the dark at the side of the road, safely away from the flames.

I called Stacy to ask her to meet me at Denny's with my daughter. Then I called Jay.

"We just unloaded all the animals," he said. "We're coming to get you!"

"No need," I said. "We're all out, and we're all OK. Meet me at Denny's."

I also called my mom, who had surely seen the news with Molli and Jesse.

When I got to the restaurant, Stacy and the toddlers were already there, settled into a booth. My gaze found Cheyanne's face, and I burst into tears, my body flooded with all the emotion I hadn't had the luxury to feel over the last four hours. I lifted Cheyanne from the high chair, and the feel of my soft baby girl in my arms soothed and rejuvenated me. I sank into the booth and let the cushions have my weight. A few minutes later, Jay and Logan came in, as fire-blackened as I was.

Jay slid into the booth next to me and wrapped me and Cheyanne in a big hug, and Logan talked excitedly about the adventure we'd just been through. A waitress took one look at us and brought us hot drinks without even asking. I'll never forget her smile or the taste of the cinnamon spice tea as it slid down my parched throat.

———

That night, after Cheyanne and I were safe and sound in a trailer on the land of the sister rescue—where the majority of our animals were being housed—Jay went back to check on our property. Amazingly, our house was still there. The fire department ordered him to leave, but he refused; he was going to see to it that we didn't lose our home. At one point the roofs of both the house and office caught fire and a helicopter dumped water on them. Fire trucks showed up off and on to help out, but they were needed everywhere at once. So Jay and a volunteer fought the fire back all through the night with a couple of garden hoses. Every time the flames were extinguished in one area, they sprang back up in another—the roots of burned-down trees and bushes so hot they reignited again and again. The flames melted the vinyl fences and burned some of the wood ones, and the wind blew other fences away entirely. Some trees burned, others were snapped in half by the wind, and still others were chopped to pieces by the firemen in an effort to remove tinder from near the house. The flames scorched the roofs, leaving the interiors of the house and office smoke damaged. And the exteriors were still being thrashed by seventy-mile-an-hour wind and debris when Jay left our property in the morning.

The following day, the Buckweed Fire—as it came to be called— was still burning, but Jay and the firemen had beaten it back to a safe distance from our land. As we figured out where all our animals were and began to make our rounds to three different locations to feed and check on them, I was exhausted and still a bit shaky, yet deeper down, beneath my sore muscles and trembling, the fire had begun to work its magic on me. In the plant kingdom, there are some species that will only germinate after a fire. The hard, resinous seeds lie dormant in the ground until a wildfire cracks them open, allowing them to sprout, grow, and flourish. I was like one of these plants. It was as though the fire had rushed through my life and burned off the debris—obstacles, doubt, fear—and cracked me wide open. New seeds would soon be sprouting all through my life—seeds of trust, surrender, and faith.

The Buckweed Fire burned more than thirty thousand acres and destroyed sixty-three structures. Fifteen other fires tore across Southern California within three days, and more than five hundred thousand acres would burn by the end, with more than three thousand structures destroyed. We were so very grateful that our house was not included in the count.

For days, the fires were in all the newspapers and were featured on local, national, and international news stations—and apparently the Gentle Barn was mentioned a number of times during this coverage. Although we talked to reporters by phone, we had no way to watch the news in the little trailer where we were staying. Besides, we were busy tending to our animals, who were scattered all over Santa Clarita. On one of his trips to feed our horses, however, Jay heard an announcement on the car radio from our mortgage company. "If you've been affected by the California wildfires and need help with your mortgage, please call us." Jay called right away, and they deferred our current and overdue payments to the back of the loan. Figuring the loan company on the car might also be willing to help, he called them too, and they agreed to do the same. Our financial pressures, for the time being, were lifted.

Slowly we began assessing the damage, filling out insurance claims, and getting workmen in to mend the fences. Once the shelters and fencing were secure enough to keep the animals safe—a couple of weeks after the fire—we were able to return with our animals and our children, but there was still so much damage that needed attention. Much of the fencing was charred or melted and would need to be entirely replaced, the exteriors of the house and office were wind-scarred, the inside smelled like smoke, there were holes in the roofs, and the land was black and barren as far as the eye could see. On the day we returned, news stations met us at our gates and got footage of our scorched land and the animals being unloaded. They asked us to explain what the Gentle Barn was all about and to talk about our experience during the fire.

"We're just so relieved that we got all the animals out," I told the reporters. "And we're incredibly grateful to the firemen and everyone else who helped us."

It was true. Despite the damage and the work that lay ahead, the emotion that kept washing through me was gratitude. Fences and roofs seemed so unimportant compared to all the lives that had been spared. The animals themselves seemed surprisingly unperturbed; they settled in as though nothing had happened and resumed their lives, once again serving as models of how to live with grace and ease.

When Jay was able to get back in front of a computer, he discovered that donations had been coming in through our website for days. Some from California, others from around the country and even from other places in the world. Checks started arriving in the mail, too. People who had seen us on the news were moved by our plight and were sending monetary help—which we would need more than ever because we'd just discovered that our place was underinsured.

From the end of October to the end of December 2007, all our focus was on repairing and rebuilding (and waiting for insurance money to arrive). Our at-risk youth program and visitor Sundays were canceled until we got settled back in. With delays in insurance money and glitches in the repair process, the roofs on the house and office would take nearly ten months to be reconstructed, but that wasn't going to stop us from reopening the Gentle Barn. Two months after the fire, when all the fencing and outside structures had been repaired, we held our first public event—a Winter Wonderland. We had snow brought in and invited people to come with their kids to play in the snow and meet the animals. We also invited the fire department and thanked them publicly for saving the Gentle Barn, and we dedicated the new cow barn to them.

In the weeks and months following the fire, it slowly sank in: There were now people all over the world who knew about us and cared about our mission. When I'd insisted that a miracle was going to find us, I'd had no idea it would ride in on the back of a wildfire. But what an amazing miracle it was. Not only did every single animal come out un-scathed, as did all the people who had worked with such courage to get them out, but kindness and generosity had met us at every turn. The donations in those first couple of weeks proved to be only the begin-ning of a flood that would continue for months, helping us fully restore our property. The fire had given us a breather from our financial pre-dicament and it had put us on the map in the animal-loving world— a widespread community that wanted to support our work now and in the future. It was impossible to doubt the worth of what we were doing with so much support flooding in, and this energy carried us forward.

But the most remarkable growth took place inside of me. I was moved and inspired and forever changed by the fire. In the face of such a force of nature, I had been derailed from my habitual patterns of try-ing to manage and control the outcome. It was so big and so power-ful and so scary that I was forced to surrender and be guided—forced to allow others to help. It was in that surrender that I found a new strength unlike anything I had ever experienced. I felt held and safe and provided for. I was not alone after all; I was just a tiny current in the large, gorgeous flow of life. I came away with a knowing so deep and so unshakable that I could handle anything life threw at me, and anything I felt truly called to take on, because I wasn't doing it alone. I had the huge, crazy, beautiful universe backing me up.

CHAPTER 13

Three months after the wildfire, we were still riding the wave of awe and surrender—saying yes to all of life—when we got a call from the sister rescue who had come to our aid during the fire. They had gotten access to the property of an animal hoarder in Lancaster and needed help pulling out two hundred farm animals who were being horribly neglected and abused. There are all types of hoarders—people who try to fill up the emptiness inside them by collecting things. Some hoard newspapers or books, some hoard candy wrappers, others hoard animals. Animal hoarders collect far more animals than they can possibly care for properly; some hoarders are also abusive toward their animals, and this was the type in question.

This sister rescue was planning to evacuate the animals the very next day and had come up shorthanded. After all the people at this

rescue had done for us, we were thrilled to be able to show our gratitude by helping them out. Jay and I couldn't both go; someone had
to run the at-risk youth program, take care of our animals, look after
Cheyanne, and pick up our older kids from school. We decided Jay
should go, and he was happy to help.

All day, Jay helped lead and carry malnourished and terrified farm
animals off the hoarder's property. As he worked he passed dog kennels by the side of the dirt driveway—a sea of cages on a huge slab of
concrete with no shelter whatsoever. Every kennel was filled with several dogs, some dead from starvation, illness, or attacks from the other
dogs, others still alive but emaciated or torn apart. There was no food
or water in any of the kennels, and the cages had not been cleaned of
feces or urine in a very long time. When Jay asked about the dogs, he
found out another rescue operation was handling it.

"I don't know, Jay," I said after he'd told me about the dogs and the
devastation he'd witnessed. He was so upset by it, he had wept as he'd
described the scene.

"They told me it was being handled," he said, wiping away his
tears.

But I felt in my gut that something was not right. Why were the
dogs still there at the end of the day? The next morning I asked Jay to
call and make sure the dogs were being taken care of.

"They assured me," he said.

"Please just call and double-check."

When he got off the phone, he showed me the name and number of
the woman handling the situation. "It's covered," he said.

I asked him to please make another call, to touch base with the
woman and see how things were going. "I just have a bad feeling
about it."

It turned out the woman was completely overwhelmed. She didn't
have the resources or space to handle that many dogs. She ended up
begging Jay to step in and take over.

"We don't have the resources either," Jay said to me. "There are two hundred dogs out there."

So we set about trying to find a larger, more established rescue operation to take it on—an organization that was more well-known and more well funded than we were. We called every rescue we could think of in the Los Angeles area—at least fifteen organizations. And one by one, every rescue declined. Most said it was just too big a case for them to handle. One said they'd stepped in once before with this guy; he was a habitual hoarder and very unstable, and they weren't interested in going back.

"We have to do it," I told Jay.

"Are you crazy? We don't have the staff for this. We don't have the funding for this. We don't have experience doing this."

I had been a dog rescuer most of my life, long before I'd ever handled farm animals. It was at the core of who I was. I may not have pulled two hundred dogs at once, but I knew my way around dog rescue as well as I knew my own heart. "We have two choices," I said. "We take it on, or we go to sleep tonight and pretend it never happened and let those dogs starve to death or kill each other off."

With everything we had just been through in the fire and everything that was happening in its wake, I knew for certain—at the very center of my being—that if we took this on we would be provided for along the way. "I am called to do this," I told Jay. "I feel it in my body; I feel it in my mind. I want us to go in there fearless, and I want you to trust me." With this I won him over.

I was torn apart knowing I would not be able to be present until the ugliest part of it was over; I was the one with the background in dog rescue, but I couldn't take a two-year-old into the trenches of a hoarding situation. I was also clear that I wasn't going to leave Cheyanne with other people in order to take care of animals, as I had done with Jesse. My commitment to being a consistent presence for my daughter had deepened as I'd learned more and more about the parent-child bond. It was critical that the primary caregiver be present for a child day in and day out until she was at least three; the longer I could keep Cheyanne home with me, the healthier she would be emotionally.

So Jay would be the one taking the lead in this rescue, even though he didn't have experience rescuing dogs. He'd be the one flying this thing, and I would have to stay behind, like a pilot on the ground guiding him through it.

The night before Jay headed back to the hoarder's site to begin the dog rescue was also the night before my fortieth birthday. Jay, the master of elegant, well-planned celebration, looked worried. "What are we going to do about your birthday? This is an important one. I should be throwing you a big party or taking you out of town."

"The only thing I want for my birthday," I said, "is for you to go rescue those dogs."

It was going to be a lengthy process, and it would start with stabilizing the situation. With Jay at the site doing the hands-on work, I coordinated from home, rounding up help and getting supplies donated. When they learned we had taken the lead, some of the rescue operations that had declined to take this on lent a hand by putting out a call for volunteers in their own communities. Within four days of Jay first spotting the sea of kennels, a hundred volunteers were helping him clean up the waste and dead animals. Mobile vets signed on to treat the sick and wounded dogs on site and locate safe houses for the sickest dogs. We sent truckloads of dog food, blankets, and doghouses, and some broken-down doghouses on site were repaired. A doghouse was provided for each and every dog, and each house was filled with warm blankets. With the help of the other rescues, we got more volunteers to sign on to take shifts so there was supervision 24/7 to keep the kennels clean and the water bowls filled, and to make sure the dogs weren't fighting. If there were fights, Jay and the volunteers shifted dogs around until everyone was getting along. I carried my cell phone around with me all day, and Jay and I stayed in constant touch about what was going on. He would call to update me about a fight he had stopped without getting bitten, or he'd let me know he had just done an interview with a news station or trained some volunteers to clean up properly. One time he called to say there was a dog whose face was so swollen that she couldn't lift her head off the ground; she looked like she'd been brutalized by other dogs. After taking her to the nearest animal emergency hospital, where she was stitched up, her eye was removed, and she was loaded up on antibiotics, Jay brought her home to me so I could nurse her back to health.

As the dogs began healing physically and understood that regular meals were going to keep arriving, the situation started to stabilize. I kept all the other rescues updated; as the dogs recovered, I asked them to step in and take whatever dogs they could. The breed rescues took the purebreds. The small-dog rescues took the small dogs. A collection of mutt rescues took the pregnant dogs. Before long, we were left with 130 large mutts out of the original 200.

Before I got to see the dogs, a new complication was thrown into the works. The hoarder, who had been banned from the property, snuck back in and was caught trying to poison the well with arsenic. We called the police out and brought in a security team, but the hoarder kept finding ways in and attempting to poison his dogs. Rather than sitting on a target and hoping not to get hit, we decided to move the dogs to a safer location. We found a boarding facility near the Gentle Barn and began raising the funds to cover the cost.

It was now three months in. With the 130 remaining dogs at the boarding facility, the situation was truly stabilized, so I felt comfortable taking Cheyanne with me to visit for my first encounter with the animals. There was every imaginable mutt mix, and all of them were filthy. Shortly after the dogs arrived at the boarding facility, a handful of groomers volunteered their time, and they began the process of bathing and grooming the dogs; it took weeks to get to all of them. As the groomers cleaned the dogs up, I began working with them emotionally.

With Cheyanne on my hip or playing nearby, I identified who was aggressive, who looked scared, who needed rehabilitation, who needed to be spayed or neutered, and who was ready to be adopted. The process of rehabilitating and placing the dogs took months, and all along the way my heart ached for these lonely, terrified animals.

"I promise we'll find you a home soon," I would tell the dogs every time I left them, their sad eyes following me from behind the bars of their kennels. I wanted to take home every last one of them and put them in my bed, but there wasn't room in my house—let alone my bed—for more than a hundred dogs.

After several months of dog adoption days, applications, phone calls, and home checks, we were down to about fifteen dogs who clearly had been born on the hoarder's property and had never known kindness. You could tell because even with all the work I'd done with them, they still didn't know how to receive a human touch or even wag their tails. This was the type of dog who needed years of rehabilitation for hours every day. Although this was exactly what I was best at, I was the mother of young children; it just wasn't the kind of project I could take on.

Finally, after much searching, we found a couple of organizations to come and take these feral dogs. These were agencies with lots of land, lots of staff, and plenty of time to allow the dogs to heal at their own pace. When the last of these dogs were picked up, I exhaled for the first time in a very long while. After ten months, the Lancaster rescue had finally come to completion. We had taken on what looked like an impossible task, but we had pulled it off. Every last dog was safe and sound.

As difficult as it had been for me to take a backseat and let Jay take charge in the first three months of this rescue, it also helped both Jay and me grow in unexpected ways. Throughout my life, I had operated under the belief that if I wanted something done, I had to do it myself. I just didn't trust anyone else to do it right. But Jay had proved me wrong and given me more trust in my fellow human beings. He had thrown himself into this rescue, body and soul, and had done an amazing job. My absence on site for the first stage had allowed him to step more fully into a leadership role and to shine. His heroism proved once and for all—most important, to himself—that he was not just the errand boy for my dream. From this, a new system of teamwork began to take shape; Jay would go in and liberate the animals from a horrific situation while I coordinated from home. Then I would step in to heal and rehabilitate the animals. He the warrior, me the nurturer. This was the new balance of our work at the Gentle Barn for all rescues to come.

That Thanksgiving, Jay and I had more to be grateful for than usual. We had just finished saving and placing two hundred dogs in loving homes. We finally had a new, watertight roof over our heads, and new green shoots were pushing up through the ashen land surrounding our house, bringing our year of recovery from the fire to a close. And, now that we were on the map in the wider animal-loving community, the Gentle Barn was finally getting a financial foothold.

"Do you want to do an event to celebrate?" Jay asked. We had not held a Thanksgiving celebration yet on our new land. We'd been too busy building, then having a baby, then recovering from a fire.

We thought about it, but then both decided we needed a break. Some downtime with the family over the holidays.

"Let's at least rescue some turkeys," I said. "We can celebrate that way."

Jay called around to find a local place that sold live turkeys and found one in Canyon Country, just a few miles from the Gentle Barn. When he contacted them, they said they had four live turkeys left.

"Let's get all four," I said.

Jay headed out there, and an hour later he called me on his drive home. I could hear in his voice that he was shaken.

"It was the worst thing I have ever seen," he said. "If you had been there, you would have gone postal. I can't even begin to describe it."

"I'm so sorry I wasn't there with you, Jay. I'm sorry you had to go through that alone."

When he got back with the four rescued turkeys, who were filthier than any I'd ever seen, Jay was quiet and withdrawn. It took him a couple of hours before he started to talk about it, blurting out bits and pieces of the story as though trying to cleanse his soul of what he had witnessed. Over the course of the afternoon and evening, Jay showed me pictures he'd taken with his phone of some of the animals and filled the story in, bit by bit.

He had driven the last couple of miles on a rutted dirt road. The place was tucked into a hillside, and the pens were fenced with scraps of wood, barbed wire, and old doors, strung haphazardly together. Less than five minutes into his visit, he was standing on a mound next to one of the makeshift barriers, and the guy called to him from the hillside below, where he was rounding up the turkeys. The guy was waving his arms and yelling. Finally, Jay made out the man's words, "You need to move. You're standing on top of Betsy." Jay looked down, his feet sinking slowly, and he stepped back, off the spongy earth, and realized that a very large animal was buried just inches under the dirt. Paying a lot more attention, he began walking around the place, making mental notes of what he saw. In the pens were cows, goats, pigs, turkeys, and chickens, all in dismal shape. The cows were emaciated, their ribs sticking out, even the ones who looked pregnant. He didn't see any hay on the property, not even the remnants that commonly cover the ground after a feeding; neither was there any other type of feed visible. The animals' waste hadn't been cleaned up in weeks or months, and there were dead and dying animals alongside the live ones. In the area where the guy did the slaughtering, there were filthy serrated knives and chain saws. A vat behind that area was filled with water, hides, and other remnants of the slaughters, and Jay said the smell throughout the place was atrocious.

Clearly he had more than a simple turkey rescue on his hands.

This was no ordinary backyard butcher—which in itself was an illegal operation. Something awful was going on, and Jay realized he had to "befriend" the guy so he could learn as much as possible about all that went on there.

So when the man, Manuel, boasted about his "show pigeons" and directed Jay to a shed to view them, Jay played along and went into the shed.

"The energy in there was terrifying," he told me. "It stank like death and it was dark and dusty, with a little light coming in between the slats in the roof—just like in a murder mystery. I don't know, Ellie, I just felt like I'd walked into the place where I was going to die."

"Why, Jay? What was in there?"

He sat there a moment. Then finally he said, "There were heads, Ellie, lots of heads . . . from all different kinds of animals. He was keeping them in cat carriers all over the walls."

The next day, Jay began making calls to the authorities—the Health Department and Animal Control—both of whom knew about the place and had been trying to rectify the situation. In between his calls Jay retreated into his silence, but I could see this thing weighing on him. Every so often, he'd shake his head, like he was trying to shake the images out. When he started talking about it again, he seemed especially focused on the cows.

"You have to go back and at least save a couple of them," I said. "This is just torture knowing what's going on and doing nothing at all." Although the authorities were supposedly handling the situation, we knew from experience that the process could take a very long time.

Before Jay went back to the site a couple of days later, he called the Health Department again to check on the status. "What are your intentions?" I heard him say into the phone. "Because I'm going to pull some cows out, and we want to know if you're planning to shut him down."

We knew we had to pay for the animals; this guy wasn't going to

relinquish them for free. But as a rule, animal rescues and farm sanc-
tuaries don't buy animals from abusers because it enables them to buy
and abuse more animals. We'd come up against this challenge before, and there wasn't an easy answer. Do you stick to the rules and
walk away from suffering animals, or do you help the animals because
you've seen their faces and felt their pain and it's haunting you? We
figured if the place was going to be shut down, it would be all right to
buy some cows.

The woman from the Health Department said that although there
was not an imminent closure, they had given Manuel specific instruc-
tions on how to clean up his place. He was forbidden to buy more animals until he complied. That was good enough for us; we were going to
save some of the animals we couldn't stop thinking about.

So Jay went back and bought two cows. They were both skinny and
terrified of humans. He backed the trailer right into our cow pasture
and opened the trailer gate so they could come out on their own, and
we gave them lots of fresh water and hay. One of the cows—who we
would later name Karma—was particularly agitated. All through the
night she bellowed without cease. At the first glow of dawn, I ran down
to the cow pasture to check on her and reassure her that things were
going to be OK now. Then I saw the milk dripping from her udder.

"No wonder you're so upset," I said to her. "You have a baby somewhere." I ran back up to the house and told Jay, and he called the guy
right away.

"What's the deal?" I heard him say on the phone. "You didn't tell
me she had a baby."

Manuel admitted he had her calf, but that he had promised it to a
family for their Christmas dinner.

"That's not right," Jay said. "The mom's going crazy, and we need
that baby for her to calm down."

Manuel protested, saying the calf was already on his truck, and in
fact would be on its way to the customer right now if his truck hadn't
broken down.

At that Jay hung up the phone and jumped in his truck with the trailer hitched to it. When he got to Manuel's place he blocked the driveway, where the big truck was parked. The driveway was on a steep grade, and Jay recognized quickly what was wrong with the truck: if you park a heavy vehicle on a hill and you don't put on the emergency brake before putting it in park, the load weighs on the gears instead of on the brakes and you can't shift the truck into drive.

"I'll fix your truck in exchange for the calf," Jay told Manuel.

Manuel looked at my gringo of a fiancé and laughed. "Right. You got a deal."

Jay tied a rope to Manuel's truck and hitched it to his own, pulled the big truck half an inch up the hill, then unstuck the gear.

"Shit," Manuel said.

Ten minutes after that, Jay was driving home with Karma's baby.

He called me from the road and I went out to wait for him on the driveway with Cheyanne on my hip. As soon as Jay's truck drove in through our gates, Karma began bellowing again. And I could hear a calf's small cry answering back from the trailer hitched to the truck. Jay got out and led the calf toward his mom, who was trying madly to get through the fence to her baby. Twice the calf passed out and fell to the ground, weak from hunger and stress. But finally Jay led the calf through the gate, and within seconds this baby was nursing as Karma licked and nuzzled her son.

As I watched the calf nurse and nurse, making up for lost time, I hugged Cheyanne tighter and couldn't stop crying. I related so deeply to this mother; we both loved our babies and were driven by love and instinct to nurture them. But I got to keep my babies; no one had the right to take them from me. Because of Karma's species, a man had the right to tear her baby from her without a second thought, leaving the two crying out for each other. I wanted to bellow, like Karma had bellowed all night; I wanted to cry out to the world from the rooftop, to tell all who would listen how wrong this was. Karma was only one of thousands—hundreds of thousands—of such mothers, and most did not get to experience this happy reunion. I vowed in that moment to try, in any way I could, to right this wrong.

———

For the next two weeks, Jay and I were haunted by the cows who were still suffering in that awful place.

"I have to go get them," Jay said finally, and he went back to the backyard butcher and brought home the rest of the cows. Among this group of six was another baby, this time not separated from her mother. We now had nine malnourished and terrified cows. They got along with Buddha and Vegan just fine, but their only contact with humans had been abusive. It was going to take a while for them to learn that some of us could be trusted.

I had never worked with frightened cows; I would just have to feel my way through it. I knew I couldn't simply leave them alone to steep in their fear; they had to get that terror out of their bodies. But as with any frightened animal, I also knew I had to take it slow. Each day, when I entered the cow pasture, the nine rescued cows fled as fast and far from me as they could. Moving slowly and giving them plenty of room, I cleaned up the yard, filled water buckets, and distributed fresh hay, singing to them so they could get used to my voice. They also got to witness how comfortable Buddha and Vegan were with me. Sometimes I just sat in the pasture and read a book. Slowly, slowly—over many days and weeks—the new cows would begin to wander a tiny bit closer. It took months before they would finally come close enough to sniff at my head or my shoe, then eventually to chew on my shoelaces or lick the pages of my book. It was important that I not reprimand them or stop them from any exploration they wanted to do. I wanted them to know that I was safe, and that their own desires and curiosities were safe.

Although we had removed all the cows from the backyard butcher, there were still many other animals who were suffering at Manuel's hands, and there would likely be more to come. There wasn't a day that passed that we didn't think about those animals, and we continued to stay in touch with the authorities. The Health Department seemed to be staying on top of the situation, and we felt certain that because public safety was at stake—with this guy selling tainted meat—the situation would be taken care of. I hoped and prayed that one day the safety and well-being of species other than our own would be taken just as seriously.

Each time a group of at-risk kids visited, I took them to the cow pasture to see our new animals. But before I led them down there, I spent time preparing them for the visit. I told them the cows' story and explained how badly they'd been treated and why they were so frightened.

"We need to calm our bodies and move slowly to help the cows feel safe," I would tell them. "I'm trying to teach them they can trust humans, and I need your help to be successful at that."

For some of these kids, quieting their energy was a chore—they were used to acting out, being loud—and it took them some time to figure out how to calm themselves and find this meditative space that would allow safety for another creature.

One group of eleven- to seventeen-year-olds from a gang-prevention center showed up for the first time when the calves were just beginning to be curious about me. As always, I prepared the kids for the visit. "If we sit really quiet," I told them, "the babies might even come over and check us out."

"There's babies?" one girl said, her eyes wide with excitement.

"Yes. Two of them."

We walked down to the pasture, and we all sat down along the outside of the fence. I watched the kids trying to move slowly and then to sit still. Occasionally one of them would whisper at the others to be quiet or stop moving. When the group really settled into stillness, sure enough, the calves inched closer, sniffing at the air. Then one calf would jump and gallop away and the other would follow. But moments later they were inching toward us again.

After a long while I moved back a bit from the fence and asked everyone to gather around so they could hear me.

"What do you think of the babies?" I asked them. "What words would you use to describe them?"

"Adorable," one girl said.

"Full of life," said another.

Others chimed in with the words "cute," "smart," "playful," "beautiful," and "perfect."

We watched the cows quietly for a while, and then I asked everyone if they ever talked to themselves with unkind words. "What are the worst things you say to yourself?"

They giggled and squirmed, and then one boy said, "I don't think about myself at all."

"Well, do you guys always think positively of yourself, or are there criticisms that you give yourself once in a while?"

After a long silence, one girl said, "Well . . . I think I'm stupid."

This gave others the courage to speak, and one by one they admitted their private self-criticisms: *Ugly. Fat. My ears stick out. Not popular. Selfish.*

"So, I'm wondering if you've always felt that way about yourselves. Have you always thought you were stupid or fat or ugly?"

Some of them shrugged.

"We're watching these perfect babies, just a few weeks old." I nodded toward the calves. "They're so beautiful. And I wonder, when you were just a few weeks old, what people thought when they looked down at you, just tiny and new. What do you think they saw in you?"

"That's a hard question," one boy said.

"I know, it is a hard question. But it's worth thinking about. You can take your time." I let them sit silently for a moment to contemplate this. Then I said, "All you see in these babies is perfection and beauty and intelligence. When you were tiny, what do you think people saw?"

"Maybe they saw the same thing we see in these baby cows. Like, cute and smart and stuff."

I nodded. "I think that's right; I think that's what they did see. So, how do you think you came to see yourselves as ugly and fat and stupid, and all the rest?"

"My mom says I'm stupid," said one girl, "so I guess I just thought she knew."

Another girl said her uncle joked that she was ugly, and a boy said the other kids at school called him Fatty.

"So, if we gathered around these two babies and told them, 'Your ears stick out' or 'You're stupid' or 'You're ugly,' do you think they would believe it over time?"

"No," a boy said.

"Why?"

"Because they wouldn't pay attention to it."

"Then why are we paying attention to what other people tell us?"

"I don't know."

"Well, here's my vote," I said. "I vote that we know how beautiful and intelligent and holy we are, just like those babies. And I vote that we not listen to what other people think of us, that we just *know* who we are, that we just know we're perfect and no one can change that." I put my hand in the center of our circle. "Who's in?"

One by one, they put their hands into the center on top of mine, all of them beaming.

The food and vet bills for the cows started accumulating fast. Although we were getting about fifty visitors every Sunday and were receiving donations for our work from our new, wider base of supporters, it still wasn't enough to cover all the bills associated with the new cows. So we decided to hold a fund-raiser to help defray the cost.

About three hundred people showed up, and as Jay and I toured them around the property, with a focus on the cow pasture, everyone kept oohing and aahing over the two calves and asking what their names were.

"We haven't had a chance to name them yet," we explained.

A half hour later, when everyone was gathered around the picnic tables, Jay came over to me and whispered in my ear that we should hold an auction to name the baby cows.

"You think people will pay to name them?" I said.

"Absolutely."

I wasn't so sure. Why would anyone pay for something they couldn't take away with them? I pictured us up there waiting for an opening bid, and people just blinking back at us. But I decided to go along with it if Jay would be the one to get up and do it.

Jay made the announcement and then asked for an opening bid of a hundred dollars. To my surprise, someone's hand shot up immediately. "A hundred dollars right here!" she shouted out. Then someone outbid her at two hundred dollars. Then another person offered three hundred. People were bidding and outbidding one another and all the while were laughing and enjoying the process. In fewer than five minutes someone had paid $500 to name the first calf. Then the naming of the second calf went up for auction, and again people jumped right in, topping one another's bids right on up to a thousand dollars. In ten minutes' time, we had raised $1,500. I looked at Jay, my mouth hanging open. He just smiled back at me, a grin that said, *I told you so.*

The two winning bidders each gave the naming opportunity to their children. A young boy named Karma's little red calf Mr. Rojas (*rojas* means "red" in Spanish). And a young girl named the other baby Night Goddess. Two fabulous names and money to help pay for their care. Jay had stumbled across a fund-raising gold mine that we would surely revisit in the future.

As I moved forward with the rehabilitation of the nine cows, not only did their trust in me grow, but so too did my confidence in my own ability to work with them. I was seeing that my instincts were just as much on target with cattle as they were with horses or dogs. And Jay and I began to feel that we had officially stepped into the role of cow rescuers. So when we received a call early in 2009 from the owner of an auction house—a place where ranchers and stockyards from all over Southern California brought their livestock to sell to slaughterhouses—we were ready. A new law had just been enacted in California that prohibited the selling of downed animals—those who were too sick to stand—for human consumption.

"Would you be willing to take some downed animals off our hands?" the guy asked Jay on the phone.

"Absolutely!" Jay said, his new confidence as a cow rescuer erasing any doubt he might have had just a few months prior.

We knew many of these downed animals would be calves pulled from veal crates. A baby who has been separated from his mother at birth and isolated in a small, dark box is, necessarily, sick—often so severely he can't stand. These sick babies are a by-product of the dairy industry.

Cows are no different from any other mammal. Just like dogs have milk for their puppies, but at no other time, just like I had milk when I had my babies, but I don't have milk now, cows only have milk for their babies. It's breast milk, just like that of other mammals. Since you can't have milk without the baby, the industry impregnates the cows. Then when the cows have their calves, the babies are taken away immediately, and the milk is stolen for humans. In order to make a profit off of all these billions of babies, the dairy industry has created the veal industry, which takes the baby cows away from their moms and puts them into a dark box where they can't move and their muscles don't develop. If the veal industry can keep them alive for eight weeks, the babies are then killed, and their meat is sold as veal, which is a soft meat served in French and Italian restaurants.

There are many meat eaters who won't eat veal because they think it's so inhumane. But what they don't know is that it's the dairy industry that's at the root of the suffering. When I'd learned the truth about the dairy and veal industries, shortly after I'd started the Gentle Barn, I immediately stopped eating milk products, going from vegetarian to vegan. I got it that if cow's milk stopped being produced, there would be no veal; there would be no veal crates; there would be no calves too sick to stand.

Unfortunately there was still a dairy industry, so we were now expecting babies. And although they would never get to have the reunion with their mothers that Mr. Rojas had had with Karma, we would try our best to fill their mothers' shoes.

In preparation for the call we knew would be coming soon, we contacted other rescues who had taken in veal calves to find out any secrets they could share with us—special supplements, treatments, or other tips that would help the calves pull through to health.

"The first thing you need to know," one rescuer told me, "is that they're not going to make it."

"What?" I said. I was sure I'd heard him wrong.

"Just be prepared. No matter what you do, they just don't live."

Other rescues pretty much agreed. The calves who survived were a rarity. Most were just too bad off to pull through.

"I simply am not going to accept that," I said to Jay after I got off the phone. I was going to apply every type of healing I could think of, every alternative treatment and supplement. I would even be calling out energetic healers. I was not going to accept death as a sentence for a baby.

When we got the awaited call in April 2009, we were armed with tubs of algae superfood powder, crates of milk replacer formula, lots of oversize baby bottles, stacks of towels, bottles of rubbing alcohol, and thermometers. We had a vet on call, and I had a list of alternative heal-ers who knew the babies were on their way. We also immediately put out a request through our community for volunteers.

No babies in the animal world—especially mammals—are left alone; the mothers are constantly licking them, nursing them, and fussing over them, and we intended to do our version of the same. It was a matter of giving these calves reason to live. We would have someone with them 24/7, singing to them, bottle-feeding them, pet-ting them, even reading to them. There would be four shifts—two in the day and two at night. One volunteer would fill each shift to keep all six calves company. As a mother and someone who owed my very life to animals, I was driven to do everything I could possibly think of to give these babies a shot at life.

When Jay brought the six eight-week-old calves back from the auc-tion house—a two-hour drive from the Gentle Barn—our new local vet, Dr. Morrison, was already waiting to examine them. She took their vital signs, writing down a description of each calf, so we could all tell them apart. There were two girls and four boys. All six calves had pale gums—a sign of anemia—skin funguses, pneumonia, and raging fevers. They were barely able to get up off the ground. One appeared to be blind. Dr. Morrison gave the calves their first shot of antibiotics, and then she mapped out the plan for their care while Jay and I took notes.

"You'll take their temperatures three times a day. Normal is be-tween 101 and 102. Right now, they're all over 104. Whenever it goes that high, or even over 103 and a half, you're going to pour rubbing alcohol along their spine in an effort to bring the fever down. It'll draw the heat out." She demonstrated this on one of the calves, and Jay and I tried our hand with the five others. "You'll need to wipe their noses and around the eyes frequently to keep them clean. And do your best to keep the flies off them."

We started teaching our first group of volunteers later that day how to do all of this, as well as how to prepare warm formula, with algae mixed in, and how to bottle-feed—not so obvious with babies this big. We began giving the calves two bottles a day; they also had plenty of fresh hay. Jay and I came down to help with all the feedings; it took more than two hands to bottle-feed six babies. We also did all the temperature taking, and we administered antibiotic shots once every three days. Dr. Morrison would be coming by once a week to check on the calves. Until the calves were cleared of pneumonia, we had to hold them in strict quarantine. They were not contagious to humans, but they were contagious to our other cows. Anyone who had contact with the calves was not allowed to wander the property, but instead had to go straight to their cars. After Jay or I spent time with the calves, we had to shower and change our clothes before feeding or visiting our healthy animals.

From the moment of the calves' arrival, we applied our secret ingredient—paying as much attention to these babies' emotional needs as their physical needs. One volunteer spent the first half of the night with the calves—starting at seven p.m.—and was replaced by the second volunteer at one a.m. Each night-shift volunteer brought a sleeping bag and slept right in the stall with the calves. When there was an open shift, Jay covered it himself, and even when he wasn't with the calves, he got so many calls during the night from the volunteers that we hardly slept for the first month.

Every night, when it was time to say good night to the fever-hot, runny-nosed babies, I felt a terrible ache in my heart. They were so sick and so weak; I yearned desperately to be the one nurturing them through the night. But I had my own babies to take care of, my own house full of children who needed me. It was the dilemma I found myself in again and again ever since I'd been crazy enough to think I could be both a rescuer and a mother. As painful as it was, I knew the calves were in good hands with Jay and the volunteers, and I was proud of myself for following through one more time on my commitment to do the right thing for my own children.

It was weeks before we saw any change in the calves, with their fevers consistently higher than 104, sometimes up to 105. They spent a lot of time lying on the ground; when they did manage to stand up, their heads hung low, as though they simply did not have the strength to lift them. Their appetites were weak as well; they'd suckle at the bottle but with no gusto, and sometimes they showed no interest in food at all. One calf was particularly weak, and his fever always outranked the others'. We decided to name him Chi, for "life," and every one of us was rooting for him—Jay and me and our kids and all the volunteers. Dr. Morrison gently broke the news to me that she didn't think Chi was going to make it and suggested we put him down, but I didn't feel we were there yet. "We have to give him more of a chance." I asked the energetic healers who'd signed on to double their efforts with him, in particular, and for a few days, he seemed a bit better. But then he started sliding downhill again. I talked to him daily, whispering to him about how good life was going to be here for him; he'd have plenty of fresh water and hay and space to run around with his friends, and lots and lots of love. But he stopped eating entirely and soon his lips and nose began to turn blue; he wasn't getting enough oxygen.

As excruciating as it was, I had to admit that it was time.

Before the vet gave him the injection that would help him out of his weak, failing body, I lay down next to him and cradled his head, gazing into his eyes. "I'm so, so sorry, Chi. It wasn't supposed to turn out this way. You don't deserve this." We had wanted to give these babies a living apology, a life of freedom and health and joy that would make up for the terrible start they'd gotten. But Chi was leaving too soon, and our gift would go unreceived. I felt as helpless as this little blue calf, straw stuck to my tear-streaked face. As I watched Chi's light go out, I promised, in the name of his spirit, that I would do all I could to let people know about the devastation left in the wake of the dairy industry.

Chi passed away only two weeks after his arrival, and I was terrified the remaining five calves would follow in his footsteps. For a good
month, they never strayed far from death's door. I ran down every
morning at the crack of dawn. *Today their fevers will be gone*, I'd say
to myself. *Today's the day.* But every morning, the thermometers read
104, 104.5, 105.

"You've got to stick around," I told the calves. "There is such a
good life waiting for you on the other side of this."

Finally, finally, the fevers started to abate. The babies still spent
another month hovering around 103 degrees, but a little more life was
visible in their eyes. For the first time, we could see a possibility that
they might actually make it.

At two months in, after hundreds of six-hour volunteer shifts,
dozens of antibiotic shots, and endless bottles of green milk formula,
the fevers finally broke. Every volunteer, and certainly both Jay and I,
walked around with huge smiles on our faces. The calves seemed to
be in celebration, their true, lively selves coming out of hiding for the
first time since their arrival. Their hunger switched on and the calves
were suddenly wildly ravenous. By instinct, when a calf nurses, she
head-butts her mother's udder to help the milk let down. Now, with
the calves' energy back, this instinct was in full force. Standing in for
the mother's udder, we had to be careful how we held the bottles; I had
more than one bottle go flying across the barnyard. The men especially
had to be sure to stand to the side of the calf, not directly in front of
them, for the calves' heads were right about at crotch height. And once
these babies had finished a bottle, they'd circle like sharks, ready for
another. But I wouldn't have traded these challenges for anything in
the world.

Once the quarantine was lifted, we decided to bring over a surro-
gate mama cow for the new babies. One of the cows rescued from the
backyard butcher, Buttercup, had had her baby, Halo, three months
after her arrival on our property. Halo was now a few months old, not

far in age from our five rescued calves. Amazingly, Buttercup patiently nursed every one of the five orphaned babies along with her own.

We continued to have someone stay with the calves 24/7 for a full four months, and it was a good while longer before we integrated the calves into the herd. All five ended up making a complete recovery, establishing a new paradigm for what was possible with calves rescued from veal crates. We went on to do two more veal calf rescues after this, and all the calves made it. Clearly we were onto something with this unusually high success rate, and we hoped that in the years to come we would be able to revamp the rehabilitation process for veal calves everywhere.

I never stopped being touched by the effort of the volunteers who offered their time and presence to help these calves survive. The request for support that we'd put out through our community for our first veal calves had brought in more volunteers than I ever would have imagined. Although we'd had our handful of volunteers before that rescue, I had always felt hesitant about asking for people's time. It felt intrusive or like I would be burdening them with my own needs, my own troubles. But during this rescue, one volunteer after another thanked *me* for the opportunity to do this work. They would be glowing after staying up all night with these babies and they'd tell me how much the calves were doing for *them*. They felt a greater sense of purpose in their lives and were honored to be a part of something so important. Here I had been trying to protect them from my burden, and instead I unwittingly had been withholding a gift. Now that I knew, I began stepping aside more and more to let people help. Even after the calves had recovered, we started putting out regular calls for volunteers. Every time we did a rescue and every Sunday, we asked for volunteer support, and our handful turned quickly into a fleet of a hundred.

This expansion outward, and especially allowing other people in, gave me one opportunity after another to loosen my grip—to step back, accept help, and release control. It was not my natural instinct to do so. It made me nervous to hand over to strangers the thing that meant the most in the world to me. But the more times I allowed others to step forward and shine, the more times they did. They entered into our fold and into our trust, and their lives were forever changed. One of the volunteers who'd helped out with the calves took a special interest in the healing process: Mike was highly attentive and devoted to the calves' well-being. He worked with the blind calf, Faith, teaching her how to walk a straight line instead of the tight circles she had learned from the veal crate. Later he became our head calf person, which would eventually grow into a paid position. And for the first time in his experience, he felt he was living the life he was meant to live.

Our fleet of volunteers kept expanding, and slowly, as funds would allow, we also began building a staff in the office and on the grounds. The Gentle Barn was growing up before my eyes. I was no longer alone in this endeavor. The animals who had always touched my life were now touching the lives of hundreds.

CHAPTER 14

Before 2009, the concept of "social media" was nowhere on my radar. I didn't know what the word "blog" meant, I avoided Facebook like the plague, and a "tweet" was the sound a songbird made. But in August of that year I went with Jay to see the movie *Julie & Julia*. It was about a young woman who loved to cook, and she wrote about it daily on her blog; she ended up having tons of people reading everything she wrote. About food. I sat there during the movie with the wheels spinning so hard in my head I could have sworn steam was coming out of my ears: *If some young girl can get herself a following for writing about food, just think what I can do with the amazing stories about our animals!* The moment we got home, I said, "Jay, set me up a blog!"

"Well, you already have a Facebook page."

"I do?"

"Yeah, remember I set up a page for the Gentle Barn last March?"

I had not remembered. I had posted one time (with Jay's help) and then the veal calves had arrived the following month, and we'd been busy trying to keep them alive. I had forgotten the page existed. Plus, I'd had no clue at that time just how amazing this social media thing could be.

Jay walked me through how to post on the Facebook page, and he also set up a Twitter account and showed me what buttons to push.

I got busy immediately. I had loads of stories to tell and lots of Facebook posting and tweeting to catch up on. I started with our cow Karma—the one who had arrived as a new mom and had been reunited with her son, Mr. Rojas, the following day. It turned out that Karma must have been impregnated—again—right before we rescued her, because nine months after her arrival she had a second, unexpected, baby who we named Surprise. This new calf was now a week old, so my first post was about how Surprise was doing. The next day I filmed the little red calf discovering what his legs could do as he ran around and around the cow pasture at just seven days old. I got Jay's help to post the video, and now the rest of the world could see it too.

I was hooked. I started posting several times a week, sometimes twice in one day. Little by little people began finding us on Facebook. I was thrilled each time someone "liked" my post, and especially when someone commented in response. I read each and every comment carefully and responded with my own comment as often as possible. Slowly our Facebook readership grew and people began following my tweets too. Some of these people had been to the Gentle Barn and were grateful to have a way to stay informed about the animals they'd met, but most of our followers simply were animal lovers and were touched by the stories I shared. I couldn't believe perfect strangers were reading about the ins and outs of what went on in my little world. These people felt not like strangers at all, but like distant cousins all over the country, and eventually all over the globe. It was as though I'd finally been put in touch with my long-lost family—the family who cared as much as I did about animals.

———

At the beginning of September there was another fire nearby. Luckily we were safely out of range, but Jay went through the threatened area to check if people needed help. We let everyone know we were available to assist with the emergency transport of animals, and we ended up hosting several animals who had to be evacuated from the fire area. All through this, I kept our extended community informed through our Facebook page.

For days the air smelled of smoke and ash, and our cow Buttercup's baby, Halo—now seven months old—was not doing well with the poor air quality. Buttercup had been malnourished through most of her pregnancy at the backyard butcher, and Halo had been born weak, with underdeveloped lungs. The smoke and ash in the air was putting him over the edge and he was struggling. We put him and his mom in the infirmary with air filters running, but pneumonia settled in and Halo never bounced back. The day after Buttercup's little fawn-colored calf left this world, I shared the sad news with our Facebook fans:

Halo just lost his battle. His dedicated mom, Buttercup, is grieving, her heart is broken completely. Hearing her cry is even more painful than losing Halo. We wish we could do something to console her, but all there is, is time.

More people than ever commented, sending their condolences, and shared the post with others. I sat crying in front of the computer reading each and every comment, some more than once, and it buoyed me to know others were right there with me—even if only virtually. The next day I posted a picture of Buttercup licking Halo right before he left us. In the photo, he lifts his head toward her, and it looks like she's whispering good-bye in his ear. Comments and "likes" poured in, and I felt surrounded by kindness. I had grieved alone so many times in my life with no support, sometimes with others mocking me. Now people I'd never even met were sending me words of encouragement and even grieving with me. I didn't have to explain or justify my sadness; they totally got it. I was in love with my new extended family, and I thanked everyone again and again for their kind words and support.

Over time I settled into a rhythm of posting twice every day, once in the morning and again in the afternoon. I thought about my Facebook family even when I wasn't in front of the computer. I'd snap a picture with my phone when an animal did something funny or inspiring and I couldn't wait to post it for my online community. I began recognizing the names of people who had commented before; it would bring a smile to my face to see their name, as though I were running into a friend on the street. Sometimes people who lived in other states wrote that they were saving money to come visit. "We've been following you for a while," one woman wrote. "We're planning to visit the Gentle Barn for our thirtieth anniversary."

More and more people started approaching me on visitor Sundays to introduce themselves. "Hi, I'm Kathy. I've met you on Facebook— well, not *met,* but I've read all your posts." We would hug like the long-lost cousins that we were. I was thrilled to be meeting my true family in person—here from all over the United States. Before long people were visiting for a week at a time. They'd get a private tour and then come each day to volunteer. Eventually we even had visits from England, Germany, Singapore . . . These long-distance visitors usually came for a whole month, staying at a little motel down the road from us and volunteering each and every day of their visit. "I'll feed the animals, I'll shovel manure, anything you need help with." I was blown away by how generous these "strangers" were—here all the way from the other side of the world on a trip they'd spent a year saving for, and all they wanted to do on their vacation was *work* at the Gentle Barn. Was my life that special that people wanted to do my daily chores on their vacation? But I had learned with the veal-calf rescue to step aside and let people help, to not withhold the gift. Actually, I was stunned by how similar these people were to me; before I'd started the Gentle Barn, volunteering with animals would have been my dream vacation too.

One of the most touching stories was from a woman named Gwen who visited one Sunday from Arizona. She told me she'd been following the Gentle Barn on Facebook for months, looking at each and every post and drawing inspiration and courage from the animals and their miraculous healing. Reading my posts helped her get through each day, for she had been undergoing chemo and radiation for a cancer she wasn't sure she would survive. "These animals have triumphed over so much hardship," she told me. "If they could do it, I thought maybe I could too." She had promised herself that if she beat the cancer, she'd come meet the animals who had inspired and encouraged her. And here she was standing before me, beaming.

***

Whenever we undertook a new rescue, I kept people in the loop through our Facebook page so they could experience each new development right along with us. When we did a rescue in Ohio to stop the mass euthanizing of a pound full of dogs—with Jay in the field and me coordinating from home—I used Facebook to receive applications, do home checks, find transporters, and place every last dog—more than sixty successful home placements done entirely through the Internet! When we rescued our next group of veal calves, this time we not only had round-the-clock volunteers staying with the calves, we also had thousands of people following the rescue online, reading about the daily challenges the calves were facing and the incremental signs of healing. When the calves recovered, we did not rejoice alone with our

volunteers this time; our global online community joined us in our relief and triumph.

The rescues inspired people personally, and they educated the
public about how animals were being treated behind closed doors.
When we intervened in an abuse case, our followers learned how badly
some animals were mistreated. When we saved farm animals, people
learned about factory farming and the atrocious abuses inherent in
that system. There was never a need to preach. We simply let the animals' stories speak for themselves, just as they always had. Only now
it wasn't just our live visitors hearing the stories; the animals and their
tales were reaching a global audience through the Internet.

I began to see the effect of this wider reach when people shared
how they had been touched and changed. Many spoke of shifting to a
plant-based diet, some requesting suggestions for how to do it health-
fully. Others shared about their own endeavors to help animals. One
woman in England, who had been following us for some time, posted a
comment that one of the neighboring farms where she lived had a little
boy sheep who had just been born. She said the farmer had no use for
him and was going to leave him in the pasture to die. "Is it possible to
save a baby that young?" she wrote. "I want to take him in but have no
idea what to do." Touched by her desire to help, I talked her through
the whole thing in Facebook messages—how to bottle-feed, when to
start him on hay, how old he should be when she got him neutered.

"Because he's a herd animal," I wrote, "he'll have the highest
chance of survival and happiness if you have another sheep with him."

So she went out and found another baby boy sheep, and with my
guidance she raised the two of them. Periodically after that I would get
a message from her: "Just so you know, my boys are big and strong and
doing wonderfully. Thank you again for all your support."

Our Facebook community was equally affected by the work we
were doing with the at-risk and special-needs kids. I often posted after
an inspiring day of working with a group, recounting the big and small

triumphs and sharing how the animals had softened and opened up even the toughest kids. People would write in that they were touched and inspired. Many said they understood firsthand the healing effect of animals. Some expressed the desire to do the same kind of work in their own town, and I encouraged them to go for it.

Alongside my posts about the animals, the rescues, and how things were going at the Barn, I used Facebook as a fund-raising tool; it was the perfect arena to request donations for newly rescued animals or to invite people to come out and visit on a Sunday. Early on I established a special ongoing posting, featuring one animal at a time—alphabetically by name—telling that animal's story and inviting people to sponsor a member of our barnyard with a monthly donation.

Then one day I got a new idea. We had rescued a beautiful golden cow who didn't yet have a name. I decided to ask our Facebook fans for help, and use it as a fund-raising opportunity. Instead of having the naming privilege go to the highest bidder—as we had done in our live naming auction—I decided to make it more accessible to lots of people by hosting a raffle online. On a morning early in November, I introduced the idea in a post, along with a photo of our unnamed cow:

> Cow naming: We rescued this cow and she needs a name. She has had no positive experiences with humans until now and she is very scared of us. She needs a name that is soft, sweet, humble and brave. Donate $20 and suggest a name in the notes box. At the end of the week all names will be put into a hat and one will be drawn. All proceeds will go to her care.

I kept everyone in the loop about how the cow was doing and shared about her growing trust in us. On the day of the drawing we had received close to sixty donations, some of them higher than the requested

$20. We printed out all the names and cut the list apart so each name was on its own strip of paper. Jay took a picture of me pulling a strip out of the hat, and I posted that photo along with some words of gratitude:

> Thank you so very much to all of you who suggested a name for this sweet cow. You guys raised $1,275 for her care and we are grateful! We put all the names in a hat and pulled one out, her name is Serenity. Good one, Alie!

In the spring of 2010, a year after our first veal-calf rescue, an anonymous donor gifted us with a second property expressly to allow us to continue rescuing cows. The fifteen-acre parcel was located just ten minutes up the road from us and was covered with grass just waiting to be grazed by our growing herd of cows. But we had to finish up a few last things to get the place ready. We sent out an e-mail asking for help painting the fences, and a dozen people signed on, with a staff member heading the project. The volunteers worked hard and gave every last fence post and rail a fresh coat.

At the end of the day, one of the volunteers, Marissa, asked for a tour of our main site. It was a weekday; generally we opened our main site to the public only on Sundays, or by prior arrangement. But we decided to follow our instinct on this one and gave Marissa a tour ourselves. We took her to both the upper and lower barnyards and introduced her to the animals, telling her some of their stories. We also told her about our at-risk youth program. And all through the tour she took pictures.

Before she left, Marissa expressed how touched and impressed she was by the work we were doing here. "I have a friend who's a celebrity," she said. "I'm going to tell her about you guys."

Jay and I didn't think much about it. *Who doesn't "have a celebrity friend" in Los Angeles?* we thought. But Marissa's friend turned out to be Portia de Rossi—an actual celebrity and an actual friend of Marissa's. She e-mailed Portia that night with pictures of the animals and raved about us and the work we were doing.

Three weeks later we got a call from the producers of *The Ellen DeGeneres Show*. They wanted to do a segment on us. Jay and I were beside ourselves. I couldn't wipe the ridiculous idiot grin off my face for weeks. I kept stopping in the middle of whatever I was doing— mid-stir of the pigs' breakfast or while I was brushing the cows—to let it sink in. *I can't believe it. We're going to be on* Ellen*!*

"This is going to really put the Gentle Barn on the map," I told Buddha, leaning into her embrace. "What a way to get our message out!"

The producers and directors visited on April 30 in preparation for the filming, and I gave them a guided tour (still wearing my idiot grin). The only time that grin fell was when they told us they'd only be interviewing me, not Jay.

"But Jay and I run this place together," I said. "He's done all the hard work right alongside me."

"It's better for the show to have only the founder," one of the producers said. "Just to keep it simple."

Although Jay didn't show it, I knew him well enough to know he felt left out. But as disappointed as we both were, we were going to have to adjust to what worked for TV, and it wasn't the last time we'd have to face the issue. Jay, however, was an incredibly good sport and was present and supportive throughout the entire thing.

The producers and directors were scheduled to come back with Portia and the whole film crew on May 3. The production crew arrived first, and we all went out to the driveway to wait for Portia. My stomach was filled with butterflies. I'd never really met a celebrity before and I didn't know how to be with her. Should I shake her hand or give her a hug, or maybe just wave hi? I even asked the producer what he thought.

"Whatever feels right," he said. "Whatever feels natural."

As soon as Portia arrived, the butterflies vanished without a trace. Her sweet, authentic demeanor put me instantly at ease. We hugged hello as though we'd met before, and I relaxed into the experience. I gave Portia a tour of our place and introduced her to the various animals, and the film crew followed us around. Portia petted and fed pigs and sheep and chickens, got to experience Buddha's hug, and asked me really good questions. The production crew followed us everywhere we went and captured our natural interaction on film.

Throughout the week surrounding the filming, I was posting and tweeting more than usual. Not only was I keeping our Facebook and Twitter family in the loop on the developments of the upcoming *Ellen* show, but I was simultaneously trying to drum up support for a dairy-cow rescue—sixty cows, half of them pregnant, who were going to be sent to slaughter because the dairy was going out of business. We wanted very much to take all sixty cows, but we needed to build a new barn on our second property in order to house that many cows in addition to those we already had. It would cost $100,000 to build it.

When Ellen and Portia learned of our mission, they started posting their own requests for people to help us, with a link to our website on theirs. Within a day the amount we had raised leapt to $10,000.

Three days after Portia and the film crew had been to the Gentle Barn, the producers called to let us know the date the segment was going to air. I let our Internet followers know that the Gentle Barn would be on the *Ellen* show on May 25, 2010. The segment itself was being edited from the footage they had taken during their visit; the video would be shown to the live audience—and ultimately to TV viewers—as part of Ellen's show. The Friday before the taping, one of the producers called us.

"We got to see your world. Now we want to invite you to come see ours. We'd like to have you in the audience to watch the taping of the show."

"We'd love to," I said, the huge grin back on my face.

"Great. We'll send out a car to get you Monday at one."

I hung up the phone and yelled, "Oh my God, we get to be there!" I jumped up and down like a teenager, the dogs watching me with their heads cocked to the side. I had never actually seen the show—I never had time to watch TV—so I had no idea what to expect. But we were going to Hollywood! And I couldn't wait to see what they'd put together from the footage they had taken on their visit.

"Can we come too?" Jesse asked.

"Yeah," Molli said, "can we?"

"Sorry, guys, just the adults were invited. And besides, it's a weekday; you have to go to school."

"I wanted to ride in a limo," Jesse said.

"Yeah," said Cheyanne, even though she had no idea what a limo was.

"This is not one of those stretch limos," I assured them. "It's just like a regular car."

An hour later the kids—now twelve, eleven, and four—had forgotten all about it and were swallowed up again in their own world of friends, video games, and bike riding.

Monday morning Jay and I got up early. We had a lot to do before we got ready. When I returned from driving the kids to school, I did my morning posting and tweeting to remind everyone the show would be airing the next day. Then I supervised the feeding in the barnyard and worked with the shy animals to further their rehabilitation and help them trust humans. I double-checked that all the hay bins and waters were clean. When I got back up to the house, Jay was just returning from our other property, where he'd been fixing a broken fence. The two of us had to scrape the dirt and manure off our boots, then clean them up with a damp cloth. This was a big deal; we had to be presentable. Finally I got in the shower to wash the barnyard out of my hair. As the steaming water poured over my head, I thought, *What on earth am I going to wear for the* Ellen *show?* My next thought was: *I get to wonder what I'm going to wear for the* Ellen *show!* When I looked in my closet, I realized I had absolutely nothing appropriate. Most of my shirts had stains or holes chewed in them by the cows. So I jumped in the truck and made an emergency run to the closest clothing store to find a nice, western-style shirt. I got back just in time to cut the tags off, throw the shirt on, and go outside with Jay to greet the car.

We hardly ever left the Gentle Barn, other than for rescues. And here we were, riding down our lane in the back of a town car headed for Hollywood, the smell of hay and manure wafting in through the open windows.

When we got to the Warner Bros. studio, they took us back to the green room, where they had nice snacks and drinks out for us. We took some bottled water and sat on one of the couches.

"Do you think Brad Pitt sat on this couch?" I said to Jay. "Or maybe Obama!"

Jay got up and sat on another one of the couches. "I think the guy from the Allstate commercial sat on this one."

We settled in and enjoyed our *Ellen* water and stared at each other in disbelief. This was really happening, wasn't it? I was thrilled to be on this adventure, and even happier to be on it with Jay.

After a while, someone came and got us and led us to our seats in the audience. Before he walked away, he said, "By the way, Ellie, after they show the segment, Ellen might want to pull you up onstage and ask you some questions."

I felt all the blood instantly drain out of my head, and I had to focus very hard to not throw up. I didn't hear anything that was being said onstage, and I don't remember who was up there with Ellen before our segment, or whether there was anyone up there with Ellen. My focus was entirely on the words in my mind: *Please don't barf, please don't barf.*

Sure enough, when they broke for a commercial, the producer came and got me. I was grateful my knees didn't buckle as I followed him down the steps from the audience and up onto the stage. I sat carefully on a sofa next to Portia, with my knees together in ladylike fashion. I was incredibly relieved that they started rolling the segment right away, so I could try to take a few deep breaths before I had to say anything. When the segment was over—which I would have to watch again later, because I could hardly focus on it—everyone in the audience clapped. Ellen and Portia talked for a bit, and I prayed to God to get through this without sounding like a total idiot.

Then Ellen said, "Ellie, why don't you tell people about who comes to the Gentle Barn."

Thank God I had talked about the work we did with animals and at-risk kids thousands of times over the years—to Sunday visitors, newspeople, anyone who would listen. I opened my mouth to answer the question, and autopilot took over. Ellen did a good job of helping me along by asking several more perfect questions (i.e., ones I knew the answers to). And my autopilot flew me through the whole thing because I was still out of my body with nervousness.

At one point, Ellen introduced Jay in the audience, saying that we ran the Gentle Barn together, and I was grateful to her for doing that.

Then she said, "We want to help you out," and to the audience: "because they need money and they're helping so many animals that need to be taken out of horrible situations, so . . ." And Ellen reached over the side of her chair and pulled something up off the floor, a big, flat rectangle covered in red cloth. Not having watched the show before, I was unfamiliar with Ellen's shenanigans and had no clue as to what was coming.

"We have some friends at Tonic.com," she continued, "that have been so extraordinarily generous with us for any occasion when they know somebody needs money." She turned to me. "I know you're trying to raise $100,000 for some dairy cows." And she pulled the cloth off of the rectangle as she said: "They're giving you $50,000 right now toward that." And she set this huge cardboard check for that amount on her knees. It was made out to the Gentle Barn.

"Oh my God," I said, and my hand flew to my heart. Now my

nervousness miraculously vanished as I was flooded with shock and gratitude.

Ellen asked the viewers to help us reach the rest of our goal.

After the show Jay and I kind of floated off the set, headed to get our stuff from the green room, and then down the hallway toward the parking lot, when one of the producers called to us. "Wait. Wait up. Ellen wants to say hi to you." We were ushered to Ellen's private green room, where her chef had made a vegan meal. Ellen hugged us, and she and Portia invited us to sit down and eat with them. We had made a book of photographs and stories for them about the cows we had rescued, and this was the perfect opportunity to present it to them.

At one point Portia asked me what I had done before the Gentle Barn.

"I was rescuing dogs and cats," I said.

"Yeah, but before that."

"Well, way before that, when I was really young, I was an actress."

"I knew it!" Portia said. "I just knew it. You do so well in front of the camera."

Apparently my autopilot was pretty good.

———

Ellen's show with our segment aired the next day, a Tuesday, at four p.m., and that night we saw our Facebook fan base explode before our eyes. People were posting like crazy and donating through our website. By the next morning the number of fans on our Facebook page had more than doubled. Giddy with disbelief I made my first post of the day:

> Welcome to all our new fans from The Ellen DeGeneres Show and from Tonic! Thank you for all your support and generosity! Because there are so many posts we can't respond to each of them, but wanted you all to know that we have read every one of them and

are so grateful for all your kind words and your generous contributions! Thank you for being part of our gentle family!

Throughout the day I kept running back to the computer to read the new comments coming in, and to make more posts. I was suddenly aware that nearly twenty thousand people were reading my words, and I felt self-conscious and exhilarated all at the same time. I posted about a cow we had rescued a couple of weeks before. Then I posted to publicly thank *The Ellen DeGeneres Show,* then another post to thank Tonic for their incredible generosity. I wrote a post about the young woman visiting us from England to volunteer for a week (she had found out about us through Facebook). Before I went to bed, I reposted the welcome to all our new fans. I felt like I'd thrown a party and thousands of people had come.

In the days following the *Ellen* show, I spent more time at the computer than I ever had in my life. I was just so excited by how big my family had suddenly grown and I wanted to spend as much time with them as possible. I ended up writing several posts a day for that entire week, and I spent hours reading all the comments from people all over the world. Phone calls were flooding in, keeping everyone on their toes, and the office staff kept an eye on the incoming donations; we were getting closer every day to our $100,000 goal that would buy the cows their new barn.

We put out a call for extra volunteers for the Sunday following the show. We usually got fifty to sixty visitors a week and had ten or fifteen volunteers helping out. We kept e-mailing our community until we'd collected a team of nearly forty, just in case. And it was a good thing we did because 350 people showed up at our gate on Sunday morning. We didn't even have the space to fit all their cars in our parking area; people had to park on the road and walk in.

I walked through this huge crowd on my own property, thinking, *Thank you, Ellen. Thank you, Ellen.* It wasn't just that we had so many visitors, which was amazing in and of itself. But the whole energy was different. People kept coming up to Jay and me and hugging us and crying and thanking us for doing this work. They understood our mission; they got it because they were just like me. We traded stories about what animals meant to us and the grieving we'd gone through and the celebrating we had done. Their eyes glistened with tears just like mine and they laughed from their whole heart just like I did. After so many years of being mocked and misunderstood and judged as crazy for how passionately I cared about animals, I had finally found my tribe. I was humbled to meet each and every person who came up to me and so very grateful to Ellen for spreading the word.

We had never intended Sundays to be profitable; it was more community outreach than fund-raising. But because of the numbers of people, our sales in the snack bar and gift shop quadrupled, and by the end of the day, our shelves were bare. And that on top of the $5 entrance donation from 350 people. If this kind of turnout kept up, Sundays would bring in a quarter of the donations we needed to run our place and take care of our animals.

Donations kept coming in online as well, and a month later we had raised the $100,000 for the new barn. It took a while for the barn to be built, and when we called the dairy to let them know we were ready to receive the cows, they informed us that they had found a way to stay open. The sixty dairy cows would not be coming to us after all. So we pledged to all our donors to keep rescuing cows from slaughter until we reached the number sixty. This was the first time since we had moved to Santa Clarita where we found ourselves with more space than animals. We had come to dread the daily calls from people who had a pig or a horse that we didn't have space for. It felt awful to say no and pass them on to another agency; it was equally difficult to scramble in panic mode to try to make the space and come up with a budget. But now that we had this land and this barn specifically for cows, it was a joy to receive calls about cows needing to be rescued; we had ample space and shelter to welcome any cows who needed us.

One such call was from our connection at the auction house. Only this time it was not a request to come pick up downed animals. He was calling to fill us in on a new trend he was seeing. With dairy farms going out of business in the difficult economy, the auction house was getting a lot of dairy cows headed for slaughter. Because dairy cows are almost constantly pregnant, many of them went into labor and dropped their calves right there in the auction house. The buyers had no interest in the calves; they only wanted the meat from the mother, so the calves were left to die on the concrete.

"Would you be willing to come take these newborn calves off our hands?" he asked.

Jay told the guy yes, but we had something else in mind. Not only did we want the newborns, we wanted to take the mothers as well to keep that relationship intact. But after Jay drove the two hours to the auction house to intercept some of these mother-newborn pairs, no births occurred that day, and he called me with the update.

"I'm about to go into the bidding room," he said. "I'm going to see if there's anyone else we should bring home." In the background I heard the horrifying din I always heard when he called me from the auction house. This was not mooing, this was mother cows *screaming* for their babies, babies screaming for their mothers, friends and relatives screaming for one another. And the screams were filled with terror and a depth of angst that I would never be able to erase from my mind.

While Jay was there, there were four animals who went down—too sick to stand any longer. Two of them were teenage cows and two were eight-week-old calves.

He called me again from the road to let me know who he was bringing home. "Start contacting volunteers," he said. "Two of them are veal calves."

I started calling and sending e-mails immediately, rounding up a support team for the orphan calves. It also occurred to me to let Portia and Ellen know that two babies were on their way home. When Ellen got the news, she decided she was well overdue for the visit she'd been meaning to make to the Gentle Barn and she scheduled to come three days later.

Like all calves raised in veal crates, the two calves arrived very sick and very weak. They were malnourished and anemic, both had pneumonia and high fevers, their coats were dull, their stomachs distended, and one could not walk because she had been stomped at birth to keep her from walking. In the next few days we discovered that the other calf had an infected puncture wound in her side, likely from a pitchfork used to prod her to stand up and get moving.

When Ellen and Portia arrived, they were so moved to meet these baby girls. They sat in the straw with them and stroked their heads, then helped me remove the auction stickers from their backs.

"You're not a number anymore," I told each calf. "You'll get to have your own name now." Then I turned to Ellen and said, "It would be a real honor if you named them."

She sat for a moment, looking at the calves, then said, "I think that one should be Holy."

"Wow, that is so beautiful."

"Like, Holy Cow," she said.

And I broke out laughing. Ellen DeGeneres was doing comedy in our barn.

"And the other one, she can be Madonna . . . and we'll have to get her a cone bra."

And thus our calves were named.

In the following weeks I kept Ellen and Portia informed of the calves' progress with a weekly e-mail, typing "cow update" in the subject line. *This week, Madonna bloated and we had to stay up all night and pump the air out of her stomach. But she's OK now.* Or: *Madonna and Holy have turned into lap cows. They're just so comfortable with people now.* After several weeks of this, Ellen began doing an update on her show: "Ellen and Portia's Weekly Cow Update," introduced by a big mooing sound.

Over the following months, Ellen mentioned the Gentle Barn often on her show and on her website, and eventually she put a "Donate to the Gentle Barn" button on her site and even designed a Gentle Barn T-shirt. I felt like I'd been adopted right along with the calves.

She and Portia came out to see us and the animals again, and Ellen even sent her brother and nieces and her mom and her mom's friend. It felt like the whole Ellen clan was becoming part of the Gentle Barn family. On her show, in her tweets, and even to us, Ellen would talk about what the Gentle Barn meant to her, saying how much we were contributing to humanity, how we were giving both animals and kids a second chance at life. I would listen to her, equally captivated and baffled. Here was this huge celebrity who had the clout to support anyone she wanted; she could have chosen some big, well-established organization, but she was choosing us, vouching for our work, and calling me an angel. Tears would flood my eyes. The little girl in me who had never been supported for my passion to help animals, who had been viewed by my parents as a nut with a weird obsession, who had been laughed at by the kids at school, was now being showered with the highest praise for doing the very things that had garnered such judgment.

One time, after hearing Ellen speak about the Gentle Barn, I quipped, "OK, I'm good. Ellen just healed my entire childhood."

Everyone present laughed. But it was true. A deep, wounded part of me was mending.

I had imagined that Ellen's support would follow a typical Hollywood trajectory: a big flash that faded away, to be replaced by some other fad or cause. But to our amazement and unending gratitude, Ellen stayed loyal to the Gentle Barn, coming up with one brilliant, off-the-wall plug after another. One day, when she had the heartthrob Channing Tatum on the show—who had also become a fan of our cause—she told everyone: "Go visit the Gentle Barn, because you never know when Channing Tatum will be there with his shirt off." The following Sunday, we had nine hundred visitors.

We were absolutely thrilled with the increase in visitors, private tours, supporters, Facebook fans, and donations, as well as the stream of other celebrities who followed Ellen's lead and got on board with the cause. The animals, however, were not as thrilled as we were. We had not been prepared for how to deal with this increase in traffic through the barnyard. We had the same system in place that we'd always had, where people could wander through the barnyards at their own pace, with our volunteer chaperones stationed at each area of each barnyard, making sure that the animals' voices were heard. We had more than doubled the number of chaperones to deal with the increased crowd, but that didn't fix the problem. Tons of people would end up crammed into the upper barnyard with the pigs and goats and chickens. By one p.m., the animals—who normally sought out attention from visitors all day long—had decided they were done and began asking people to leave them alone. The volunteers had to apologize and ask people to please not pet the animals. Something had to be done to keep this the happy haven it had always been for its residents.

The increased crowds had come because of Ellen, and the answer to how to deal with the crowds came through Ellen as well. Ellen's mother's friend, who worked for Toyota, seemed to be the one who had gotten us nominated for the 100 Cars for Good giveaway. Rallying our Facebook fans to vote for us, we'd won hands-down, and Toyota had come and presented us with a beautiful new hybrid Highlander. Wanting to help us further, Toyota had built us an amphitheater just above the upper barnyard.

The amphitheater! The answer to our crowd control. We would

take fifty people at a time into our amphitheater, where they would listen to a presentation about how we'd gotten started and what our mission was, as well as guidelines on how to listen to the animals' requests. Those fifty people would then get to go into the upper barnyard to be with the animals. No one else would go in until those people had come out, keeping the crowd to no more than fifty at any given time, and keeping the animals happy and sociable throughout the day.

In the middle of all this growth—with our Facebook fan base reaching 100,000 and with Ellen selling a lock of Justin Bieber's hair on eBay for $40,000 to support the Gentle Barn—Jay and I actually managed to find a moment to do something special for ourselves. In truth, it was all Jay's doing. Ever since he had proposed, six years earlier, I had cited one reason after another for postponing the wedding. We hardly had a minute to sit down and take a breath; we had three kids to raise, a hundred animal "kids," with new ones coming in all the time, and all the programs we were running at the Barn. How were we going to fit a wedding into all that? Jay and I sometimes talked about what our wedding might look like, but to me we were just fantasizing; it didn't seem like it would ever really happen. Neither did I even need it to. Jay and I were good just like we were.

Apparently Jay had different ideas about the subject.

The day after Thanksgiving in 2010, Jay said to me, "Come on, let's take the kids and go pick up my mom in Burbank and let's all go to a museum."

What a nice idea. I hadn't been to a museum in years.

On our way to the car, I realized it was colder out than I had thought. "I'm going to go back and get a jacket," I said.

"No," Jay said. "Stop! You have a jacket in the car. Let's just get in the car."

"I just want to get a jacket, Jay. And make sure the dogs are set up right, since we're going—"

"No!" he said again. "The dogs are set up. Just get in the car."

What is his problem? I thought. *Jeez.* But I got in the car, along with the kids.

As we neared Jay's mom's house, he said, "You know, we're running a little early. I don't want to rush her, so let's go get some lunch." And he detoured away from her house. Several blocks later, I saw a Chinese restaurant that had a neon-green sign in the window with the word VEGETARIAN. Jay and I had an agreement that if we ever saw a vegetarian or vegan place, we would eat there to support them.

"No, no, no," he said. "I want to look for a Togo's."

"A Togo's?"

"We need something quick." But he kept driving around and around, saying, "I saw a Togo's here before. I know it's here somewhere."

This didn't make any sense at all. "You never get lost," I said. "You have a great sense of direction." Then my stomach started to growl. "We could have been eating spring rolls by now."

But Jay was sticking to his stubborn course, taking us down streets that were more and more filled with traffic.

"You're going to end up at the Burbank airport if you're not careful," I said.

And sure enough, we ended up at the Burbank airport.

"What are you doing?"

Jay looked over at me and said, "Will you marry me?"

"Yeah," I exclaimed, annoyed and confused, "but they don't have a Togo's at the airport!"

In that voice of his that could go suddenly smooth as silk, he said, "We're not going to Togo's. We're going to Vegas to get married."

"Come on!" I said. Why was he messing around like this?

"No, really," he said. "Kids, is that right?"

And my children, who had been unusually quiet in the backseat through the whole drive, burst out with their answer: "Yeah, Mom, we're going to Las Vegas!"

"What are you talking about? I didn't pack."

"I packed for you," Jay said.

"But I don't have a dress."

"I bought you a dress." Then he pointed out the window and said, "Look, there are your friends."

There in front of the entrance to the airport were my two closest girlfriends with their husbands and kids, all standing on the curb. One of my friends held up the most beautiful wedding gown for me to see.

"Oh my God," I said, "I—I—I didn't bring any makeup."

"Don't worry, I've got it all covered," Jay said.

"I didn't bring any shoes."

"I bought you shoes."

"I didn't even shave my legs."

After a beat, he said, "I can't help you with that one."

By the time we got to Vegas, the whole thing finally had sunk in. I was getting married to the man I loved. Jay put us all up at the Venetian; I had never seen anything like it. Inside the hotel, there were clouds and stars in the "sky" and canals with bridges and gondolas. That night we went and got our marriage license, and then we all went out to a show. The next day, Jay had arranged for all of the women and girls to get our hair and makeup done, and had included a beautiful diamond clip he had bought for my hair. He ushered us to the salon at the hotel, and then went off with the guys. All of us with straight hair got it curled, and everyone who had curly hair had it straightened. And all the fussing made each of us feel special. After the salon, I put on the dress, and it fit me like a glove. How he had done that was a mystery to me. When we were all finally ready, my girlfriends and our daughters took the elevators down to the main floor.

"It's over there," one of my girlfriends said.

"Where?"

"At the other side of the hotel."

"But that's, like, miles away," I said. "There are acres of casinos and restaurants between here and there."

"Come on," she said, "we're going to be late."

"I can't walk through all that."

"Why?"

"Because there are tons of people, and I'm all dressed up like a bride." I was never embarrassed to be out in the world covered in barn dust and smelling like goats . . . but dressed in a wedding gown? This was just too conspicuous.

"Come on, Ellie. You're going to be fine."

I figured maybe I would just half-close my eyes till we got there. But as we turned the corner and walked into the casino, everyone in there burst into applause. We couldn't walk ten feet without people stopping us to ask if they could take our picture. "Would you mind holding my baby?" one woman asked before she put her infant in my arms and set off her flash. Someone else flung her parents at me. "Will you be in a photo with my mom and dad?" All along the way, people clapped and called out, "Look at the bride. Congratulations!"

It was the longest fifteen minutes of my life. And yet by the end of it, I kind of felt like a movie star.

The bridge where Jay and I would stand to take our vows was beautiful, with white roses woven all through the railings. I stepped up onto the bridge, which spanned a large canal. Jay was already there at the center of the bridge, and I couldn't believe how handsome he was. I hadn't thought I needed to do this; a ceremony that had proven the first time around not to be so binding after all. But in this moment, as I stepped in front of Jay and stood on the precipice of a public commitment to this man, my love for him went to a whole new level. Tears started streaming as I said my vows, and as Jay said his. I was sure my mascara was running all down my face, but I didn't care. None of that mattered. What mattered was the depth of love I felt for this man who had toiled by my side to manifest all that we had created together.

To applause, we descended from the bridge and were whisked away by a gondola. I was a princess in my own fairy tale, and there was nowhere else I would have rather been.

CHAPTER 15

We returned to daily life at the Gentle Barn, with our emergency calls and rescues and the daily hubbub of caring for a barnyard full of animals and a house full of children. Nothing had changed, and yet everything had changed. The commitment Jay and I had made seemed to amplify the support I felt. The man I loved was truly by my side, caring for our enormous Gentle Barn family right alongside me.

I had always needed animals like I needed oxygen. They were my very breath, and every time I saw one of them suffering, it was like someone was holding their hand over my own mouth. But for most of my life I had felt alone in these feelings, and like I had to prove that the animals I cared about mattered. I had to fight against my parents, push against my first husband, shove my way through the founding of the Gentle Barn. And in hindsight, perhaps part of all this proving and pushing was me trying to persuade the critic that lived inside my very own head, the one that had always wondered—just a little bit—if all of them were right that I was crazy.

But here was Jay, showing me I wasn't the only one who cared this deeply about animals, and proving to me once and for all that I didn't have to do this work alone. The fire had burned the fear right out of me and deepened my faith; the Internet had connected me to a fabulous, global, animal-loving family I'd never dreamed existed; and Ellen had validated me and my work in front of the world.

The next thing that happened made me feel, for the first time in my life, like a true grown-up—one who no longer needed to prove anything at all.

It was August 2011, a scorching month in our little high-desert valley. We were working with a filmmaker named Tim to create a short film about the Gentle Barn. Sitting in the shade of a pepper tree, we were trying to look like we weren't melting from the heat as I explained why we no longer rode our horses, and that we didn't want to participate in the domination over any animal. Besides, it was much more satisfying and intimate to just walk by their sides on a mutual adventure.

Then Tim asked us to name each rescue we had done and tell the accompanying story. We tended to forget all we had accomplished in past rescues, focusing instead on what was in front of us—because there was always so much in front of us. Talking about the rescues brought back all the emotion we'd been through at the time—feeling the animals' pain, experiencing the relief of removing them from a bad situation, and then the triumph when the animals had healed.

"Oh my gosh," I said to Jay at one point, "we've been through a lot of adventures together, haven't we?"

When we got to the story of the backyard butcher, Jay said, "We handed that one over to the Health Department. They were working on shutting him down or making him get his place in order. He wasn't supposed to be selling meat anyway; you have to be a slaughterhouse to do that. And this guy was selling *contaminated* meat."

Jay had occasionally seen Manuel at the auction house over the years, and had even gone back to his place a couple of times to check on conditions there. For a while, it had seemed that the pressure from the Health Department was helping. But Jay hadn't been there in many months.

"We don't actually know what finally happened with that place," I said to Jay when we took a break from filming. "Maybe we should go check on it, to make sure they really did stop the guy."

Jay decided to drive out there later that afternoon. When he got home a few hours later, he did not look happy. "It's way worse than ever," he said.

Jay started talking with the authorities again, asking why they hadn't shut the guy down. The Health Department told him they had been working to get Manuel to comply and bring his place up to code.

"But after all this time he's *not* up to code," Jay told them. "And the guy is selling tainted meat."

The woman from the Health Department told Jay that if the man was butchering and selling meat, it wasn't the Health Department's jurisdiction. She'd have to pass the case on to the USDA. We didn't hear anything back for days. When Jay contacted the Health Department again, the woman told him the USDA could not take the case on because Manuel was not an actual slaughterhouse; they only regulated legal slaughterhouses.

"Well, then, isn't it back in your hands?" Jay asked.

The problem, they told him, was that they had never been able to gather any evidence that Manuel was selling meat.

"But they always announce they're coming," Jay reported back to me. "They set up appointments for reinspection." Manuel thus had enough warning to be on his best behavior, to make sure not to have any customers show up at the time of the inspection, to clean his place up and remove any of the dead animals Jay had witnessed when he'd been there. Jay had seen animal carcasses rotting in the pens or being eaten by the other starving animals.

When Jay called Animal Control, they said they had been there a number of times, and there was always fresh hay out for the animals. We suspected they announced their visits too. In response to the sick and starving condition of the animals themselves, apparently Manuel had provided them with documentation that he'd just brought those animals home from auction. Jay knew otherwise.

Frustrated and at our wits' end, Jay called the Health Department again. "Can't you do some undercover work to catch this guy in the act of selling meat?"

The Health Department said it was not their mission to entrap anyone. Their mission was to regulate and give guidelines, helping people rectify any problems and setting them up to succeed in bringing their place up to code.

Throughout these dealings with the authorities, I was restless and angry. How could something so blatantly wrong be allowed to happen? How could people simply turn their gaze away? I kept imagining the sick, starving animals crying for help and getting no response. I'd find myself awake in the middle of the night, the wheels spinning in my head. *There's got to be a way to stop this guy. Should we call the press? What reporters do we know?*

Then Jay had a brilliant idea. "The next time Tim comes out to work on the film, he should come with me to the backyard butcher and capture that place on camera."

I could feel the excitement stirring in me. This might really work. But I was worried about Tim. "He's never seen anything like this before. Are you sure you want to put him through that?"

"Tim will be fine," Jay said. "And it can serve double duty. It's perfect for the film, too."

But we weren't sure of the best way to go about it. I couldn't imagine the backyard butcher agreeing to have himself or his place filmed. We thought briefly about trying to hide a camera, but we didn't know anything about undercover work.

"I might be able to convince him to let us film," Jay said. Jay had taken photographs with his phone before, telling Manuel he wanted to show some pictures of the animals to his wife. Because Jay had built a "friendship" with the guy, Manuel had always said, "Sure, man. No problem." Jay had told him about our program that brought inner-city kids out to work with animals as a way to help the kids. "I think he's going to let us do it," Jay said.

I wasn't as convinced as Jay was. The entire time Jay and Tim were gone I was nervous and distracted. What if the guy got angry that they wanted to film? Clearly he was violent toward animals; was he also a danger to people?

A few hours passed before Jay finally called. "He let us film everything. He said stuff on camera that— Well, let's just say he might have just shot himself in the foot."

Jay and Tim had gotten footage of the dead and dying animals, the filth, the slaughtering area, and most important Manuel himself boasting about how many animals he had killed, how much meat he had sold and to what kinds of people. In one of the shots Tim showed me, I saw one goat who was a heartbeat away from death. She was like a little skeleton barely able to hold her head up.

"Oh, Jay, you've got to go back and get that goat."

But when the guys went back the next day, that goat had passed away, and her poor little body lay unburied in the pen, in the same spot she had been lying the day before.

There was no shortage of animals who needed rescuing at the backyard butcher. Jay called me on his way back and said, "I pulled three goats. We're going to take them straight to the hospital; they're really, really sick." At the hospital they received subcutaneous fluids and had blood work and X-rays taken.

When they arrived home, all three goats went straight into strict quarantine in our infirmary. They had high fevers from staph infections in their lungs and they were so emaciated that their hips jutted at sharp angles and you could count every rib. There was no spark whatsoever in their eyes, not one iota of hope.

"I wonder what that is on their faces," I said to Jay. Their muzzles were covered with black gunk stuck in their hair.

"It's probably the rotten tomatoes. That's all he had out for them to eat."

Goats didn't normally eat tomatoes. To eat rotten ones, a goat had to be on the verge of starving to death.

We set to work immediately on healing these three girls, coordinating a plan with the vet and giving them their first shots of antibiotics and their first doses of superfood algae. And of course we made sure to have plenty of fresh hay and clean water out for them. They had arrived so terrified of humans, I had to move as slowly as possible in order to not further traumatize them. For the first week, I needed help from one of my barnyard staff in order to give the goats their medicine and supplements. The easiest way to contain a goat, and the least stressful for her, was to get her to walk into the corner of the twenty-by-twelve-foot infirmary, without any need for chase or force. We did this with the help of the goat's natural response—as a prey animal—to "pressure." Several feet from her, I would stand just a bit forward of her shoulders to keep her from bolting ahead; my assistant would stand just a bit to the back of her hind end to keep her from turning and bolting in the opposite direction. With arms spread wide, we'd move very slowly toward her, adjusting our positions according to her movements, to stay on these "pressure points." Through this gentle maneuvering, we'd end up in the corner with the goat in our arms, and my helper would gently hold her still while I administered the medicine and supplements.

"This is going to make you better," I would coo to them. "You're going to get strong and healthy and go outside to play with the other animals in the sunshine." But in truth, for the first couple of weeks, I didn't know for sure if they would. I would hold my breath each time I approached the infirmary, not knowing whether I would find them alive or dead. It took almost two weeks for their fevers to break. Slowly they began to understand that what I was giving them was making them feel better. Not only did they stop fighting the supplements, they also started to trust me just a little bit. Eventually they turned into superfood-algae junkies, waiting for me to arrive with their "treats." Their appetites improved, and they slowly began to gain weight. I sent Ellen three choices of names for each of the goats and asked her to choose. She selected the names Sassy, Joy, and Divine.

A week into healing these goats, I finally saw the video Tim had edited from the footage he'd gotten over the two visits to the backyard butcher. Jay tried to dissuade me from watching it.

"I don't think you want to see the whole thing," he said.

"Please just show it to me," I said. "I want to know."

But I watched with my hands half-covering my eyes. Even worse than the visuals was what the guy said. He had not only slaughtered animals; he flaunted how many animals he had tortured and the details of how he had done it. He was the go-to guy for groups involved in ritual torture and sacrifice. At the end of the video, I sat there frozen in shock and horror.

Not only was it hard to believe anyone actually did such things, but here he was, openly admitting to it. And they had gotten it all on film without even hiding the camera.

"That's the sickest part," Jay said. "He was happy to have us film it all. He has absolutely no clue how twisted and wrong it is."

Manuel didn't think what he was doing was wrong because he was not the first to do it; it had been handed down from his father, and before that his grandfather. Three generations had let animals starve to death and left them out to rot, slaughtered animals in plain sight of the others, tortured animals for money, and manipulated and deluded the authorities. And now Manuel was in the process of teaching it all to his own children.

"We have to stop him, Jay," I said. The shock had given way to a grief and anger so fierce I could hardly breathe.

"I'm right there with you, babe," he said. "I am so right there with you."

We sent our footage to both the Health Department and Animal Control. For a couple of days we didn't hear anything, so we called to follow up.

"We've passed it on to our Major Case Unit," the guy from Animal Control said over the phone. At first I thought it was another blow off, but the next day we got word from the Unit directly. The Major Case Unit was the department of Animal Control that handled particularly bad cruelty cases. They would be starting a major investigation immediately, visiting the backyard butcher to collect evidence, and pulling animals that were in particularly bad shape. These animals were brought to us to heal, including one newborn calf whose mother was in such bad shape, the officers had had to euthanize her. It would take months for them to build their case, and I hated to think of the animals that would suffer in the meantime, but it was a relief to know someone was finally taking this seriously, and I was grateful they were keeping us in the loop. They also asked for our help, requesting that Jay provide written documentation describing what he had witnessed on his several visits over the last few years. We were pretty certain we'd be receiving more animals once they shut the guy down.

It helped to spend time with the three rescued goats. At least then I felt like I was actively doing something to help make things right, rather than simply waiting for news. Each day, the goats grew to trust me a little more. Sassy—a La Mancha goat with little elfin ears—was the first to start showing her true colors. When I sang to the three girls, Sassy started coming over to me and nibbling my nose; then she'd lie down right next to me and fall asleep. My guess was that she had been someone's pet before ending up at the backyard butcher, making her the quickest to heal emotionally because she'd had an earlier experience with human kindness.

I kept our Facebook followers up to date on the progress of the three goats, but I posted next to nothing about the backyard butcher himself. I didn't want to tip him off that we were working with the authorities to shut him down. The less on-guard he was, the better.

A month after we'd rescued the goats, all three were cleared of lung infections and were let out of quarantine. Watching them frolic in the barnyard and meet the other animals gave me a small glimmer of hope that this backyard butcher nightmare might actually get resolved. I wrote a lengthy piece that day about them on my blog, ending with these words:

> I am deeply in love with all three of them. . . . To me, they are not just goats, they are heroes; they have overcome the absolute worst lives, worst experiences that could have ruined them. Yet they have found a way to forgive, to be courageous and welcome me in, to move on and accept a new life. Their lives could have easily crushed them, body and spirit, but they have risen above it and let it go. . . . They do not sit around and think about where they have come from and the torment they have gone through, they sit in gratitude and blessings. We have learned so much from them already, and they have only been here for a month!

Finally, on April 2, 2012, we got the call we had been expecting. The case against the backyard butcher was at last complete. The Major Case Unit told us they were going to do a raid on the place the next morning. Manuel would be arrested, and the Unit would pull every last animal. "Can we bring them to you?" they asked.

Yes!

Because all the incoming animals would have to be kept separate from our current animal residents for at least twenty-one days, we needed to create separate pens for them, immediately. But we didn't know how many animals to expect and wouldn't know until the next day; we'd just have to make our best guess. We called the Fence Factory—who had built the temporary village for our animals when we'd first moved to Santa Clarita. They came out again and, in four hours, built temporary pens on our second property that were large enough for a few dozen animals. We would use these outdoor pens to triage the animals—one holding pen where each goat or sheep could be examined, one pen for the goats and sheep who were healthy, one for the sick animals, another for the very sick animals who needed to be in strict quarantine, and an iso-pen for the goats and sheep who were even contagious to other kinds of animals, including humans. We also sectioned off part of the pasture, where the rescued cows would go.

That night I could hardly sleep. I was so amped up—a mixture of excitement that something finally was going to be done to stop this monster and anxiety about how the next day would go. Did we have enough space for all the animals who were going to be confiscated and brought to us? Did we have enough separate pens? How many of the animals would arrive pregnant? Were we going to be able to save everyone?

The next morning, we hurried over to our other property to meet our vet, Dr. Morrison, and make sure everything was ready. We checked if there was enough straw out for the animals to be comfortable. We double-checked that the feeders were securely hung in each pen and that the waters were clean. And we kept looking at the gates, expecting any minute for the officers to arrive.

Finally, around midday we got a call from the Major Case Unit. They were at the backyard butcher's place. Manuel had been arrested by the police, and the Major Case Unit officers were starting to pull the animals. "There are a lot of them, maybe thirty," the guy said on the phone. "They're very sick. Be ready."

Thirty animals. We had never taken in that many at once. The hour it took before they arrived seemed like forever. I kept staring at the gate and then at the clock, and then running to double-check the pens. To help pass the time, I finally decided to make a Facebook post to get a jump on rounding up the support we were desperately going to need.

Remember Sassy, Divine and Joy from the backyard butcher? The gross abuse going on over there has finally been stopped today! He was arrested and all the animals there have been removed and are on their way to the Gentle Barn. This is a huge victory in shutting down backyard butchers, their extreme cruelty and their tainted meat. The animals are arriving now. Please help us! Go to www.gentlebarn.org to make a donation.

This time when I looked up to check the gates, they were opening.

"They're here!" I yelled, my heart pounding. And Jay, the vet and her assistant, a barnyard staff member, and I gathered along the driveway, watching as the first truck pulled in through the gates. It was a big white truck pulling a long trailer that stirred eddies of dust into the air. Then another truck followed the first. Then another. And another. I started weeping as I watched five, six, seven big trucks pull their trailers along our driveway. They really were here. They had believed us.

The trucks stopped, filling the full length of our gravel drive, and the officers jumped out. There must have been around eight of them, all in their khaki uniforms with shiny badges. As we started looking inside the trailers to see what kinds of animals had arrived and how sick they were, the officers approached us to shake our hands.

"Thank you so much for what you've done," one of them said. "It's an honor to meet you."

"This is the worst cruelty case I've ever seen," said another.

We had talked with a number of these officers on the phone and all were eager to meet us face-to-face. I wanted to be present with each one of these men and women, but I also wanted to get my hands on the animals and start helping them.

In one trailer I saw the tiniest baby goats with runny noses. In another trailer there were goats with such bad eye infections their eyes had turned an opaque red; if they weren't already blind, they were headed in that direction. There were five terribly skinny cows. And there was a horse. We hadn't expected a horse at all; where were we going to put a horse? Then I saw chickens and dogs and cats. We hadn't expected them, either.

Together with Dr. Morrison, we decided to start with the cows. But once we let them out it would be impossible to corral them to do the needed tests, so Dr. Morrison had to climb into the trailer to examine them.

"Be careful!" I said to her. She was not a very big person, and she was going to climb right into a trailer with a bunch of big, scared cows, some of them with horns.

"Oh, I'll be fine," she said, ever soft-spoken.

She talked quietly to the cows as she squeezed in between them. There were five of them in a relatively small trailer, so there wasn't much room to maneuver. "OK, guys, I'm just going to have a look at you." She examined them, drew blood, and ran fecals, handing vials out to her assistant. All of the cows were emaciated and had open sores on their hides, but none had fevers or present symptoms of pneumonia. They likely had parasites, but we'd have to wait for the tests to confirm it.

After Dr. Morrison climbed out of the trailer, we backed it straight into the sectioned-off cow pasture and opened the trailer gate. It was as if the cows understood immediately that here they would finally be safe. They ran into the pasture and jumped and sprang through the grass. When Jay and I turned around, all the officers were heading our way. One after another, they hugged us, tears streaming down their faces.

"We never get to see this," one officer said. "We only see the awful places."

"It's amazing how happy they are," another said. "They have a future. They're going to be OK here. Thank you so much for the work you do."

We moved on to the goats and sheep, many of whom were in much worse shape than the cows. The officers unloaded one animal at a time into the holding pen, where Dr. Morrison and her assistant recorded the animal's gender and distinguishing marks, took vital signs, drew blood, administered a dewormer, and determined which pen each animal should go into. It took two hours to triage the rest of the animals; there were thirty in all, many of them so sick we didn't know if they'd make it through that first night. There were many with very high fevers, and all of them were emaciated and riddled with parasites.

For the unexpected horse, who looked the worst of any of the animals, we had to quickly come up with a shelter by making a corral with some extra fence panels that was partially covered by an awning. The Animal Control officers would take the chickens, dogs, and cats to their shelter for care and neutering. But they promised they would bring back to us any who didn't get adopted.

When all the animals were finally in their pens, we sat down with Dr. Morrison to go over our plan of action. After she left, we took the first steps toward creating appropriate indoor accommodations for all these animals. There on our second property, we had a large warehouse filled with hay. We would move all the hay out and raise the money for insulating mats, feed buckets, lots and lots of straw, and fence panels to be able to create separate indoor pens; these animals were just too sick to stay outside for long. As soon as I got back to the house, I headed for the computer to update our Facebook followers. The comments were already pouring in in response to my earlier post. "Great news. Gentle Barn, you are AWESOME!" "Donation made. Thanks for all you do!!!"

I continued to keep our wonderful community in the loop, and they continued to support us, with both donations and moral support flooding in daily. I also kept Ellen and Portia informed, and they went to bat for us once again, boosting public awareness of the Gentle Barn and the backyard butcher case, and asking people to help us out with contributions. The following Sunday many visitors asked about the animals rescued from the backyard butcher, and now that Manuel had been arrested, we could fill everyone in on the details of all we had witnessed. Volunteers started calling and e-mailing right away to let us know they were available to take shifts with the animals. We were so very grateful for their willingness, but because of how terrified these animals were of humans, we decided the best way to proceed was to let them settle in for a couple of months with as few humans around as possible; only two of us would go into their pens twice daily to take temperatures and administer treatments.

In addition to the individual contributions, Sun Chlorella, the maker of our superfood algae supplement, stepped in with a huge grant so we could finish upgrading the warehouse and turn it into a proper, temperature-controlled healing center with an exam room.

Even with all this support it was several months of very long days—sometimes staying up half the night—trying to save these animals, working as hard as we could to raise the thousands of dollars we needed to heal them, as well as taking care of all of our other animals and our own children. But every one of the animals confiscated from the backyard butcher pulled through. Healing them emotionally was going to take even longer. But we'd get there, and eventually these animals would be able to be integrated into our herds.

This rescue went far beyond helping these particular animals. So many times when we rescued animals, we remained powerless to rectify the horrifying situation the animals had come from, and those who had caused the harm could go on to do more harm. This time was different. This time we had interrupted the cycle of abuse, not only stopping an abuser, but stopping him from teaching the abuse to his children. Manuel Guerra was tried and sentenced to ninety days in jail and five years of probation. He was ordered to pay $4,000 restitution, complete forty-eight animal cruelty classes, and was forbidden from ever owning another animal in his life.

For the first time ever, I felt truly supported by the authorities. They had taken us seriously, backed us up, gone in there and raided the place, and then thanked us, their faces wet with tears. I got to see that the officers themselves cared deeply about animals and had surely gotten into this line of work to help them. All that time that Jay and I had been frustrated with a system so overloaded with red tape and politics, the individual officers had probably been just as frustrated as we were. In the end, we were supported not only by Animal Control but by the county board of supervisors, who thanked us, along with the officers of the Major Case Unit, in a public ceremony in downtown Los Angeles.

I had come a long way from my little half-acre, where it was me and Mary against the world. It no longer felt like the world was opposing me, or that I had to prove that what I was doing was important. Instead, I felt absolutely supported. We had hundreds of thousands of people across the globe saying yes to the Gentle Barn, yes to the work of helping animals and kids. My work was valuable. My thoughts were valuable. I finally had earned my place in the world.

I also recognized that my relationship with the Gentle Barn had shifted. At the very beginning, I *was* the Gentle Barn. The Gentle Barn did not exist without me, and I felt I couldn't exist without it. But the success or failure of my organization was no longer riding entirely on my shoulders. Neither was I the only one reaping the joys and triumphs of the work we did. My little organization had grown up and become so much bigger than me. The Gentle Barn had a life of its own. It was time for me to open my hands and let it fly. For it no longer belonged to me; it now belonged to the world.

EPILOGUE

I took my dogs out into the spring afternoon for a walk. We hiked up the hill behind our house, waist-high in wild grasses sprinkled with purple and yellow flowers. A full year had passed since the backyard-butcher rescue, and all the animals pulled from that place were healthy and thriving. At the top of the hill I sat down, and my dogs romped around me through the grass. The air was just right, warm with a light breeze, and the long shadows of late afternoon fell across the terrain. I gazed out over the Gentle Barn, dotted with barns and sheds and held in the deep green embrace of the pepper trees, finally coming to maturity. The animals, just finishing up their dinner, congregated around their feed bins, searching for any missed bits of food. In that moment, as the sweet air caressed my face, it dawned on me how truly happy I was.

I was in love with, and now married to, my best friend, and we had mastered the art of running a business and raising a family together. My parents and I were getting along better than we ever had, and they had come to see the importance of my work and were actually proud of my accomplishments. And the Gentle Barn was flourishing. Every year, we rescued hundreds of abused animals and helped hundreds of at-risk kids. We had 170 animal residents, and that number was slowly growing. Our fleet of volunteers had reached a thousand. Hundreds of visitors showed up at our gates every Sunday, and well over 200,000 fans followed us on Facebook. People supported us and came and visited from every corner of the world.

Yet the happiness I felt was not from some outside source. It emanated from the center of my being. I no longer had to go outside myself to find that still, deep feeling of peace and contentment—not to men or a substance or even into the woods or a field full of butterflies. That feeling was now inside me; it had become part of the fiber of my being. I felt like I was covered in butterflies every day.

The healing was complete.

That didn't mean my work was done. To the contrary. I wanted more than ever before to share this gift with the world. I wanted as many people as possible to receive the healing power of hugging a cow or giving a pig a tummy rub or meeting the gaze of an animal and feeling truly seen. These animals had healed me, and I had witnessed countless others being healed too. Now I wanted to share the healing on a much grander scale. I had begun a plan to open Gentle Barns all across the nation—and eventually all across the globe. If everyone had the chance to connect with animals, perhaps they would come to understand something I had been fortunate enough to know all my life. That we may all look different on the outside, but on the inside we're all the same.

With Gentle Barns all over the globe, in just one generation, perhaps the world will become a kinder place.

Please visit us at www.gentlebarn.org.

ACKNOWLEDGMENTS

First and foremost, I would like to thank my husband, Jay. He is my partner, my best friend, my soul mate, and my other half. He sees me, he understands who I am and what makes me tick, and he has sacrificed everything for my dream. He is a great friend, a wonderful father, and a hero, working by my side to save animals who have no one else and nowhere else to go. I always wanted this life and this dream, but I didn't know I would have someone to share it with. Thank you, Jay, I am so grateful!

I want to thank my children, who have been very patient with me, and who have at times not lived the most normal lives. They have tolerated late nights, early mornings, farm animals in the house, and animal emergencies that have taken us all over the country. Molli, Jesse, and Cheyanne, you inspire me, make me want to be a better human being, and teach me every single day—I love you!

I would like to thank my agent, Sasha, who has been with me since the beginning, and who was the catalyst for this book. You are so easy to talk to and always know what to do. You made this process easy. I would like to thank Nomi, who got inside my head, found my voice, and enabled me to tell my story—thank you! I never imagined it could be so fun to write with someone else; you are a true artist, a genius, and I can't wait to start writing our second book! Thank you so much to the great folks at Crown: Mauro, Leah, Amanda, Ellen, Christina, and the rest of the team who helped us structure the book and make it wonder-ful. You all are so good at what you do; I thought we made a great team and it has been an honor, a privilege, and a blast working with you. I have enjoyed each delicious moment of this process!

To my parents and friends, thanks for believing in me, for loving me, and for sticking with me, always!

ABOUT THE AUTHOR

Ellie Laks was born in Israel and raised in the States. She has always loved animals and from the time she could walk she headed into the woods daily to be with them, sometimes bringing them home—much to her parents' chagrin. In 1999, Ellie founded the Gentle Barn, an animal sanctuary that rescues and rehabilitates severely abused and neglected farm animals. Once the animals are healthy, they help Ellie heal at-risk, inner-city, and special-needs children. Ellie lives on the property outside of Los Angeles with her husband, who runs the Barn with her, and their three children. Learn more at www.gentlebarn.org.